Leaders and Lea
in Educatio

Helen Gunter is Senior Lecturer within the School of Education at the University of Birmingham. Before entering higher education Helen was a secondary school teacher (history and politics) and manager for 11 years. She has teaching and research interests in education management, biographical methodology, and the professional development of teachers. Helen has published articles and books on theory, educational leadership and appraisal. Her particular research interest is in the history of the field of education management, and she has recently completed a study into the intellectual history of the field.

Leaders and Leadership in Education

Helen M. Gunter

P·C·P

Paul Chapman
Publishing

First Published 2001

 Paul Chapman Publishing
A SAGE Publications Company
6 Bonhill Street
London EC2A 4PU

SAGE Publications Inc
2455 Teller Road
Thousand Oaks, California 91320

SAGE Publications India Pvt Ltd
32, M-Block Market
Greater Kailash - I
New Delhi 1 10 048

A catalogue record for this book is available from the British Library

ISBN 0 7619 5492 9
ISBN 0 7619 5493 7 (pbk)

Library of Congress catalog record available

Typeset by Anneset, Weston-super-Mare, Somerset
Printed and bound in Great Britain by Athenaeum Press, Gateshead

Contents

Acknowledgements

Without Barry this book would never have been written. Thank you.

This book has its origins in *Rethinking Education* (Gunter, 1997) where I issued the following invitation:

> You are cordially invited to contact me and to participate in this ongoing research. Your account of your professional life history, the choices you have made, the nature of your work within your past and current professional portfolio and your views on the development of the field of education management are all of interest and central to our collective concerns. (p. 114)

I have very much enjoyed the dialogue that resulted and I am delighted by the positive feedback. I would like to pass on my thanks to the reviewers as this stimulated me to take the arguments forward. In this book the conversation continues . . .

If leadership is not about having a vision, then how might we best understand what all the fuss is about? The argument that dominates this book is that leadership is not an 'it' from which we can abstract behaviours and tasks, but is a relationship that is understood through our experiences. Consequently, leadership is highly political and is a struggle within practice, theory and research. Furthermore, leadership is not located in job descriptions but in the professionality of working for teaching and learning. I have a strong commitment to educational leadership through which learning activity is a space for knowledge use and creation. Such thinking has been supported by Bourdieu's theory of practice and I would like to thank Professor Jenny Ozga for introducing me to his work and for her support for my research.

I am also indebted to my friends and former colleagues at Keele University: Gill Cleland, Barbara Cole, Professor Denis Gleeson, Professor Derek Glover, Barry Pitt, Mike Johnson, Richard Race and Pat Smith. My professional life has been further enriched by my move to the University of Birmingham, and I would like to thank Professor Stewart Ranson, Professor Peter Ribbins and Dr Desmond Rutherford for their tremendous support. Teaching has always been important to me and my thanks also go to the Doctor of Education (EdD) Leaders and Leadership in Education course members who are making postgraduate work so exciting and challenging. I am grateful to Professor Anne Edwards, and colleagues in the Centre for Sociocultural and Action Theory Research at Birmingham, for introducing me to Activity Theory.

Recent events have suggested to me that this book has a deeper origin. In 1998, along with my school year group I turned 40, and we had a reunion. Not an unusual event, but as I looked around the room at over 200 people who had but had not changed, I realised the importance of our experiences. We were all victims and beneficiaries of educational structures. In 1969 we all failed the 11+ and hence the structuring of education had limited our life chances. We were to be prepared for a particular working life that fitted in with others' plans for children like us. However, in 1972 the school became comprehensive, with new teachers, new buildings and new opportunities. The school now had a sixth form, I was in the second sixth form group, and the optimism was infectious. For the first time we were not intellectually impoverished through labelling. Looking around the room at the reunion, at people who in a high unemployment area were working, had raised families, gained professional qualifications and ran their own businesses, it was a crime to have failed us at 11 years of age. It was comprehensive education that gave us all a second chance through inclusion. We are now living at a time when trying to be optimistic about education is difficult, and the current government seems to be on track to end comprehensive education. In my 11 years of being a school teacher I never changed my view that comprehensive education is the best way to enable effective governance in our society. I wonder if the current modernisation of education will have the same positive effects on the attitudes and outcomes of children's learning as my generation experienced from comprehensivisation? We will have to wait and see. The creation of diversity between schools, rather than enabling diversity within the comprehensive school, is dangerous for a country where the democratic settlement continues to be vulnerable. This book is dedicated to the class of 1969.

Helen M. Gunter
University of Birmingham

Abbreviations

AERA	American Educational Research Association
APU	Assessment of Performance Unit
AST	Advanced Skills Teacher
BEAS	British Educational Administration Society
BELMAS	British Educational Leadership Management and Administration Society
BEMAS	British Educational Management and Administration Society
BERA	British Education Research Association
BBC	British Broadcasting Corporation
CASE	Cognitive Acceleration through Science Education
CCEA	Commonwealth Council for Educational Administration
CCEAM	Commonwealth Council for Educational Administration and Management
CEO	Chief Education Officer
COSMOS	Committee on the Organisation, Staffing and Management of Schools
CPD	Continuous Professional Development
CTC	City Technology College
DES	Department of Education and Science
DfE	Department for Education
DfEE	Department for Education and Employment
EdD	Doctor of Education
ESRC	Economic and Social Research Council
FE	Further Education
GCSE	General Certificate of Secondary Education
GMS	Grant Maintained Status
HEADLAMP	Headteacher Leadership and Management Programme
HEI	Higher Education Institution
HMCI	Her Majesty's Chief Inspector
HMI	Her Majesty's Inspectorate
HRM	Human Resource Management

ITT	Initial Teacher Training
ICSEI	International Congress for School Effectiveness and Improvement
IIP	International Intervisitation Programme
ILEA	Inner London Education Authority
IMF	International Monetary Fund
ISEIC	International School Effectiveness and Improvement Centre
LEA	Local Education Authority
IQEA	Improving the Quality of Education for All
LFM	Local Financial Management
LMS	Local Management of Schools
LPSH	Leadership Programme for Serving Headteachers
MCI	Management Charter Initiative
NAHT	National Association of Head Teachers
NDC	National Development Centre
NPQH	National Professional Qualification for Headteachers
OfSTED	Office for Standards in Education
OTTO	One Term Training Opportunities
PANDA	Performance and Assessment
PhD	Doctor of Philosophy
PRP	Performance-Related Pay
PSSR	Primary School Staff Relationship
RCT	Randomised Controlled Trial
SATs	Standard Assessment Tasks/Tests
SCRELM	Standing Conference for Educational Leadership and Management
SENCO	Special Educational Needs Co-ordinator
SMS	School Management South
SMT	Senior Management Team
SMTF	School Management Task Force
STRB	School Teacher Review Body
TTA	Teacher Training Agency
TVEI	Technical and Vocational Education Initiative
WSCD	Whole School Curriculum Development
ZPD	Zone of Proximal Development

1

Challenging Leadership

News headlines continue to tell us that there is a crisis in education: '4,000 teacher jobs cannot be filled' (Dean, 2000a), 'Schools policy crisis as third superhead quits' (Carvel and Mulholland, 2000), and, 'Poverty no excuse for failure, says Blunkett' (Carvel, 2000). It seems that what we need is more leadership of educational institutions, with superheads being drafted in to turn 'failing' schools around. The questions I explore in his book are why leadership and why now? And, is it *educational* leadership? This is problematic for leadership watchers and practitioners because, even though popular models seem to suggest that we have settled the debate, it is still the case that we know little about the realities and possibilities for leaders, leading and leadership in educational settings.

I focus on how particular positions regarding leadership in educational studies can be revealed through an examination of research and theory, and how this interconnects with the education policy context. I ask the question: how can we best describe and explain the emerging field of educational leadership? Investigating knowledge production enables a range of issues to be explored: what is a field and what positions are there within and between fields? How does membership of a field create and resolve debates about theory, practice and research? This allows us to dig deeper and ask: in what ways is the production and organisation of knowledge within a field related to dominant group interests and values? This enables professional practice to be related to systems of control and considers the interplay between the agency of the knowledge worker and the structuring effects of organisational location within an educational institution.

This book is about and is the product of intellectual work, and my contribution is to theorise leadership in education through the use of Bourdieu's theory of practice. By thinking with Bourdieu's thinking tools of habitus and field I present the leadership territory as an arena of struggle in which researchers, writers, policy-makers and practitioners take up and/or present positions regarding the theory and practice of educational leadership. This provides opportunities to reveal positions that are being written into and out of the working lives of educational

1

professionals. Furthermore, it enables a historical as well as a contemporary perspective to identify a range of approaches to understanding the everyday work of educational professionals. I draw on intellectual resources from around the world to enable particular questions to be asked about the growth of the field and interconnections with educational restructuring. In order to illuminate the interplay between structure and agency I use site-based performance management in England and other nations of the UK, with a particular focus on schools, as the prime location. The emphasis is on large-scale mapping and contours, rather than on charting of each intellectual pathway. In exploring boundaries I show the messiness and dynamism in the positioning and repositioning of work. I am well aware that much will remain uncharted, and I hope that through reviews and continued dialogue the terrain will be further opened up.

The leadership terrain

The leadership in education terrain is very busy. By using the metaphor of a field we can identify this space as a place of struggle over and within theory and method. Activity is structured, entry and boundaries are controlled. Leadership knowledge workers who engage with what we know and generate new knowledge about what we need to know are located in a range of employment and organisational settings, from teachers in classrooms through to professors in higher education institutions. It is a territory where answers to particular leadership problems are sought, and it is also an interesting site for the exploration of enduring questions about human beings. All are represented in this book, but differences within professional portfolios and the setting in which knowledge production takes place does mean that enabling what we know about leaders and leadership to be made visible is highly problematic. The real-time real-life nature of educational work means that capturing, understanding and theorising the dynamism, even by those directly involved, is challenging. This does not invalidate the project but, instead, provides us with the opportunity to ask who the knowers are, why they are deemed to know and, perhaps significantly, where are the silences?

This book draws on a range of theory and research from knowledge workers who undertake work around particular intellectual positions on the leadership terrain:

- *Critical studies*: concerned with power structures, and how educational professionals experience work.
- *Educational management*: promotes improvements in the leadership, management and administration of educational organisations.
- *School effectiveness and school improvement*: identifies the characteristics of effective schools, and the processes that will bring about improvement.

Even in attempting to describe these positions I am adding to boundary disputes, though the simplicity of these categories becomes evident as the book unfolds. At the moment all I wish to say is that knowledge workers who have identified their work as being located in one of these areas of activity are increasingly interested in leadership. Consequently, networks are developing that are bringing together interesting alliances or are making clearer the boundaries. However, before I can reach the stage of describing this positioning I need to establish some conceptual underpinnings. In particular, I need to be explicit about the authoring process and to problematise my own position.

An intellectual journey

Bourdieu (1988) argues that any attempt to try to be anonymous and to be neutral or to hide behind method 'is doomed in advance to failure' (p. 25), and so my position within the unfolding analysis is open to scrutiny. I begin the process of revealing the intellectual resources that make up the 'the lacework of meanings and significations' (Seddon, 1996, p. 211) that shapes my orientation to this area of study and practice. My original interest is rooted in a combination of personal experience and academic discourse, and as a knowledge worker in both a school and, more recently, a university setting, I have observed and I am a part of the growth in the field from the early 1980s. This involvement has gone through a number of interconnected, and often parallel, phases involving working as a teacher of history and politics in a secondary school through to a university lecturer in education management. This experience of positioning my professional practice and interests within the field, and securing employment within a higher education institution (HEI), has raised a number of questions about how my own professional identity has been challenged and reshaped. Not least because I have become increasingly networked into other fields both through my research and writing, and it is difficult to escape the dominant language and discourse of 'effectiveness' and 'improvement'. The question I ask is: how do I come to be professionally located where I am today? Exploring this raises the importance of lived experience and how I understand my professional practice and make sense of my situated context. This can be revealed through professional life stories in which choices and decisions, to work here or there, to teach this or that, to write on this topic or that, can enable an understanding of how clusters of people can come together to create and develop an area of activity. Underlying this is an understanding of what it means to be a member of a field in which professional practice is shaped through association with others, and what happens when particular questions are asked, research issues are focused on and debates about theory take place.

Since becoming a student, and then a researcher, I have developed a sense of being within a field of study and how I see my position and how others seek to position my work. This may appear, with hindsight, to be neat and tidy. However, within any person's professional biography there are contradictions and dilemmas that have had to be faced, and these are often not revealed through the publication process. Underpinning this is the interplay of agency and structure, and issues around what it means at different times and in different situations to be able to make sense of and to live in the world. The complexity of this approach is illustrated when knowledge workers give glimpses into how they understand and handle these dilemmas. Skeggs (1997) describes how we are positioned by macro structures such as nation, class and sexuality, and these affect our access to education and employment, and what we understand as possible in our lives. Often in contradiction to this is epistemological positioning through particular theories, methodologies, funding and fashions: 'all these positionings impact upon what research we do, when and how we do it. However, there is no straightforward correspondence between our circumstances and how we think: we are positioned in but not determined by our locations' (ibid., p. 18).

Like Deem (1996a) I inhabit border territory, I simultaneously do and do not belong. Much of my professional practice is the same as other field members, but my research and theoretical interests have shifted from the common-sense problem-solving agenda to that of critical studies and, in particular, the historical setting and development of the field. During this intellectual journey I seem to have crossed Popkewitz's (1999, pp. 2–3) metaphorical room away from the 'pragmatic-empiricists' who are concerned to make organisations work better towards a position where 'critical' is interpreted as being about understanding and explaining the tensions and contradictions in why organisations work in the way they do. Being critical is not about taking an oppositional stance but is about opening up spaces for discussion about knowledge claims and production (Alvesson and Willmott, 1996).

This type of reflexive approach enables me to see the link between the dynamic and ongoing development of fields I am studying and changes within my professional identity. In doing this I am taking inspiration from Greenfield because he sees his work and writing as representing 'a groping towards understanding, not a uniform and logical line of extrapolation' (Greenfield and Ribbins, 1993, p. 269). This has considerable resonance with me as it supports my argument that this book is a contribution to a dialogue and not a claim to be encyclopaedic. This ongoing reflexive approach is what makes study exciting and worthwhile, but at the same time I am well aware that researching fields and knowledge production can be challenging. As Bourdieu (1988, p. xv) argues, what is spoken or written about 'is bound to be read differently by readers who are part of this world as opposed to those who are outsiders'. Nevertheless, making the self visible means that the 'assumptive choices' (McPherson and Raab, 1989) I have made in the design and development of this book can be opened up to debate and it returns us to the opening questions in how we seek to understand the theory and research about leadership within educational settings through position and positioning. I problematise intellectual work by making connections between the individual knowledge worker and the context in which knowledge production takes place.

Knowledge and knowing

Describing and understanding leaders and leadership in education is about knowledge production: who does it, what they do, how do they do it and why do they do it? The emphasis is not so much on the product of knowledge in the form of a fact or a theory, as the process by which there is 'a selection and organisation from the available knowledge at a particular time which involves conscious or unconscious choices' (Young, 1971b, p. 24). This problematises knowledge rather than accepts it as a given, and it sees knowledge production as connected to the interplay between agency and structure.

Agency is concerned with the subjective capability and capacity to control, for example, through the exercise of choice and discretion. In asking about the who, what, how and why of knowledge production we need to consider the skills and the will to use them. This can be related to identity and how the individual is able to position the self as *being* a knowledge worker and, more importantly, how what the individual *does* in their relationship with others makes this visible (and invisible). In this way who knowledge workers are is not just about what a role or job is or is not, but it is about what is and is not done. Identity is not homogenous and static, but is about identities that can shift within time and space, and can complement or contradict.

Identity is not just the product of the individual but is a socialised and socialising process in which identities can be received as well as shaped. Structure is concerned with external controls, for example, how technical job descriptions and/or organisational cultures define expectations of what work is and is not about, and so agency can be enhanced, moderated or stifled. Organisations are also places where external power structures are at work in which social injustices in our society related to discrimination and political interests can impact on, and perhaps determine, the exercise of agency within knowledge production. Visibility of the self as a knowledge worker may be highly public, or it could be consciously suppressed or unconsciously repressed. How the self is represented and allowed to be represented is interwoven with social and political issues of age, disability, gender, race and sexuality. In this way the individual is the object of someone else's gaze, and can be grouped according to abstract categories and essentialised as being a typical example.

This brief analysis of agency and structure enables us to investigate leaders and leadership in education by asking, for example, why did I not write this book in 1985? This could be related to how I saw and understood my work as a teacher, and how I made choices to prepare lessons and mark essays rather than write a book about the exercise of pedagogic leadership underpinning those activities. It could be that even if I had wanted to write a book (and many teachers do), I was unable to do so because of the institutional, political and social context that determined what a teacher should and should not be doing.

If such choices and directions in professional practice are to be theorised effectively, then a conceptual framework that will enable the interplay between agency and structure in the exercise of power to be at the forefront is needed. Work by researchers and theorists about knowledge production is itself a field of struggle through which position and positioning takes place, and from this work there are a number of conceptual issues that enable important issues to be raised about leaders and leadership in education.

Leadership as a paradigm shift

It could be that the growth in leadership studies is due to a new paradigm, and certainly the word 'paradigm' is being used increasingly as a means of describing change. Kuhn (1975) argues that knowledge is located within epistemic communities: 'a paradigm is what the members of a scientific community share, and, conversely, a scientific community consists of men who share a paradigm' (p. 176). What this scientific community 'share' are a number of connections related to professional identity, such as being the practitioners of a scientific speciality, absorbing the same technical literature, membership of professional societies, reading the same journals. In addition to this there is a 'tacit knowledge' that comes from the doing of science and in being trained in the rules and assumptions of the paradigm. A paradigm shift takes place when the epistemic community accepts a new way of thinking, seeing and defining the world. Such changes are incremental and are rarely the product of one person. The most important aspect is how these changes are disseminated in journals and eventually reach the lay person through their impact on teaching and textbooks: 'what were ducks in the scientist's world before the revolution are rabbits afterwards' (ibid., p. 111).

This approach enables us to see that knowledge, and what is or is not the truth, is related to those who produce it. However, it is a rather elitist view of knowledge production because it presents intellectual and manual work as rational and separate. A privileged epistemic community is able to control the progress towards, and the acceptance of, what is the truth through a top-down transmission of what is to be known. It seems that leadership as a paradigm is only helpful if you want to impose a model of leadership. For the field to gain a better sense of itself and its purposes, then, we need a way of understanding knowledge production that not only enables the struggle within and over knowledge to be visible, but also to be more inclusive of who the knowers are.

Leadership as academic tribes and territories

Becher (1989), who like Kuhn (1975) is interested in knowledge communities, broadens out the focus to consider the relationship between disciplines and professional identity: 'the ways in which particular groups of academics organise their professional lives are intimately related to the intellectual tasks on which they are engaged' (Becher, 1989, p. 1). Becher (1989) uses the example of discovery and describes how it is very important in some fields of enquiry and less so in others. For example, discovery is very important in molecular biology but not so much in taxonomies of plant life. In mechanical engineering it has been replaced by invention. Discovery is out of place in other areas of enquiry such as history. Becher argues that these differences are not just sociological but lie within the nature of the work of the academic, and this leads him to provide a multidimensional framework to investigate the epistemological features of knowledge:

1. *Abstract and reflective or hard and pure*: the natural sciences and maths in which there is linear development by building on previous work. Outcomes tend to be concerned with universal and value free truths.
2. *Concrete and reflective or soft and pure*: the humanities and social sciences in which there is debate about the type of the questions to be asked and the nature and validity of outcomes. There is emphasis on an iterative process and the use of findings as illuminative.
3. *Abstract and active or hard and applied*: the science-based professions, e.g. medicine and engineering, in which trial and error approaches dominate. Progress may or may not take place, and the emphasis is on mastering the natural world through the use of a practical and problem-solving method.
4. *Concrete and active or soft and applied*: the social professions, e.g. education, social work and the law in which the intellectual roots are reinterpreted and developed, and so there is no accumulation of knowledge which is agreed and accepted. This domain is concerned with understanding the complexity of human relationships and interactions, and so is unstable and open to change. Outcomes are focused on identifying the best ways of doing things and in arranging human interactions, and can be judged according to pragmatism, or, utilitarianism or ethics.

Becher goes on to show how these knowledge domains are evident in the creation, evolution and reproduction of tribes of academics and the territories they inhabit. Terrain is marked by the spatial characteristics of which parts of the campus you visit, through to the stereotyping of disciplines and how new entrants are inducted into professional attitudes and values. The academic within the academy is conceptualised as pursuing recognition as a means of power and this is displayed in rituals to do with citation, and the pecking order of departments.

Becher's work enables the university as a site of knowledge production to be focused on, and using his categories means that leadership studies are concerned with knowledge claims that are 'soft and applied'. Becher (1989) acknowledges the increase in external regulation through directed investment and research grants which is causing 'epistemic drift' (p. 137) as tough choices have to be made regarding the generation of income and the knowledge requirements of those who are funding research. If, for example, funders want knowledge about leadership to be 'hard and pure' then this challenges the epistemology and professional practices of those who see leadership as an alternative way of knowing. However, Becher's analysis does not take this far enough, he does not locate the professional practice of 'academic tribes' and the 'territories' they inhabit within debates about the 'structures of privilege and power relations as a condition of knowledge production' (Skeggs, 1997, p. 20). What we need is an approach to knowledge production that engages with issues around how economic and political interests can create and sustain the structures that ensure particular tribes and territories and particular types of knowledge claims are protected while others are excluded.

Leadership as a power structure

Leadership in educational studies can be seen as the process and product by which powerful groups are able to control and sustain their interests. Such an approach to leadership studies enables the connection between facts and values to be made visible, and establishes that 'the political positions of knowers are significant factors in the construction of knowledge' (Griffiths, 1998, p. 52). In this sense, seeking to understand the production of knowledge requires a description of structural power and dominant elite groups, combined with an analysis of the processes of transmission and learning.

Young (1971a) argues that there is an explicit relationship between elite groups and how knowledge is organised. Knowledge is stratified in the sense that the value of knowing one thing rather than another is linked to power structures that determine what is to be known, and what it is worthwhile knowing. The transmission of this knowledge is controlled through access to learning in a particular institution, the structure of the curriculum within that institution and the power relations that structure pedagogy. Curriculum change and the entry of an alternative way of knowing into the school or the HEI is linked to power relationships, and change will or will not happen dependent on how elite groups perceive the type and level of challenge to their values and power base (Young, 1971a; 1971b; 1998). A useful starting point is to focus on how knowledge is organised and controlled through disciplines which Bernstein (1971) argues 'means accepting a given selection, organisation, pacing and timing of knowledge realised in the pedagogic frame' (p. 57). Young (1971b) argues that we are socialised into a specialised subject discipline in which learning is a 'private property' for the individual to achieve and be rewarded. Individuals are presented with what is 'high-status knowledge' which is abstract, written, received and distant from experience. Alternative knowledge that puts emphasis on the relevance of theory to practice, and on learning through talk and group activity is of low status (Young, 1998).

Relating knowledge production to power structures is an important contribution and can help to explain features such as the endurance of hierarchy in schools and so leadership can be seen to have been reworked and developed over time to sustain political and economic interests. Knowledge and the truth are not neutral but are related directly to powerful interests, and intellectual work is highly political in seeking to support or challenge this dominance. However, this approach does tend to objectify, and so it can limit agency because in being essentialised the complex identities that grow through the individual's experiences and struggles over time and in a range of contexts may be lost. The post-structuralist writer Foucault (1972) moves us forward by arguing that power is diffuse and is visible through discourse. Discourse is presented as being about what can be said and thought, and 'who can speak, when, where and with what authority' (Ball, 1994b, p. 21). Meaning comes from power relations, there are exclusions and inclusions, claims are made, and positions taken. Finally, discourse is complex and dense, and is about how the world is seen and understood, and the assumptions that structure what can and cannot be said. There are sites in which a right to speak is known and understood, and education can be identified as a site of discourse development. In this sense a teacher or lecturer does not create, develop, communicate and transmit knowledge separate from context, and practice is linked to issues of power, status, recognition and value judgements about worth and validity. This approach is conceptually productive because through discourse the structuring of power is visible, and intellectual work can be seen as complicit within the 'regime of truth' about and for particular forms of leadership (Ball, 1994b). Developing this approach to knowledge production needs to consider the struggle over knowledge through practice, and how position and positioning is central to what can and cannot be said.

Leadership as praxis

Knowledge production through professional practice is central to action research. As Winter (1989) states: 'in action research practitioners reflect on their work in such a way as to generate insights which will open up new practical developments, and from these new practical developments fresh insights are derived which subsequently open up further practical innovation, in a theoretically endless spiral' (p. 193). This relationship between theory and practice is a matter of debate and Hirst (1974) makes a distinction between 'forms' of knowledge and 'fields' of knowledge. Forms of knowledge or disciplines are concerned with knowing the world, compared with fields of knowledge which are action orientated. Forms of knowledge have central concepts forming a logical structure, with techniques and skills, and 'distinctive expressions which are testable against experience' (Hirst, 1974, p. 44). In contrast a field or 'organisations' of knowledge 'are not concerned, as the disciplines are, to validate any one logically distinct form of expression. They are not concerned with developing a particular structuring of experience. They are held together simply by their subject matter, drawing on all forms of knowledge that can contribute to them' (ibid., p. 46). Therefore engineering and medicine as fields are dependent on foundational knowledge from the natural sciences; and, education is a field based on the social sciences.

Usher and Edwards (1994) argue that this has common-sense appeal in its neatness and tidiness, but they agree with Schon (1983) that the application of the Hirst model distorts practice because disciplines are within practices: 'education cannot "draw from" disciplines in a Hirstian sense because it is already "in" disciplines – disciplines are already implicated in education' (Usher and Edwards, 1994, p. 49). Carr (1993) argues against the theory–practice divide, and against the superior–subordinate implication of that divide: 'by making the twin assumptions that all practice is non-theoretical and all theory is non-practical, this approach always underestimates the extent to which those who engage in educational practices have to reflect upon, and hence theorise about, what, in general, they are trying to do'. (p. 162). He goes on to argue that we need to locate concepts within their historical and cultural context, and he demonstrates that praxis as defined as 'morally informed or morally committed action' is currently being marginalised. Emancipatory praxis requires the practitioner to be the subject and not the object of change, and pedagogy as a leadership relationship is within the tradition of educational practice (Smyth, 1989a). However, the ability of the teacher to engage in self-reflection and collaborative critique is limited by their self-censorship rooted in contextual settings.

Teachers are currently positioned as curriculum technicians (Ball, 1990a) and followers of charismatic leaders (Gronn, 1996), and so it seems that what we need is an approach to knowledge production that focuses on the use and production of knowledge in which the knowledge worker in the classroom and the university can engage in dialogue about the same questions, participate in the same networks and engage in both radicalism and practicalities at the same time. Gramsci's (1973) contribution is to connect domination by the state (political society) with hegemonic control through culture (civil society). Gramsci (1971) sees knowledge production as more than a deterministic link between an economic base and a social infrastructure, and he conceptualised intellectuals as being essentially concerned with material issues rather than the lofty concerns of the truth. Hence his work is important in the location of the intellectual between structures of power and the actual workings of the education system (Brym, 1987; Swingewood, 1987). 'Traditional intellectuals' (Gramsci, 1971, p. 9) are historically located and enduring with privileges and dominance over society, but face challenge from organic intellectuals who are produced from the workings of a new social class as it grows and develops. Change takes place through a social group developing its organic intellectuals as a means of achieving an 'assimilation and conquest' of traditional intellectuals (ibid., p. 10). What seems to be of interest in this analysis for investigating theory and research about educational leadership is the importance of the formation of organic intellectuals, their social location, mobility and preparation through the workings of education systems. This challenges us to ask questions about how teachers are, or are not, or could be, prepared through their personal and professional lives to be organic intellectuals sustaining leadership practice that is integral to pedagogy.

This is supported by feminist critiques and interpretations of knowledge production, and Gramsci's work has informed research that aims not just to understand what is known, but also to challenge and to transform (Lather, 1986). In particular work around issues of social injustice is central here such as work on gender (Skeggs, 1997; Stanley and Wise, 1993) and interconnections with struggles over and about democracy and rights in post-colonial societies (Yeatman, 1994). In this way leaders and leadership in education is not about the promotion of one model of effectiveness, but is about seeking to understand and transform how we present leadership in ways that challenge assumptions. In this way what we need is an inclusive approach to intellectual work, that prevents the 'othering' of people, ideas and ways of living, and enables difference to be recognised (Blackmore, 1999). In this way knowledge production about leadership is understood to be not just about problem-solving but also about problem-making.

Leadership as intellectual work

The conceptualisation of a knowledge worker as an alienated or distanced thinker who is seeking the truth and a part of a scientific progression towards the truth has been challenged. The term 'intellectual' can be dated to the time of the Dreyfus affair in late nineteenth-century France when artists and writers took political action and were labelled by the right-wing. Connell (1983) argues that we need to stand outside the traditional power structures that have created and sustained intellectual work as an elite activity and see it instead as a labour process or a job in which there is equipment (pen and paper), manual activity (writing) and abstract activity (thinking). Intellectual work can go wrong and be involved in systems of oppression, or it can lead to enlightenment and understanding. For Connell this raises the question: what are the conditions in which *intellectual* work takes place? If a knowledge worker such as a headteacher in a meeting or a teacher in a classroom is in receipt of frameworks which have already decided the answers, and so s/he just describes rather than critically evaluates, then there is no intellectual work to be done. It is work but it is not *intellectual* work. This is because 'intellectual work is not necessarily radical, but it must always be subversive of authority in its own domain. There is nothing exotic about this, it is implicit in the very notion of intellectual *work*' (ibid., p. 250, original emphasis). The danger for Connell is that continued hierarchical relationships about the validity of different types of knowledge work will undermine both the school and the HEI as sites of knowledge production. If the university academic is privileged as knower then theory is handed down and, while it can support critical thinking, it may be disengaged from action; if the practitioner is privileged as the knower, then theory may be eschewed and hence practice fails to become praxis. Field activity can only be understood by a theory of knowledge production that enables an interplay between objectivity and subjectivity so that the binaries which establish oppositions are eliminated. Those who write and are written about, those who use theory and those who produce it, those who research about and those who research with, can all be part of the same story.

This presentation and discussion about knowledge and knowing enables the theory and practice of leading and leadership in educational settings to be problematised because it shows that knowledge production is a highly political process through the exercise of agency and the impact of determining structures. We need to give recognition to struggles for position and to position within and about the sites of knowledge production, and how this can exclude particular social and occupational groups. Furthermore, we need to see how this is located within both the local context of an institution, and the larger setting of economic and political interests which impact on and shape agency. We need ways of conceptualising agency and structure that do not present them as binary opposites but enable the complexity and reality of interplay to be visible. In the next section I argue that Bourdieu's theory of practice provides the means through which knowledge production in leaders and leadership can be explained.

Bourdieu's theory of practice

Bourdieu provides both a conceptual lens through which to investigate, combined with the thinking tools needed to explain (Jenkins, 1992). Understanding intellectual work requires a sociological interrogation of practice in order to describe and understand the complex motivations of individuals and the structures they inhabit. However, in using Bourdieu's theory of practice I am clearly on dangerous ground as the current anti-intellectual approach to teaching and learning in England means that I could be positioned as engaging in the 'adulation of great thinkers' (Tooley with Darby, 1998, p. 56). However, engaging with theory through thinking with Bourdieu is the means by which I, like others in educational studies, can stand outside such attempts to objectify positioning.

Bourdieu provides us with the concept of field in which agents take up positions in a struggle for distinction. The practice underpinning position and positioning is explained through the genesis of habitus or the disposition to act. Bourdieu bridges the subjectivity–objectivity divide by the use of habitus which is a 'feel for the game' (Bourdieu, 1990, p. 9) and can only be understood through the agent's interactions with others. It is ways of talking, moving and making things, which are not about rules but about regularities in social actions which are both socialised and socialising.

A field is a competitive arena in which struggles are not just about material gain but also symbolic capital, or authority, prestige and celebrity status. This is linked to who is accepted as having legitimate views, who is listened to, who is published, who is read and who is talked with and about. Books, papers, articles, keynote speeches and seminars are all part of a field in which position and social relationships sustain or condemn. Citing, quoting, acknowledging, giving reference to and reviewing enables us to see the meaning and distinction attached within a field. Agents want to preserve or improve positions in relation to how the capital is defined, the relationship between position, for example, through the symbolic form of a book or conference paper, is a means by which the link between the agent and the field is objectified. In other words the award of credentials such as a Doctor of Philosophy (PhD) imposes 'the universally approved perspective' within a field, and is good currency in the marketplace. The holder no longer has to engage in a 'symbolic struggle' about position (Bourdieu, 1990, p. 135). As Johnson (1993) describes, there is a complex process of investing and seeking reward in a field, and being accepted as legitimate: 'under normal circumstances, no one enters a game to lose. By the same token, no one enters the literary field – no one writes a novel, for example – to receive bad reviews' (p. 8).

Fields have boundaries that are set by the point(s) at which the field no longer has an impact on practice. Social processes are structured by a hierarchy of fields: political field, economic field, cultural field and education field, and so positions and positioning is about domination, subordination, or equivalence. The education field can seek to be dominant through struggles over, for example, pedagogy, however, it is dominated through the workings of the market by the political, economic and cultural fields. Bourdieu focuses on the educational field and shows the importance of external factors such as legislation or economic crises in their impact on what is to be taught and who has access to education. He argues strongly that struggle within a field is not just about reacting to external pressures because you must look at the 'whole logic of the field' (Bourdieu, 1990, p. 43). Changes in educational demands do not determine how field members respond when there is a mechanistic cause and effect relationship, rather, what is significant is how and why agents within the field, linked to their habitus or dispositions, give legitimacy to particular claims for recognition.

This theory of practice enables knowledge production about and within leaders and leadership in educational studies to be described and understood. It provides the language and the conceptual tools that can show how the agent can be both the subject and the object of activity. As a subject the theoriser, researcher and practitioner can position the self, and as the object the theoriser, researcher and practitioner can be positioned. The interplay and complexity of this positioning and repositioning is the stuff of struggles within and about the leadership terrain, and as someone about to embark on this process I now need to describe, as clearly as possible, my position.

Staking a claim for a position

The analysis presented so far has been concerned with exploring the possibilities for describing, explaining and understanding knowledge production in the emerging field of educational leadership. Leadership watchers and practitioners engage in intellectual work such as pedagogy, research and theory which gives them legitimacy to speak through oral and written texts regarding what is and what ought to be professional practice. As an author I am involved within existing power structures, and through the publication process I am staking a claim for distinction, as will those who read, ignore or comment upon my work. I am also entering dangerous territory, particularly in England, where intellectual work is either tolerated as eccentric or ridiculed as irrelevant. Alan Bennett (1997) best describes in his diaries what this feels like:

> 13 May. Colin Haycraft and I are chatting on the pavement when a man comes past wheeling a basket of shopping. 'Out of the way, you so-called intellectuals,' he snarls, 'blocking the f—ing way.' It's curious that it's the intellectual that annoys, though it must never be admitted to be the genuine article but always 'pseudo' or 'so-called'. It is, of course, only in England that 'intellectual' is an insult anyway. (p. 218)

In this book I stand on a metaphorical pavement and begin (or perhaps continue) a conversation about educational leadership, and no doubt I will get in the way of those who would much rather get on with prescribing the action for us. I argue that there is a preferred model of leadership in education that permeates policy texts, it is the product of laboratory science, and is currently labelled 'transformational' leadership. This model presents leadership as being a leader through appointment to a post within an organisational structure, and prescribes what that leader does by abstracting tasks and behaviours. It exaggerates agency in ways that objectifies, and hence undermines, professional relationships between headteachers and teachers, and their students. This model is more about leadership in educational settings than it is about educational leadership. I show how and why this model has gained ascendancy and how it is shaping the work of educational professionals and compromising their agency to exercise professional judgement in teaching and learning, and to work productively within communities. I show how educational leadership is conceptualised through the critical accounts of professional lives and practice. In particular, I argue for conceptually informed practice that embraces a radical professionality in which educational professionals are users and producers of leadership knowledge, and that the site for knowledge production is a collaborative and shared space for knowledge workers in schools and other settings (Edwards, 2000b).

The dynamics of power is integral to this analysis, and I use Bourdieu's tools of habitus and field to conceptualise that the practice, training, research, theory and study of leadership in education is contested. Struggle is intellectual, and is about the ideas, beliefs and the resources we use to work though our understandings of educational purposes and the type of organisations such as schools that we want to create, sustain and develop. It is about the effort and commitment we put into our work, and how we strive to work through complex issues. It is about the process or means through which decisions are made, and the dialogic nature of networks and associations that form. Struggle should not be automatically interpreted as being about the type of negative conflict and infighting that Clark (1998) reports brought the Ridings School the title of 'worst school in Britain'. Neither is it necessarily about the shift from authentic dialogue to personal attacks that followed Greenfield's contribution to knowledge claims about theory and practice in 1974 (Greenfield and Ribbins, 1993). Struggle is within the possibilities and traps we face every day, and while political interests illustrate difference, this need not be partisan or sectarian. While there is much that may divide us, there are also common interests. The social fabric is vulnerable to dysfunctional crises that show deep, enduring and mutually reinforcing divisions, but not inevitably so. This does not float free of the structuring effect of dominant economic and political power structures, and this is the particular focus of Chapter 2. The policy context is not presented as necessarily determining struggles, but as defining the setting in which dialogue is being constructed and reshaped. The book then moves on to a study of different field positions in Chapter 3 where I present the spaces and boundaries in which leadership work is currently located. Chapters 4 and

5 are about research and theory, and as such are concerned to present and analyse the particular positions around which knowledge workers cluster regarding particular epistemological questions. Chapters 6 to 9 then go on to look at what we know through these theoretical and research approaches about the pathways of those in leadership positions before going on to review: headteachers, teachers as middle and senior managers, and teachers and students as leaders. Chapter 10 returns to the central questions of leadership in educational institutions by locating the struggle over and within issues of professionalism within education. Finally, I consider possibilities for the ongoing development of intellectual work in leadership studies in education.

2

Leadership and the Performing School

This chapter presents and analyses the policy process that is sustaining a particular version of the school and the purposes of schooling. This is directing and shaping a mandated model of leadership in educational institutions rather than encouraging the development of educational leadership. In particular, I argue that there are competing versions of the performing school and the one that is dominating promotes leadership as a universal prescription rather than a context-specific professional relationship. Leadership is a conduit through which individualising markets are installed in education, rather than a dialogic process located in civic democratic values connected with social justice and equity. Nevertheless, while the terrain is being mapped, described and objectified by government as a means of achieving a preferred settlement, being a leader, undertaking leadership and trying to hold on to educational leadership is highly political.

Central to understanding the struggle on the leadership terrain is how the performing school has been, and continues to be, defined and built (Gleeson and Gunter, 2001). Even a change in government does not mean that policy will be reversed (Carr and Hartnett, 1996; Novlan, 1998). Given the proliferation of spinned policy texts, it is difficult to present alternative debates and approaches to leadership without being demonised as 'irrational ... destructive and mad' (Ball, 1994b, p. 44). Nevertheless, as Carr and Hartnett (1996, p. 175) argue, 'such settlements are always fragile, and continually being challenged by the realities of social, economic, political, moral and intellectual change'. Consequently, contestation within education is not linear, outcomes are not inevitable and at most what we can seek to do is to provide a snapshot of the current state of play. In this sense symbolic forms of capital such as books and articles on leadership that make claims regarding the 'outdatedness' of previous publications are seeking distinction that connects with the commodification of knowledge in which we are in fashion by being in the know.

The performing school

How children, parents, teachers, post-holders, headteachers and governors all perform has been and continues, to different extents, to be central to theory and research. Grappling with this can be evidenced through how mandatory requirements are interpreted within the day to day workings of human activities and relationships. In this sense policy is not implemented, legislation is not introduced, and theory is not applied to practice, but instead there is a complex process of under and overlaying (Ozga, 2000). This can be further understood through what Ball (1999) calls 'personal and institutional fabrications' in how we seek to represent our interests regarding what is accepted, rejected, fudged and put on hold. Who is staking claims for a particular version of the performing school, what those claims are, who is listened to and who receives acclaim and validation by others are all central concerns to understanding the current configuration of schools and schooling.

In England and Wales the neo-liberal version of the performing school, around which various individuals and groups have positioned themselves and have supported particular intellectual work, has the following features:

- Education is a product and service to be marketed, bought and sold, as the most efficient and effective way of organising and meeting consumer needs.
- The purposes of schools and schooling are to enable the workforce to be appropriately skilled to operate in the current and developing economy.
- Schools have stakeholders who invest their resources into learning outcomes, accountability is through measurement which enables judgements to be made about value for money.
- Leadership is about the location of entrepreneurial behaviours in the role and tasks of senior and middle management post-holders.
- Management systems in schools are designed to control and deliver education outcomes.
- Teachers are the workforce to be trained and to be flexibly trainable to deliver externally determined curricula by teaching through targets and testing.

What seem to lead to variations are the different positions taken on the role of the state between those who argue for the complete withdrawal of the state, through to those who see the role of the state as important in determining education's contribution to the moral and social order (Carr and Hartnett, 1996). Contradictions within policy is evident in the promotion by successive Conservative governments of site-based performance management, combined with central regulation of the curriculum, inspection, the restructuring of the profession through training and the control of resources through contracting.

Chubb and Moe (1990) argue in favour of schools as institutions rather than as a part of a system, because 'democratic control normally produces ineffective schools. This is how it works' (p. 227). Tooley (1995; 1996; 1999) argues in favour of markets because this enables both voice and exit to operate, whereas in a non-market context you can only complain. For Tooley (1995) the problem lies not with markets but with the failure to fully market education. This position was revealed through a reply to Ranson (1993), and the latter's reply to Tooley (Ranson, 1995), and in this debate Ranson makes the case for the critical role of education in democracy, and so alternative versions of performance are recognised. Central to Ranson's argument is that education is not a 'thing' or commodity, and putting education into the marketplace changes the product itself in ways that are not predictable, and hence the argument that the market is an efficient means of control is flawed. Furthermore, while democratic institutions may not yet be authentic, they are places where choices can be scrutinised and opposed through collective dialogue and action. Deciding to exit the market is different to that of the political system, as the individualisation of the marketplace would attempt to take the individual out of a context of collective action. It is a commercial anarchy in which 'a community is denied the possibility of clarifying its needs and priorities that are monitored, revisable and accountable to the public' (Ranson, 1993, p. 339). Ranson (1993; 1994; 1995) goes on to argue that the democratic project can be furthered through the creation of a learning society, in which participation is an educative process where the individual learns to debate, listen, negotiate, moderate and co-operate.

Versions of the performing school that are concerned with the ideals and practice of democracy tend to stress:

- Education is a public good, it is an entitlement and promotes equity.
- The purposes of schools and schooling are to educate as well as train, and to enable children to engage in the theory and practice of what it means to be a citizen in an unfolding and reforming democratic project.
- Leadership is a relationship, can be exercised by all, and tasks are achieved through negotiation.
- Teachers and students engage in leadership in the development and experience of learning.
- Schools are located within communities, and so accountability is through mutuality and a respect for difference.
- Management systems support and are integral to pedagogy.

What seems to lead to variation in this version of the performing school is the role given to the state from those who continue to stress its importance in ensuring social justice, through to New Labour (from 1997) who have abandoned structural reform in favour of maximising educational outputs.

The left failed to sustain the comprehensive school project and assumed that the fundamental values of the public sector would endure. With the rise of Thatcherism, community-based politics were labelled as the 'looney left', and they were unable to escape this position. In particular, the manufactured crisis in education was not countered (Carr and Hartnett, 1996), and the myths around falling standards and progressive education gained momentum (Daugherty, 1997). The impact has been significant and, for Hutton (1995), Britain's experience of markets has been so negative because of the failure to link reform to social and political structures, and so tensions between price and employment have been resolved in favour of the former. West et al. (1997), drawing on Le Grand and Bartlett (1993), show how school entry can be controlled through 'cream skimming' and covert selection so that able children, usually from the middle classes, are more attractive than those who are 'expensive users' of schools (West et al., 1997, p. 176). In post-compulsory education the emphasis has been more on training and keeping the working classes 'off the dole' than on education (Gleeson, 1996). The goal of diversity within the school is being resisted by the endurance of diversity between schools, and so there has been a politics of exclusion because of the failure of the left to convince the high earners in society that they have a stake in social justice and welfare systems (Apple, 1998). Boyd (1999), building on Garbarino, describes how in the USA: 'we are now raising children in a "socially toxic environment" polluted by the combined effects of poverty, the breakdown of families and communities, the neglect of children, soaring levels of violence and crime, including the proliferation of guns and shootings, drug and alcohol abuse, and the threat of AIDs' (p. 284). For Carr and Hartnett (1996) democracy has throughout history been intellectually and practically contested, and within western democracies the version which has gained legitimacy has been based on neo-liberal capitalist principles in which private interests dominate and have prevented the development of a community involvement in problem resolution. New Labour's version of the performing school with the modernised teacher is located in this enduring power structure, and rather than pursue a democratising project based on social justice it has adopted a version that has many features that are akin to the neo-liberal position.

Research and dialogue about the place of education and leadership within a democratic project still continues (Apple and Beane, 1999). Glickman (1998; 1999) and Scheurich (1998) have recently debated how democracy is differently understood and experienced in the USA, and whether promoting the struggle for rights and entitlements in the Declaration of Independence is meaningful for those who have and continue to experience oppression. Yeatman (1994) is troubled by claims about western democracy but argues that this does not invalidate an emancipatory project but instead makes the possibilities for it more real and urgent: 'postmodern emancipatory vision does not offer a utopian future, but works to develop contestatory political and public spaces, which open up in relation to existing systems of governance' (p. ix). Reality and truth are constructed through 'a *politics* of representation' (ibid., p. 31) in which questions are raised about: 'whose representations prevail? Who has the authority to represent reality? To put the question differently: who must be silenced in order that these representations prevail? Whose voice is deprived of authority so that they may prevail?' (ibid.). These types of questions support Yeatman's analysis of the positioning and repositioning of feminism and post-colonialism in its challenge to masculine and western assumptions about knowledge production. Furthermore, she presents a 'democratic politics of difference' (ibid.) as a means of recognising groups who are 'othered' (p. 86) in western-style democracies, and makes visible the historical neglect of race and class by feminism so that 'it is accepted that the needs of differently positioned women are different' (p. 53). Realising this is enabled through 'interconnected polities' (ibid., p. 89) in which difference is not articulated through niche marketing and an economic liberalism of self-interest, but through new ways in which rights are talked about and worked through in the locality. This leads to an alternative form of local management based on debates about public governance (Gleeson and Shain, 1999a), and so leadership is not just about gaining and sustaining institutional advantage for particular children but is a place of dialogue for education.

The performing school: contesting and struggling

Figure 2.1 uses Dale's (1989) chronological framework to structure how I represent the visibility of particular themes in educational restructuring. In this section I describe and analyse the restructuring of state education from the administration of education through to the impact of site-based performance management, and how this connects with the promotion of a preferred model of leadership in educational institutions.

	1944–74	1974–88	1988 onwards
Culture and Practice	Educational Administration	Organisational Management	Site-Based Performance Management
Structure and System	Partnership	Power-dependency	Regulation
Quality and Efficiency	Professional self-regulation	Stakeholder interests	Contractualism

Figure 2.1 Centralisation and decentralisation in the restructuring of education

Educational administration

Dale (1989) argues that the post-war settlement established education policy-making based on a framework of central and local interaction with very little demand from parents and industry. The 1944 Education Act located the responsibility for the provision of primary and secondary education with Local Education Authorities (LEAs), but the relationship between Whitehall and County Halls lacked clear boundaries, and is generally regarded as being encapsulated in the phrase: 'national policy locally administered'. Educational administration was located in bureaucratic structures that supported a social and educational elite who maintained the 1944 settlement, and who had developed a *noblesse oblige* orientation towards public service. It seems that the same ethos and type of person inhabited local administration, and is symbolised in the headmaster tradition in schools, and so there was no need for the centre to use interventionist powers as there was a coincidence of interests. Bogdanor (1979) describes educational administration as a strong network which sought to secure a balance in the name of the public interest. This worked as long as there was a deferral to this elite to 'act sensibly' through their professional community (ibid., p. 161).

Challenges to the post-war settlement took place from the mid-1960s, with trends towards more participation, and a pluralism of interests, often conflicting. The purposes of schools and schooling and the connections with the democratic project gained ascendance both in government and in research. Universities expanded and polytechnics were created. For schools the most significant change was the development of comprehensive education which had implications for the internal administration of teaching and learning. Up to the 1930s management was very much about strong control and discipline through 'the capacity of headteachers to keep other teachers and the pupils in a state of subordination' (Grace, 1995, p. 29), but in the post-war period there was a moral energy for change and a belief in the connection between education and democratic culture. This was the time of the 'modern professional' where the relationship between headteacher and staff was based on educational values and the ethical issues of working with children. Administration was about supporting educational objectives, and status within the profession came from pedagogy. However, the comprehensive school made the internal arrangements for the organisation of teaching and learning more complex: children were increasingly organised in mixed ability classes, the pastoral role of the practitioner was enhanced and schools grew in size. Grace (1995) argues that this led to a period of 'social democratic management' in which activities were still rooted in the values of professional collegiality, with an emphasis on participation in decision-making dependent on the management style of the headteacher. However, while the opportunity existed to develop the democratic project it was not seized upon. As Benn and Chitty (1997) have shown there were examples of democratic schools such as Risinghill and Countesthorpe, and headteachers such as Barker (1999), who have given a professional lifetime commitment to democratic values, but innovative practice was 'ring-fenced' and subjected to media and political ridicule around issues of standards. The reality is that: 'many comprehensive schools and their heads harboured the utmost suspicion of both progressive education and much democratic management, choosing instead the good old-fashioned 'tight-ship' with a captain very firmly in charge' (Benn and Chitty, 1997, p. 293).

Models of business management became and were increasingly made attractive to an education profession that sought to modernise itself at a time when class and privilege were being challenged, and private sector values were being acclaimed. The potential destabilisation of headship, through the creation of a more pluralistic headteacher caste (products of grammar schools and, later, comprehensive schools) was avoided. Management models based on traditional hierarchical control enabled the headmaster tradition to be reworked into modern leadership behaviours and practice (Grace, 1995).

Organisational management, 1974–88

The most serious challenges to educational administration came from the neo-liberal coalition, which used the opportunity of social change and economic decline to develop and promote their versions of the perform-ing school. The role of the state in the central planning and resourcing of services has never been settled, and powerful interests continued to exclude themselves from the welfare state in the post-war period. Furthermore, the failure to achieve the reform of government institutions meant that the system of democracy as it had developed was increas-ingly ridiculed and undermined as being overly bureaucratic. It seems that Britain was 'becoming harder to govern' because of overload in which 'politicians used to decide, or at least believe that they were deciding. In the 1970s they merely grope' (King, 1976, p. 25). The thesis was that the government took too much responsibility for problems that should be dealt with by the market (remember the sugar shortage in 1974 when Fred Peart travelled the world trying to find us sugar?), and also the system's capacity to cope was in question with policy U-turns, increasing civil disobedience and demands for institutional reform. The emergence of government agencies with a brief to deliver, rather than the reform of institutions through which problems could be debated and solutions agreed, has its origins in this type of context. Expressed through public choice theory, which carved out an intellectual territory that captured popular public opinion, especially the private sector middle classes, the case was made that the growth in public sector spending was connected to privileged groups such as teachers, who within a pluralist setting were able to make claims for more expenditure without direct accountability (Lauder et al., 1999; Ozga, 1995). Put more graphically, Pring (1988) presents the argument attributed to higher civil servants that education had in fact 'been too successful – we can cope with the Toxteths and the Brixtons, but we may not be able to manage future unrest. Once again we must teach young people to know their place' (p. 91).

For neo-liberals the crisis in the state had to be worked in ways that would enable cuts in public expenditure but at the same time not lose public support (Lauder et al., 1999). By packaging cuts as new freedoms, successive Conservative governments were able to make claims about governability, and at the same time relay the message of personal responsibility marketed as choice: 'the administered market in education seeks to fetter local elected representatives and professionals, as the bearers of the old order, and emancipate the middle class as the bearers of the new' (Ranson, 1993, p. 338). Establishing national requirements for public services would allow the state to retain its control of public spending and what has become the drive to push up standards, but at the same time by moving the responsibility and accountability for public services down the line to those who deliver them the government would be able to free itself from the turmoil of ungovernability (Flynn, 1997). This is the origin of the current site-based performance management, and from the mid-1970s onwards can be seen in the development of organisational management. The management of the curriculum regarding content, philosophy and pedagogy faced state regulation and the beginning of the requirement to internally manage externally required learning outcomes. Challenges to professional collegiality were already appearing as headteachers faced the internal management consequences of contraction through falling rolls. Furthermore, led and symbolised by Callaghan's Ruskin College Speech in 1976, the agenda was clearly focused on what was taught, to what standard, and what accountability mechanisms were to be used (Callaghan, 1976). A decade later, through the White Paper *Better Schools* (DES, 1985) and the changes to teachers' pay and conditions of service in 1987, the government created the climate and foundational systems for a performance management imperative.

Performance management

Neo-liberal versions of the performing school gained further ascendancy in the post-1988 period and is evident in the Conservative administrations from 1979 through to the New Labour government from 1997. The centre has increased its intervention regarding educational standards, and has done this through management agencies rather than through reforming existing institutions of governance. The Ibbs Report or 'Next Steps' (Efficiency Unit, 1988) has led to a separation of the policy-making function of a Whitehall department, from the service delivery through an agency such as the Teacher Training Agency (TTA), and the Office for Standards in Education (OfSTED). Compliance through contractualism is technical in how resources are bid for, targeted and accounted for within particular projects. While the rhetoric is humane, with talk of social inclusion and community participation, the contradictions that have arisen between achieving this and meeting contractual accountabilities mean that the drive for efficient management is eclipsing politics.

This public sector restructuring towards a strong managerialist and regulatory centre means that by the late 1980s LEAs had become, according to Brighouse (1988), 'eunuchs' (p. 102), in which the innovative role of past local educational administrators had been lost. In the post – 1988 period LEAs have faced ongoing restructuring as their traditional role has been changed, and according to the Audit Commission (1989) they were in a transition of *Losing an Empire, Finding a Role*. The nature of this role remains uncertain and often contradictory, and as Wragg et al. (1996) show LEAs were given the responsibility for teacher appraisal in 1991 at a time when other responsibilities were being delegated to schools or to agencies. More recently, the continued emphasis on standards has created an agency role for the LEA over literacy and numeracy, and a complex process of Education Development Planning has been introduced to ensure that performance can be monitored and measured.

The 1988 Education Reform Act is seen as a watershed in the structure of state education in England and Wales, though many trends can been seen in the years prior to this (Feintuck, 1994). Important changes were made to the governance of schools in 1986 (Education [No. 2] Act) in which parental (through a ballot) and community (through co-option) representation was increased and practitioner representation decreased (Deem et al., 1995). Mechanisms and processes to secure increased accountability to parents were introduced through the requirement from 1986 for a governing body to publish an annual report to parents and to hold a parental meeting at least once a year. The nature of governance and the role of governors have been changed by successive legislation in which a governing body has substantial responsibilities for setting the strategic direction of the school, and for the quality and standards of educational provision. Nevertheless, research into the reforms of governing bodies (Deem et al., 1995) shows that this has not empowered individual lay people, or revitalised their communities. It seems that recruitment to governing bodies has not been a democratising process, but a niche marketing exercise to enable business communities to select which schools to support.

The 1988 Education Reform Act illustrates this policy direction through some significant changes in the restructuring of LEA provision: the abolition of the Inner London Education Authority (ILEA); the provision for a parental ballot to enable a school to be 'opted out' of local authority control to that of grant maintained status (GMS); the introduction of city technical colleges (CTCs); the introduction of open enrolment enabling parental choice; local management of schools (LMS) through delegated budgets; and the national curriculum. Local management of schools created a form of site-based performance management in England and Wales in which there were new responsibilities for financial, human and physical resources. The introduction of formula funding meant that schools would receive their budget according to student numbers, and when combined with open enrolment this put the provision of education by the school within a 'quasi-market' which is in direct tension with public sector values based on equity (Le Grand and Bartlett, 1993). The ability to hire, fire, promote and demote staff enables the school to determine the amount and type of staffing, and the nature of contracts. The delegation of budgetary control was designed to enable the culture and practice of identifying site-based resource priorities, the planning and implementation of a budget and the monitoring and evaluation of provision. Other policy changes have impacted increasingly on this with a growing shift in the 1990s towards income generation in which formula funding remains the most significant financial input, but schools are encouraged and directed to seek funding from other sources.

Legislation has also put in place external levers to improve prescribed educational standards and to generate data on the performance of educational institutions. The 1988 Education Act introduced a National Curriculum for children aged 5–16 and national testing was introduced at ages 7, 11 and 14. These Standard Assessment Tasks/Tests (SATs), together with the General Certificate of Secondary Education (GCSE) and post-16 qualifications, were intended to provide evidence of the school's impact on a child's learning, and enable judgements on efficiency and effectiveness to be made. The 1992 Education Act established OfSTED and introduced regular inspections of schools by privatised inspection teams. The OfSTED Framework of Inspection and the inspection process require schools to produce documentation on the management systems and learning processes and policies prior to an inspection visit to the school. As a result of on-site observation and documentary analysis the inspection report identifies the strengths and weaknesses of the educational provision. From September 1997 schools began the second cycle of inspection in which the emphasis was on validating their improvement and effectiveness since the first inspection. In 1992 the first league tables for schools were published in which examination results and statistical measures on attendance and exclusions are presented. Comparisons between schools have been further facilitated by the 'Autumn Package' in which statistical information can be used to measure like with like (DfEE, 2000b). This is meant to improve target-setting for each school and enable it to meet LEA and national targets for literacy and numeracy. The government's 'Fresh Start' policy is designed to close a struggling school and reopen it with a new 'superhead' who is being paid at a high rate, has a new staff and a new school name. So far there have been four high-profile resignations by superheads, and arguments that educational change takes longer than the policy is designed to allow (TES, 2000).

Site-based performance management has changed the structure and practice of employment within schools and colleges. Grace (1995) argues that organisational management is about enabling schools to operate, compete, survive and develop within a market context, and the secularisation of schools has shifted the goals and priorities of educationalists away from learning processes towards budgets, auditing, target-setting, monitoring and evaluation. These changes have facilitated a shift towards human resource management (HRM) in which employees are a resource to be efficiently and effectively deployed in order to meet targets. Commitment to, and integration within, the organisation is achieved through recruitment processes, appraisal schemes, performance-related pay (PRP), and training. At the time of writing PRP is being introduced in English schools through the implementation of the Green Paper *teachers: meeting the challenge of change* (DfEE, 1998). This is based on a discrediting of the achievements of teacher appraisal schemes set up by LEAs from 1991 (Bennett, 1999; Gleeson and Gunter, 2001) and teacher development has been defined by Morris (1998) as performance driven rather than a morally committed process.

Teacher performance has been further promoted through centralised in-service training. In September 1994 the TTA was established and it has created an integrated framework of continuous professional development (CPD) encompassing Initial Teacher Training (ITT), the identification of expert teachers, subject leadership, the role of the special educational needs co-ordinator (SENCO), and headteacher leadership. National standards have been published for practitioners at each of these stages, and for aspiring headteachers a professional qualification, the National Professional Qualification for Headteachers (NPQH), was introduced in 1997 and restructured in 2000. For newly appointed headteachers the Headteacher Leadership and Management Programme (HEADLAMP) scheme was introduced in 1995 with vouchers for purchasing training from licensed providers. In September 1998 the Leadership Programme for Serving Headteachers (LPSH) was introduced, in which headteachers have a business mentor (Bush, 1998). Historically there has been an emphasis on voluntary and pluralistic provision, though recent changes in the funding arrangements and certification of professional development has marginalised HEIs (Ouston, 1998). The restructured 'performative' university (Blackmore and Sachs, 2000, p. 2) means that, as Miller (1995) argues, while academics 'may retain quite high degrees of technical control, they can be seen to be losing "ideological" control of their work' (p. 57). This is more than a change in language, such as from student to customer, but a reorientation of the purposes of higher education as a provider of skilled labour supported by the adoption of corporate management structures and systems.

What this analysis of the introduction of site-based performance management illustrates is that there have been three interrelated levels of change: first, the growth in management functions leading to either the relabelling of practitioner work as leadership and management and/or the appointment of people to leadership and management positions; second, the adoption of private sector management techniques and language such as strategic planning, and performance indicators; and, third, a more fundamental ideological transformation through the reshaping of relationships, values, and the redistribution of power. It seems that there has been an attempt to shift formal approaches to problem identification and resolution from leadership within governance to leadership and management functions 'so that spending problems become budget and contract, rather than political issues' (Deakin and Walsh, 1996, p. 44). The failure to focus on democratising government continues to have consequences, not least in how the continuation of the language and rituals of democracy has led to a disillusionment with so called 'democratic institutions'. This has led to the growth of single-issue pressures groups that have sought recognition through direct action rather than through community involvement. In this sense, government through management is marginalising voices that want to and must be heard, and so it seems that the ungovernability of the 1970s cannot easily be managed away.

Markets and leadership in education

What is evident from the analysis so far is that what is currently in ascendancy is a model of leadership in education which is located in neoliberal versions of the performing school. England and Wales are not unique in the move to restructure education in this way (Bottery, 1999; Esland, 1996), and there is evidence of 'policy borrowing' (Whitty et al., 1998) and 'cloning' (Dimmock, 1998) that can be in the form of global moves such as the operation of the International Monetary Fund (IMF) and the World Bank (Smyth and Shacklock, 1998a). Smyth and Shacklock (1998a) argue that it has not been difficult to make the case 'stick, that schools have "failed" ' (p. 22) and so governments have been able to distance themselves from the responsibilities for democratic development.

Headteachers are being positioned as leaders or managers, in which distinctions between these two processes are being made in order to facilitate the separation of a leadership elite from those whose work is being routinised. Leadership is being defined around notions of controlling uncertainty through charismatic behaviours and strategic tasks, while management is about system maintenance. For this version of the performing school to operate, there are three detectable and interrelated strands in the preferred leadership model for education institutions:

- *Leadership of systems*: the installation and oversight of tasks and structures to enable the control and external accountability requirements to operate, e.g. delegation of budgets, installation of management information systems, strategic development and operational action planning.

- *Leadership of consumers*: controlling the external environment of the school through the use of contract compliance. This is based on the individualising of the relationship between teacher, pupil and parent in which target-setting is about disciplining all stakeholders in the delivery of predetermined and measurable outcomes.
- *Leadership of performance*: controlling the embodied identities and approaches to work so that what is visible in tasks, behaviours, and interactions is about achieving the total integration of the school in the delivery of external policy agendas.

These strands are evident in the mandated and integrated models of leadership presented in the *National Standards* in which the headteacher 'working with the governing body ... provides vision, leadership and direction for the school and ensures that it is managed and organised to meet its aims and targets' (TTA, 1998a, p. 4). As Bell (1999) argues the current emphasis on excellence has put huge responsibilities on the shoulders of headteachers in which there is 'no concept of shared or distributed leadership' (p. 214). Compatible with this is the role of the subject leader who 'provides leadership and direction for the subject and ensures that it is managed and organised to meet the aims and objectives of the school and the subject' (TTA, 1998b, p. 4). Teachers are trained to prescribed standards (TTA, 1998c) that enable assimilation into the leadership and management structures, based on what Hatcher (1994) regards as a clear intention to achieve the compliance of the workforce by 'installing a set of management practices that prevent teachers carrying out a different agenda' (p. 55).

New Labour has continued the deprivileging of public sector groups with more emphasis on cultural than structural change, by confronting what Blair (1999) has called the 'forces of conservatism' that has a 'culture of excuses ... a culture that tolerates low ambition, rejects excellence, treats poverty as an excuse for failure'. Hartley (1999) calls the process going on in schools to achieve this as 're-culturing' (p. 311) in which the dichotomy is bridged by the internal market where the management 'sells' and the teacher 'buys into' the vision and mission. Through this 'manipulation of intimacy' (Blackmore, 1999, p. 38), relationships are controlled in order to get the job done. The emotional work involved leads Hartley (1999) to ask if this is a process of 're-enchantment' in the workplace: 'the worker/teacher may now come to be regarded as the internal customer, a customer who is perhaps even to be "delighted" by management, and who will in turn "delight" the pupil' (p. 318). This development of the flexible 'preferred teacher' (Smyth and Shacklock, 1998a, p. 107 ff) and 'endlessly re-trainable employee' (Beck, 1999, p. 228) will close the loophole of professional expertise and knowledge through the eradication of professional judgement. The differentiation in staffing through PRP will need a cultural bond of employee to employer to support it, and this will need to be embodied and symbolised through language, dress, physicality, and the breakdown in the boundary between home and work (Hatcher, 1994; Whitty et al., 1998). This is creating a 'culture of "performativity" rather than an enrichment of learning opportunities' (Whitty et al., 1998, p. 87), and the teacher as facilitator of the National Curriculum can move around and be slotted into and out of the timetable. This 'modernisation' is being presented as being about new teachers for new times, and to achieve the goal of a 'world class education system' by using funding mechanisms to 'motivate and increase the professionalism of teachers and encourage risk and ambition' (Barber and Sebba, 1999, p. 187). However, what is 'best practice' is highly political and, as Crump (1997) argues, in Australia it has been used to 'blame workers rather than management for poor productivity and profitability' (p. 46). Questions continue to be raised about the endurance of power structures and, in particular, the gendering of education policy (Leonard, 1998). Blackmore (1999) argues that improvements in equal opportunities are more about enabling management to work better than about connecting the educational process to broader democratic and social justice problems.

This analysis raises important issues about the relationship between the theorisation of these developments, and what is happening in the day-to-day realities of work. Questions need to be asked about the positioning of the practitioner through the codification and interpretation of policy texts, and Bourdieu's theory of practice conceptualises this as a struggle. Whitty et al. (1998, p.86) argue that headteachers and principals are 'generally supportive' of educational reform but staff are not and, while senior managers have been more privileged in the process, there is evidence that 'their positions have become more vulnerable as they are held more personally to account' (p. 62). There is evidence that teachers have not fully embraced the management imperative and language because there are deep contradictions in what they are being told is good performance management practice, and their experiences of what matters in their work with children and the community (Smyth and Shacklock, 1998a; Whitty and Power, 1997).

Seddon (1999) has asked us to think about change in different ways to the traditional rational approaches, and so she theorises from her empirical work that teachers and leaders are 'capacity-builders' in which they recognise their changed context but are steadfast in their commitment to the emancipatory goals of education. In Seddon's view this requires critical thinking and practice that is about locating and redefining work within the bigger organisational and policy context. In this way the future is not visioned but is worked for, a future in which it is possible to 'pick away at inequality . . . the efforts of these individuals and groups are constrained by the past and shaped by prevailing orthodoxies but they can still be directed intelligently towards willed-for and worked-for scenarios that offer alternatives to, and practical critiques of, capitalist triumphalism and its neo-liberal programs' (ibid., p. 37). This is consistent with work being done on the experiences of headship/principalship where research evidence shows that at local level there are complex interpretations regarding position and positioning over time. Work by Hall (1996), Smulyan (2000) and Strachan (1999) on women headteachers/principals shows how identity has been shaped by the interplay between the headteacher and the local/national setting in which they are working. This reveals the importance of conceptualising leadership as a social and political relationship that is visible within the lived contradictions and dilemmas brought about by the exercise of agency in tension with external policy interventions in a particular educational context.

Summary

The endurance and current ascendancy of neo-liberal versions of the performing school means that educational professionals are being objectified and stratified into leaders and followers. Leadership is being defined as particular tasks and behaviours that enable those who are responsible to be accountable for learning outcomes and measures of school improvement. This move is an attempt to structure professional identity through mandating and training the particular social relationships needed to sustain technicist job requirements. However, it does not float free of organisational and personal histories that also shape and enable agency, and how real people with real lives struggle within and through the contradictions that challenge their values. This raises questions about the origins and process in knowledge production as revealed through a critical reading of theory and research, and the people, project positions and knowledge claims being made. Of interest is the structural and institutional location of knowledge workers who research and theorise about leadership, and the habitus of 'leadership watchers' connected to questions about where their gaze falls, e.g. primary or secondary, senior or middle management, grounded theory or theory informed. Furthermore, we might ask how knowledge workers are responding to the politics of education policy and whether they are positioning their work in ways that enable policy to happen, or are they seeking to reveal and sustain alternatives?

Already in this chapter I have drawn on intellectual resources that have enabled me to show both debate and how educational change is being conceptualised, researched and theorised. These leadership knowledge workers can be revealed in more depth by analysing the various positions and debates within educational studies, and this is the focus of the next chapter.

3

Leadership in Educational Studies

This chapter is about knowledge positions and positioning around leadership through a study of school effectiveness and school improvement, education management, and critical studies. In doing this I use the labels and self-positioning adopted by field members themselves, though my interpretation and critical reading will clearly have an impact. What is also problematic is that positions change or remain stable, and not all positions may be visible or fully in focus. I present the trends and tendencies rather than objectify fixed and certain accounts. I am well aware of the dangers involved because the current anti-intellectual climate in education means that the dialogue I describe could be characterised as bickering. However, leadership is a highly political issue within which struggles over competing versions of the performing school are taking place in homes, classrooms, offices and seminar rooms. These are not technical matters but go to the heart of governance and the development of democracy. People have invested and continue to invest their lives, resources and reputations in education and, while no area of social and occupational life is immune from bad behaviour, it would be a distortion as well as bad faith to characterise debate as inevitably and unproductively esoteric, posturing and irrelevant.

School effectiveness and school improvement

Reynolds et al. (2000a) describe three main strands of school effectiveness research: first, school effects research which takes a scientific approach using input-output models; second, case studies of effective schools and classrooms using quantitative and qualitative methods; and, third, the developing change processes of school improvement. The origins of this work in North America and the UK lie in a reaction to studies that argued that educational outcomes were determined by wider social and economic factors (Coleman et al., 1966; Jencks et al., 1972). Studies such as Rutter et al. (1979) and Mortimore et al. (1988) in the UK show the importance of school effects, and case study work has enabled these effects to be studied in depth (Myers, 1996). More recent studies have been undertaken into effective departments and the role of middle management in securing improved learning outcomes (Sammons et al., 1997). Reynolds and Teddlie (2000) argue that the combination of school and teacher effectiveness provides the potential to model the complex relationship between different variables operating at different levels, and so what is emerging is an 'educational effectiveness paradigm' (p. 159). Knowledge production is based in centres such as the International School Effectiveness and Improvement Centre (ISEIC) at the Institute of Education in London. Collaboration has been facilitated by the American Educational Research Association (AERA) special interest group on School Effectiveness, the formation of the International Congress for School Effectiveness and Improvement (ICSEI), and the journal *School Effectiveness and School Improvement* (Reynolds, 2000).

Essentially the focus within school effectiveness research has been on the identification and multilevel measurement of 'key determinants of school effectiveness in secondary and primary schools' (Sammons et al., 1995) and these are shown in Figure 3.1. School effectiveness stakes its claim around an ontology of the unitary organisation combined with a rational epistemology of cause and effect connections between what schools do and pupil outcomes (Teddlie et al., 2000b). Theorising tends to be through a systems approach (input–process–output–feedback) in which outputs are the product of the organisational processing of inputs. In other words, 'effective secondary schools are not simply schools with effective teachers' (Sammons et al., 1997, p. 178), and the context (inputs) does not automatically determine outputs, because there are institutional and organisational whole-school and departmental effects: 'in terms of pupil progress (the value added) school effects are much more important than background factors such as age, gender and social class (being roughly four times more important for reading progress, and ten times for mathematics progress)' (Sammons et al., 1995, p. 6).

As Figure 3.1 shows leadership is given a very high profile, and Reynolds and Teddlie (2000) tell us: 'we do not know of a study that has not shown that leadership is important within effective schools, with that leadership nearly always being provided by the headteacher' (p. 141). Effective leaders are 'firm and purposeful' in leading improvement; 'participative' by sharing leadership and delegating; and, 'the leading professional' through their pedagogic and curriculum knowledge (Sammons et al., 1995, p. 8). The interrelationship of leadership with the other ten factors is important as headteacher impact on learning outcomes is more likely to be mediated through teachers and the conditions for learning established within the school. This is further developed by Reynolds and Teddlie (2000) who draw on Murphy's (1990) work on instructional leadership which is concerned with the management of the curriculum and learning within a positive and motivational climate for pupils and

1. Professional leadership	Firm and purposeful A participative approach The leading professional
2. Shared vision and goals	Unity of purpose Consistency of practice Collegiality and collaboration
3. A learning environment	An orderly atmosphere An attractive working environment
4. Concentration on teaching and learning	Maximisation of learning time Academic emphasis Focus on achievement
5. Purposeful teaching	Efficient organisation Clarity of purpose Structured lessons Adaptive practice
6. High expectations	High expectations all round Communicating expectations Providing intellectual challenge
7. Positive reinforcement	Clear and fair discipline Feedback
8. Monitoring progress	Monitoring pupil performance Evaluating school performance
9. Pupil rights and responsibilities	Raising pupil self-esteem Positions of responsibility Control of work
10. Home–school partnership	Parental involvement in their children's learning
11. A learning organisation	School-based staff development

Figure 3.1 Eleven factors for effective schools (Sammons et al., 1995, p. 8)

teachers. Leadership is therefore synonymous with headship and contingent upon pedagogic outcomes.

Field members have argued in favour of caution regarding the isolation and measurement of variables in ways that can produce generic and predictive statements of effectiveness. Researchers are concerned to build and develop research designs so that the stability of effects can be measured over time (Gray et al., 1999; Sammons et al., 1996a). In addition, field members argue that the school effects list is not a blueprint to be applied 'mechanically' to a school, but instead the school context needs to be taken into account (Teddlie et al., 2000c). It is argued that effectiveness research is valuable in the process of school self-evaluation and this connects how school improvement as a change process can be used to improve the conditions in which learning takes place.

Teddlie et al. (2000a) argue that those who are interested in school effectiveness research are no longer just the 'scientists' who are concerned to measure school effects, but there are two other groups: 'pragmatists' who are interested in the implications for school improvement, and the 'humanists' who are 'committed to the improvement of practice more than the generation of research knowledge' (p. 42). However, Reynolds et al. (2000b) show that referencing and citations indicate little use of effectiveness work by those who write about improvement, and in the UK there has been little collaboration in spite of the government's funding and support for effectiveness and improvement work in schools. Nevertheless, there have been projects and work that have shown the validity and appropriateness of connections between the two (Gray et al., 1999). The boundary between school effectiveness and school improvement has shifted with the case being made that the time is right for a merger to take place based on the knowledge deficiencies of each field remaining on their own.

Important research has focused on school processes and not just outcomes, and this has produced international collaborations, e.g. Stoll and Fink (1996) and Joyce, Calhoun and Hopkins (1999). Leadership in school improvement is often concerned with leader–follower relationships and like effectiveness research it is contingent on pedagogy (MacGilchrist et al., 1997). Increasingly the dominant approach to leadership is that of transformational behaviours and functions in which charismatic leaders are central to the bringing about of change (Leithwood et al., 1999). Change through a planned process is a strong feature of work around strategic development planning (Hargreaves and Hopkins, 1991; Hopkins and MacGilchrist, 1998; MacGilchrist et al., 1995). School improvement is also interested in imposed change such as how the OfSTED inspections identify schools to be 'failing', and so the field has turned its attention to ineffectiveness and the process of turning a school around (Gray and Wilcox, 1995; Stoll and Myers, 1997).

Research and theorising about change is in many ways a field in itself, and significant here is Fullan (with Stiegelbauer, 1991; 1997; 1999) and Hargreaves' research on the impact of change on teachers and their work (1994; 1998; and Evans, 1997). Illustrative of this is the *What's Worth Fighting For . . .* trilogy (Fullan, 1992; Fullan and Hargreaves, 1992; Hargreaves and Fullan, 1998) in which the authors seek to engage teachers and headteachers with the problems generated from the inter-relationship between themselves, others and changes in education and beyond, so that they can ' "fight for" fundamentally positive changes that will benefit themselves, students, and society, and do this with the full knowledge of the reality of the task' (Hargreaves and Fullan, 1998, p. xi). Integral to this is research based on partnerships between schools and members of HEIs, in which surveys, interviews, observations, feedback sessions and discussion have been used. Illustrative of this is the Improving the Quality of Education for All project (IQEA) in which leadership is one of the six conditions needed to support teaching and learning (the other five are staff development, involvement, co-ordination, enquiry and reflection, and collaborative planning [Hopkins et al., 1997]). From this work leadership is conceptualised as a shared function and the project team have taken their work a stage further and devised the classroom conditions needed to support learning: authentic relationships, boundaries and expectations, planning for teaching, teaching repertoire, pedagogic partnerships and reflection on teaching (Hopkins et al., 1997). The orientation here is to make teaching more effective, and there is a strong emphasis on processes and techniques combined with teacher professional development. Joyce et al. (1999) have worked on the connection between whole-school factors and the classroom by reviewing school structures and approaches that support learning, and take a community approach to decision-making. They argue that leadership is a collective process through what they call the 'Responsible Parties' made up of teachers, parents and the community who are concerned to inquire and seek to improve the school.

In summary, this field or fields have been struggling over the relationship between school effectiveness and school improvement, in which there seems to be a strong case for merger. School effectiveness works on developing more sophisticated modelling while school improvement focuses on school and classroom processes. This is a field that eschews politics but is in reality, like other knowledge production in other fields in educational studies, highly political. However, and unlike other knowledge workers, school effectiveness and school improvement has been officially consecrated by current government policy in which the scientific epistemology of school effects and the processes of improvement have become integrated into the political goals of New Labour.

Education management

The origins of education management lie within what was known in England and Wales (and is still known internationally) as educational administration and was developed within networks that began abroad through the IIP, the CCEA (later CCEAM), and at home the formation of BEAS (later BEMAS, and now the British Educational Leadership Management and Administration Society, BELMAS). This networking provided theorising and research opportunities to support practitioners through training. The field has grown rapidly with extensive provision in postgraduate courses, and Doe (1997) reports that 'more than 4,000 senior managers are spending £7 million and large amounts of their spare time on part-time degrees' in education management. Field members associated themselves with particular journals such as the BELMAS journal *Educational Management and Administration*, originally *Educational Administration Bulletin*, and from 1976 it was called *Educational Administration* (Hughes, 1997; Strain, 1997), *School Leadership and Management* (previously *School Organisation*) and, internationally, *Educational Administration Quarterly* and the *Journal of Educational*

Administration. Field members are actively involved in BERA and AERA special interest groups, there are the BELMAS annual and research conferences, and in 1999 the Standing Conference for Educational Leadership and Management (SCRELM) was formed.

Field membership is heterogeneous, and Fitz (1999) argues that there are three positions, the 'academic', the 'practitioner' and the 'entrepreneur', and he shows how the individual career trajectory is likely to have included all three. A field member in a university may have begun their professional practice as a school teacher, engaged in consultancy work, and currently undertakes scholarly research. The balance within an individual's portfolio of activities could be determined through the agency of interest interplayed with the requirements and expectations of employment within a particular institutional setting. The purpose of the field is the study and practice of management (Bush, 1995) and field members focus on what does and/or what ought to happen when management in an educational institution takes place. This has been particularly important in periods of educational restructuring such as comprehensivisation and, from 1988, site-based management. Training and professional development is about improving capability (Glatter, 1979) in which the practitioner can use a range of concepts and models drawn from the social sciences. Debate over knowledge claims can be seen through studying landmark texts and articles from prominent field members in the area of the preparation of educational administrators, managers and leaders (Baron et al., 1969; Glatter, 1972), theory (Baron and Taylor, 1969; Bush, 1995; Hughes, 1978; Hughes et al., 1985), research (Baron, 1979; Saran and Trafford, 1990) and the ongoing development of the field (Bone, 1982; 1992; Bush et al., 1999; Glatter, 1972; 1979; 1997; Harries-Jenkins, 1984; 1985; Howell, 1978). I illustrate the ongoing debates within the field by discussing the ongoing struggle regarding the scientific nature of knowledge generated by Greenfield's work.

Greenfield's challenge and legacy is documented in a series of papers that were brought together by Greenfield with Peter Ribbins (Greenfield and Ribbins, 1993). The collection achieved international acclaim and presents Greenfield's unfolding critique and his engagement with other writers such as Hodgkinson (1978) and Evers and Lakomski (1991a; 1991b). In 1974, at the Bristol session of the International Intervisitation Programme (IIP), Greenfield gave a paper in which he questioned the legitimacy of the Theory Movement in North America led by writers such as Griffiths (1958; 1964; 1969), Halpin (1958) and Simon (1945) who put the emphasis on creating an objective and reliable theory in which facts and values are separated. Greenfield's thesis is that organisations exist in the subjective phenomenology of the individual and are invented social reality: 'organisations come into existence when we talk and act with others. We strive to communicate with these others, to touch them, to understand them and often to control them' (Greenfield and Ribbins, 1993, p. 53). Greenfield was concerned about the technicist approach of management science and its impact on the preparation of administrators, and he argues that such an approach fails to enable the professional to engage with issues to do with power, moral responsibility and legitimacy.

The impact of Greenfield's critique of educational administration threw the field into 'intellectual turmoil' (Griffiths, 1979). This still resonates today as Evers and Lakomski (1991a; 1991b) argue that his attack on science means that we need a better science. Gronn and Ribbins (1999) argue that this rational, cognitive approach to theory excludes emotion and values and hence raises questions about how we decide what is better. We also need to note that there were some highly contentious and deeply personal attacks on him. Greenfield (1978) states: 'somewhat like St. Sebastian, I suppose, I'd rather be in pain as long as the crowd understands what the ceremony is about. But it is hard just to be written off, ignored or buried' (pp. 86–7). As Gronn (1985) shows he was on an 'intellectual pilgrimage' in which he knew that he had come from the very academy that he was criticising, but he was uncertain about where he was going. In a more recent interview with Ribbins (Greenfield and Ribbins, 1993) he recounts that his only aim was to engage in an intellectual debate about ideas which for him were not clearly formed or set in concrete. Furthermore, he admits his naivety in not realising that in attempting to engage in intellectual debate he was not only attacking ideas but also the careers and reputations of those who had supported those ideas. However, he was not prepared for the inability of the field to rise above personal attacks and innuendo: 'I discovered something about my field: its pettiness, its calcified and limited vision, its conventionality, its hostility to dissenting opinion, its vituperativeness' (Greenfield and Ribbins, 1993, p. 247). Greenfield (1978) argues that his lack of an invitation to the 1978 IIP is connected to the inability of the field to engage in a dialogue about theory and, while there is a genuine desire to talk, they do not want to be involved in 'an unfortunate battle in rather poor taste which somehow demeans theory and the past glory of the field of study' (p. 83). He shows exasperation in being unable to get his colleagues to ask different questions, and he is worried about the consequences of 'the tidy minded' (ibid., p. 90) on the intellectual development of the field.

The Greenfield debate set the tone and agenda for the 1970s onwards, and field members at the 1974 IIP conference and afterwards witnessed at first hand what happens when a field member raises epistemological questions, and what it means to be a member of a field which resolves intellectual debates through exclusion. As Hodgkinson (1993) argues 'Greenfield remains a stimulating irritant to the ranks of the professoriate. For some a burr under their saddles, for others a continuing inspiration' (p. xiv). It also seems to indicate a problematic role for the field member because debates about theory may not rest easily with the demand for efficient and effective problem-solving. Greenfield's work is in the tradition of what Hoyle (1986) terms theory for understanding in contrast to theory for action or improvement. Increasingly within the field the latter has come to dominate with a growth in entrepreneurial work that supports technicist strategic and operational problem-solving. Like the field(s) of school effectiveness and school improvement, charismatic transformational leadership and the school as a unitary organisation is often unreflexively accepted. There is very little evidence of field members discussing the knowledge claims on which 'management by ticklist' (Davies, 1990) is based, or that there are controversies which remain unsettled. It seems that the emphasis has shifted from the pre-1988 period where there was an interest in describing and understanding organisations through the use of social science theories such as the work of Cohen and March (1989) and Weick (1989), to the normative prescription of generic process collegiality such as teams and leadership vision (Gunter, 1997).

Bush (1999) asks the question whether the field is in crisis or at a crossroads, and his motivation along with that of other field members is to ask about the relationship between the policy context and field activity. Glatter (1999) is interested in how field members position themselves at a time when the TTA has centralised the provision of training, preparation and the accreditation of practitioner professional development. However, those who respect the Greenfield legacy have kept the debate about values open and Glatter (1987) calls 'for those involved in the management of education to reassert their competence not only in implementation (essential though that is) but also to contribute, together with many other groups, to the debate about values, basic assumptions, goals and policies' (p. 11). Simkins (1999) argues that rather than see theory as a range of conceptual possibilities for the practitioner, we should see theory as a contested domain on which field members take positions: descriptive or normative, bureaucratic or collegiality. For Simkins trying to make sense of the burgeoning literature produced within the field over the last 30 years is about identifying the ongoing themes of power (in the tradition of Hoyle [1982]) and values (in the tradition of Greenfield) which structure the positions taken by field members. Hall's (1999b) work on gender reminds the field that there are conceptual places where it needs to go in order to 'challenge the androcentrism of much of the discourse about leadership and management' (p. 157).

In summary, the field of education management has engaged and continues to engage in work that supports and challenges the practitioner in the strategic and operational leadership and management of educational organisations. However, there is concern that within the current policy context an imbalance is being created in which instrumentalist projects are coming to dominate and are supported by a collaboration between entrepreneurial activity and government agencies. In addition, the growing ascendancy of the school effectiveness and school improvement field(s) and the colonisation of the language of performance management is challenging the field's territory. For those in the field who cherry-pick, package and trade 'know-how' then these developments are important short-term business opportunities. For those in the field who are in the Greenfield tradition and are interested in knowledge debates within leadership experiences then there are longer-term intellectual opportunities to orientate the field around the dynamic links between management and leadership with teaching and learning (Bolam, 1999; Cordingley, 1999).

Critical studies

Critical studies is a label that captures the intellectual work in a range of fields with many specialised interests reflected in the range of journals, such as *British Journal of Sociology of Education, Gender and Education* and *Journal of Education Policy*. Those who take a critical approach to research and theory are concerned with enduring power structures and the impact these have on the lives and work of educationalists and communities. As Smyth et al. (2000) show, there are features of critical research which are about challenging accepted interpretations, focusing on those who are marginalised, locating questions within social, political and economic contexts, emancipatory in seeking equity, and inclusive of the researcher role within the process. This type of work uses research methodologies that seek to capture how leadership is experienced as a political re-lationship, and in particular how teachers and students can and do exercise leadership. Theory and theorising is central to how power is con-ceptualised, and some theorists draw on labour process theory (Ozga, 1995; Smyth et al., 2000); others use the work of particular thinkers, e.g. Bates draws on Habermas (Park, 1999), and Ball's work has been exten-sively informed by Foucault (Ball, 1990a; 1990b). Given the complexity of critical studies, I use the example of Education Policy Sociology as a way of illustrating the critical orientation.

Deem argues that there has been a 'policy turn' with a shift from narrating policy developments to a more theoretically informed and critical stance taken towards a highly politicised and large volume of education policy and legislation from the 1980s onwards (Deem, 1996a; Deem et al., 1995). Policy sociology has produced a significant body of work about education policy which is 'rooted in the social science tradition, historically informed and drawing on qualitative and illumi-native techniques' (Ozga, 1987, p. 14). This field has engaged in lively debates about the relationship between the state and policy development with conflicting views between pluralist and neo-Marxist interpretations (Bowe et al., 1992; Dale, 1989; Gewirtz and Ozga, 1990). Dialogue is concerned with the interplay between the economic determinism of the capitalist state to control education, and the ability of those at school level to control through mediation and possibly resistance. Hatcher and Troyna (1994) accept the ability of policy to be reinterpreted at institutional level, but they argue that the dominance of policy elites structures the exercise of power. Ball (1994a) argues that the Marxist conceptualisation of the state disempowers the ordinary voices of teachers, children and parents, and the significance of this should not be lost under the weight of theory.

This type of debate enables us to understand where field members position themselves regarding leadership, and whether a headteacher is positioned by the economic interests that control the state or is capable of agency through exercising professional judgement and discretion. Following on from this, critical knowledge workers have gone on to explore how teachers and headteachers are experiencing leadership in a market-driven and managerialist education system (Ball, 1990a; 1994b; Gillborn, 1994; Menter et al., 1997), and have explored the capacity of teachers to become policy-makers and exercise agency to develop alternative ways of working (Ozga, 2000; White and Crump, 1993). Teachers and students who tell their stories enable the struggles surrounding identities, relationships and meaning to be made visible (de Lyon and Widdowson Migniuolo, 1989). Mac an Ghaill (1994) tells the story of being given a bunch of flowers by a male pupil. A fight broke out in the playground involving the pupil, and in the staffroom he faced ridicule. On being called to the headteacher's office and being told 'he had gone too far this time' he realised that the concern was not with the playground fight but the exchange of flowers between two males, one a teacher and one a pupil, one white and one Muslim. This seemed to threaten the institutional logic of how teachers and pupils inhabiting particular roles should behave and be seen to behave: 'in this school, the white dominant teacher perception of Muslim male students was that they were intrinsically more sexist than white males. These teachers were undoubtedly confused by the fact that the student who gave me the flowers was a Muslim' (ibid., pp. 1–2). It seems that dominance in leadership and management is the means through which social and political power structures can be maintained. Central to critical work is not only to reveal this but also to shift our gaze towards alternative understandings of leadership within pedagogic relationships between teachers and pupils (see Chapter 9).

Grace's (1995; 1997) work on critical leadership studies is helpful here as he argues that the current model of charismatic transformational leadership lacks the necessary radicalism needed to pursue issues of equity, because there are enduring features that help to shape headship in England such as the headmaster tradition. Illustrative of this is teacher professional autonomy and Ball (1987) shows that it is in the gift of the headteacher rather than a professional entitlement of the teacher. Consequently, it is a myth to argue that professional autonomy has been used by teachers to defend themselves against modernising teamwork imperatives. Professional autonomy has always been relative to both the macro and micro context in which teachers' working lives are located, and as Ozga (1995) has argued relations between teachers and the state have always been problematic. At the micro level, the headteacher can and will withdraw resources or block a change if s/he sees that the rules of the game are being challenged in some way: 'as soon as discussion becomes oppositional, it is redefined as subversive and disloyal – very powerful concepts. Such redefinition serves to factionalize the staff and stigmatize and isolate opponents' (Ball, 1987, p. 137). This is not only an English issue as Hsieh and Shen (1998) show that when teachers talk about leadership they tend to 'use "they" rather than "we" when discussing the skills, knowledge and value of a good educational leader' (p. 118). The endurance of the headmaster tradition, that Ball (1987) identifies as being central to the denial of authentic professional autonomy, is currently being reworked as an executive function regarding teacher and student performance. Teachers who lose out in the contest over what is the 'preferred teacher' (Smyth and Shacklock, 1998a) are no longer just isolated in meetings and staffrooms, but are being moved on, made redundant and given early retirement. It is argued that the separation between headteacher and teachers pre-dates 1988, and site-based performance management has exacerbated the growing separation between managers and managed.

In summary, critical knowledge workers engage in what Morley and Rassool (1999) describe as 'policy archaeology' (p. 131) to uncover the workings of power structures by charting and theorising the experiences of those who inhabit them. This work is concerned to theorise the interplay between agency and structure, and to use theories of power as a lens through which to describe, understand and explain. In Ball's (1995) terms, theory enables us to 'begin from what is normally excluded' (p. 267) by providing language and conceptual tools to question. As Ball argues, not any theory will do, and he is both critical of theory that is instrumental and about making things work better, as well as a traditional form of social science theory that is pure and hard, and seeks to dominate. He goes on to argue and use theory that 'rests upon complexity, uncertainty and doubt and upon a reflexivity about its own production and its claims to knowledge about the social' (ibid., p. 269). This challenges the traditional view of intellectual work and shifts the emphasis away from an elite caste to being 'a cultural critic offering perspective rather than truth' (ibid., p. 268). Consequently, through a commitment to the development of democracy, the detrimental impact of restructuring on the working lives of teachers can be revealed and alternative understandings of educational effectiveness and improvement can be presented.

Boundaries

In presenting the analysis so far there is an assumption of clearly defined boundaries. Certainly, boundaries are visible through journals, networks, the validation of postgraduate courses, job titles and the designation of chairs, the focus and title of research centres, and peer review processes in appointments, publications and research. These boundaries are also reinforced by how enduring economic and political interests, as evident through government policy processes, give support to and consecrate particular preferred knowledge production.

There is cross-border traffic, for example in who is invited to write in edited collections (e.g. see Busher and Saran, 1995a; Gray et al., 1996). Greenfield's work is a resource that a range of knowledge workers draw on for inspiration (Grace, 1997; Greenfield and Ribbins, 1993; Park, 1999). What seems to underpin the movement across boundaries is epistemological orientation in knowledge production, and this impacts on positions regarding agency and structure. There is a strong scientific approach to knowledge production in leadership studies that could lead to a description as a 'movement' or, given the evangelical nature of much of the writing, as a 'cult' where you are either in or out (Ouston, 1999). Stakes are made here by school effectiveness researchers who are concerned with objective cause and effect relationships, and this is a place where many in the field of educational management are also epistemologically comfortable and this is illustrated by work about organisational effectiveness through technical systems and processes such as how to market and how to plan. Perhaps the popularity of this position merely reflects the point made by Anderson (1996) that there is one dominant approach to knowledge, and: 'while debates about alternative paradigms are carried on around the margins of the field, the structural–functionalist mainstream continues to remain dominant by absorbing these new perspectives into its discourse' (p. 948). In this way leadership could be an example of what Hartley (1998) describes as a 'modernist makeover' (p. 154) in which new language and the relabelling of work is absorbed but the knowledge claims underpinning models of good practice are essentially modernist rational control systems.

An alternative position is humanist, about moral values, and for some knowledge workers it is philosophical. The orientation tends to be concerned with describing and understanding the experiences of those who are working within leadership roles in schools. This position is attractive to many in school improvement and educational management, and is illustrated by collaborations across boundaries, the widespread engagement with Fullan's work on educational change, and the use of qualitative/biographical methods to gather leadership experiences. While the emphasis on action is evident (schools have to be led and managed on a Monday morning!), those who are located in a critical epistemology are more concerned with how power structures within and outside educational institutions impact on the actions that can and cannot be taken. In other words, are educational leaders victims of oppressive systems or can they exercise agency and retain their professional capacities? This type of question does lead to boundary skirmishes, and school effectiveness has been criticised from a broad range of knowledge workers in educational studies, e.g. Hatcher (1998), Harber and Davies (1997), Ouston

(1999), Morley and Rassool (1999) and Slee et al., 1998. It is argued that the failure of school effectiveness to have an explicit theory of power leads to work that shows how the field is implicated in enduring and existing power structures. Morley and Rassool (1999) argue that: 'school effectiveness and school improvement are powerful policy condensates, demanding consensus and orthodoxy' and they go on to say: 'they exemplify the steering at a distance trend in public policy whereby education is more overtly tied in to national economic interests while giving the appearance of site-based autonomy' (p. 135). As Thrupp (2000) shows, field members have raised concerns that their work has been 'abused' by governments and, given the global nature of activity, 'they cannot be held responsible for everything done in the name of school effectiveness' (p. 16). Nevertheless, Thrupp identifies the contradictory situation that affects positioning in the difficulty of being both critical of education policy but at the same time seeking funding that is about implemention.

Border clashes between education administration/management and critical studies have also been about how epistemological assumptions have led to charges and counter-charges of ideological commitment. The field of education management has been critiqued for its highly technicist nature (Angus, 1994; Ball, 1995; Ozga, 1992), and a debate has opened up between Caldwell and Spinks (1988; 1992; 1998) and a range of international scholars (Grace, 1995; Gunter, 1997; Smyth, 1993; Whitty et al., 1998) regarding the politics of site-based performance management. In the late 1970s Glatter (1979) analysed the relationship between management studies and policy studies as a macro–micro continuum, and he argued that the division between the two was one of convenience rather than conceptual. Viewed from the 1990s this continuum seems to have fractured and Ball (1995) argues that there is now a distinction between policy scholarship that seeks to use theory to be 'destructive, disruptive and violent' (p. 266), and policy science that provides the technical answers to received problems. More worrying still is the growth in policy entrepreneurship where the intention is: 'not to research practices, but to change them into the image of policy' (p. 265). Ball argues that the flourishing of policy science and policy entrepreneurship means that the 'academy is tamed' (ibid., p. 259) in which there has been a repositioning in the relationship between the teaching, and research, within higher education and the state.

It would be very easy to write these debates off and characterise the occasional bad temper as normal to academic work and, so, irrelevant to getting the job done in schools and classrooms. Such an approach is an attempt to tidy up complex issues around epistemology and theorising in ways that support endemic pragmatic action at the expense of knowing about and developing alternatives to that action. We need to be aware of how the positions and positioning that seek to be dominant in their own terms may be dominated by the interests they serve. What is particularly interesting is how particular epistemological positions are popular places to be, and the competition over knowledge claims reveals not only the habitus underlying position, but also asks questions about how political and economic interests position and marginalise other leadership work. As Carr and Hartnett (1996) argue, 'ideas count' (p. 130) but how they are weighed and made to matter is connected to enduring power structures. These structures may be global (Bottery, 1999) in the promotion of generic ways of working, and can be in our language so that we adopt words like 'improvement' in ways that mean we are doing the ideological work of particular interest groups (Smyth and Dow, 1998; Willmott, 1999a). Such dilemmas facing knowledge workers in HEIs are not new, and work by Hammersley (1996), Whitty (1985) and Young (1998) on the rise and fall of the sociology of education but the endurance of sociological enquiry in education, raises issues about how knowledge workers are able to make their own choices regarding their professional practice or the extent to which those choices are made for them.

While we know that the work of the academy has changed through the mechanisms for the funding of research and the introduction of performance systems, it would be a misrepresentation to argue that there is a direct connection between the dispositions of a knowledge worker in an HEI and government policy. At the same time, as Ball (1997) argues, it would also be a distortion to claim detached objectivity through a 'scientific vocabulary' (p. 264). We need to understand how educational problems are constructed, shaped, identified and worked on: 'the idea that human sciences like educational studies stand outside or above the political agenda of the management of the population or somehow have a neutral status embodied in a free-floating progressive rationalism are dangerous and debilitating conceits' (Ball, 1997, p. 264).

Language and labelling

Dialogue enables us to investigate the labelling of people as leaders, and their actions as leading and leadership. It could be argued that leadership and management are about the same thing, but Figure 3.2 shows how they are currently being distinguished. This divide assumes that leadership is strategic and is about enabling particular personal attributes and behaviours to build followership within an organisation, while management is more about technical activity of system maintenance, monitoring and evaluation. Hodgkinson (1991; 1996) argues that there is a distinction between administration and management, in which the former is about values and the latter is about facts, and that leadership is within administration (he is using administration in the sense of policy-making). While discussing and clarifying the language we use and the meanings we attach to it are important, what we also need to ask is why do we want to call what we do leadership, who wants this type of label and why? When and why did we start talking about governors, students

Leadership	Management
'Building and maintaining an organisational culture' (Schein, 1985)	'Building and maintaining an organisational structure' (Schein, 1985)
'Establishing a mission for the school, giving a sense of direction' (Louis and Miles, 1992) 1992)	'Designing and carrying out plans, getting things done, working effectively with people' (Louis and Miles,
'Doing the right thing' (Bennis and Nanus, 1985)	'Doing things right' (Bennis and Nanus, 1985)

Figure 3.2 Distinctions between leadership and management (MacGilchrist et al., 1997, p. 13)

and parents as stakeholders rather than as democratic citizens? These types of questions require historical work, because as Hartley (1997) argues management theory is 'situated in time and space' (p. 48) and is influenced by structures and culture at the time. Could it be that we are now beyond leaders and leadership, and are living at a time of performers and performing? Looking at the intellectual history of a field, then, we can see labelling is a place of struggle, and central to this is whether there is just a change of name or whether knowledge claims underpinning the label have changed.

In the 1960s Baron and Taylor were concerned to establish and debate the meaning of educational administration and a significant text that dominated thinking and practice through the 1970s, was *Educational Administration and the Social Sciences* (1969). The book is the product of contact with the mature field in North America and its relevance to understanding what was required to develop the field in England and Wales. Taylor (1969) describes the work of the educational administrator as being both about what we would now call management: 'concerned with the acquisition, control and distribution within a social system of scarce educational resources', and what we now call leadership: 'decision-making, communicating, evaluating, supervising, and so on' (p. 207). Taylor argues that administrative work is undertaken by headteachers, deans and heads of department in universities and colleges, and by Her Majesty's Inspectorate (HMI), local authority advisers and inspectors. Field leaders had been professionally socialised into seeing management as activity connected to the lay governance of Board Schools and then primary schools (Baron and Howell, 1974).

The main educational change in the 1960s and 1970s that led practitioners to seek support regarding changes in their work was comprehensivisation, and it was increasingly recognised that headteachers were uneasy at being called administrators (Baron and Taylor, 1969). Educational restructuring led to demands for professional development opportunities, and Taylor worked with headteachers to develop in-tray exercises and simulations in which to investigate management issues and, in particular, planned change. A worry expressed at the time was the danger of too much pragmatism, and the possibility that practitioners would not see the importance of theory. In particular, Taylor (1976) was concerned that short-term, supposedly 'relevant', management training should not replace the broad-based education legacy within administration because it: 'includes a good deal more than is usually encompassed by education management, taking in ideas from sociology, political science, history, economics and other social sciences that are often either missing from or presented in a highly derivative manner from the management literature' (p. 49). However, the term 'management' was increasingly accepted (including by Baron and Taylor) as more applicable to the practitioner in England and Wales, with educational administration reserved for international networking (Gunter, 1999a). Management was seen as a distinct activity (Bennett, 1974), and increasingly a superior form of activity (Morgan, 1979) and headteachers were describing their professional practice in management terms (Barry and Tye, 1975; Peters, 1976; Poster, 1976). At a time when purposes, standards and performance were coming under scrutiny practitioners wanted the emphasis to be on the 'what' and 'how' of doing things better.

This clash over terminology is pertinent to current debates. When practitioners argued in favour of management in the 1970s it was for a way of working and having their work understood by others that would enhance their status. It could be argued that what we now call leadership is what we used to call 'management' and prior to that 'educational administration'. Following on from this, labelling can be seen to be linked to struggles over how field members want to present themselves and their work in ways that enable it to be understood and appreciated. It could also be argued that in leaving behind educational administration the links between schools and elected representatives at local and national level have been severed in ways that have injured the development of democracy. Indeed, Bolam (1999) argues that the continued use of educational administration 'enables us to adopt a broader concept of the field, and thus to embrace policy studies as well as institutional management' (p. 194). Perhaps by accepting a modernised identity as managers and, more recently, as leaders, headteachers are seeking the acclaim and respect of the private sector.

An alternative reading of history could be made by arguing that educational restructuring, through comprehensive education and, more recently, site-based performance management, brought about new tasks and processes in schools that make labels such as leadership and management appropriate for headteachers and senior and middle managers. However, the continued emphasis on behaviours and functions of administration, leadership and management has itself been challenged. Gronn (1999a) argues that being appointed to a role and being a leader are not the same thing, and being given the task of visioning does not of itself constitute leadership. For Gronn (1999a) leadership 'is an ascribed or attributed status' (p. 5) and so this assumes that leadership is a relationship. This connects with work undertaken by critical approaches in educational studies where issues of power are central to how we understand the practice of leadership as a struggle (Smyth, 1989a). Furthermore, critical studies raise the issue that much of what is written and assumed about leadership and management is content free, and that leadership and management in education is not necessarily concerned with education (Grace, 1997). For leadership to be educational then it needs to be integral to pedagogy in which teachers and students engage in a leadership relationship where the emphasis is on 'problem-posing' as distinct from 'problem-solving' (Smyth, 1985).

Summary

The study and practice of leadership is a dialogic relationship, and this chapter has outlined field and epistemological positions where teachers, headteachers, governors, parents, children, researchers, consultants and publishers have and may position themselves, and be positioned by others. Shifts and changes in language are not just about fads and fashions but make statements about purposes, and, ultimately about how we want to live together and govern ourselves (Gray and Jenkins, 1995).

Seeking the spaces and places where intellectual work can continue to thrive at a time when the dominant model of effective and improving leadership seeks to totalise who we are and what we can do is a central issue. This clearly needs more investigation and the next two chapters take this forward by investigating debates about research and theory.

4

Research and Researching

This chapter presents ways in which leaders and leadership in education is being researched. A central focus of this chapter is to investigate the divergence between positivist epistemologies based on quantitative surveys, qualitative work based on 'situated portrayals' (Ribbins, 1997b), and critical accounts (Ball, 1990a; 1994b). Inevitably given the volume of work this chapter is selective, but the particular emphasis is on how claims are made about how different methodologies enable knowledge and understanding of educational leadership to be revealed, and this is connected to current debates about educational research. In particular, scientific approaches dominate, even though, as Hall and Southworth (1997) argue, claims about how and why headteachers make a difference are more about assertion and belief than evidence based. While humanistic approaches that seek to understand what it feels like to be in a leadership post are officially tolerated, the importance and the recommendation from knowledge workers of more long-term case studies is not being advanced. Research that takes a critical approach to the impact of neo-liberalism on professional identities and the control over work is being marginalised, even though this work is essential to our understanding of how preferred models of educational leadership are being sustained and developed. In being a leader watcher we must also be field watchers, so that our understanding of research is such that it does not float free of the political (and often Political) interests and goals of those located within it.

Struggling for research

Educational research is a contested political arena in which struggles have been taking place between researchers, and this has led Oakley (2000) to argue that differences between quantitative and qualitative methods 'seem very silly' (p. 293) and that 'too much time and effort is going into paradigm warfare' (p. 302). She goes on to argue in favour of systematic enquiry that

49

is free from the baggage of historical position and positioning so that the positive association of qualitative work with the emancipation of the oppressed is challenged, and experimental work is rehabilitated by showing that statistics are not necessarily power over processes which are anti-women and anti-human. In other words, ways of knowing based on both statistical and experiential data can become a major part of the strategies developed and used to answer research questions.

This argument is currently being used in government policy-making in which the emphasis is on HEIs telling the government 'what works'. Given what we have come to know about BSE, the sinking of the *Belgrano*, and the Dome, decision-making in government does need to be more open so that choices at the ballot box are based less on habit and more on dialogue. However, what is missing in the 'what works' debate seems to be the transparency needed to enable us to see the evidence that leads to the judgements about what is deemed to work and why. Without this governments could be charged with duplicity as much reform has taken place in education based on dogmatic positioning disguised as instinct or common sense, rather than evidence. The stripping away of theory (sociology and psychology) in the training of teachers is a good example of this, but theory just will not go away because, as Atkinson (2000) shows, teachers do use and produce theories which may not be articulated because of the anti-intellectual climate that has been created in education.

There is impatience with this type of discussion, and it is very easy to be positioned as 'serving academic careers' (Oakley, 2000, p. 323). According to Milliband from the Policy Unit researchers need to stop being commentators and become 'engaged in debate beyond the confines of academic journals' (Lloyd, 1999, p. 13). Blunkett (DfEE, 2000a), in his lecture to the Economic and Social Research Council (ESRC), argues that: 'the Government has given a clear commitment that we will be guided not by dogma but by an open-minded approach to understanding what works and why' (p. 2). In tandem with this, Sebba (2000) describes how the Department for Education and Employment (DfEE) has been implementing the action plan put forward in the Hillage et al. (1998) report:

- *National Forum for Educational Research*: aims to develop a strategic and coherent approach to research agendas and to improve impact on policy and practice.
- *Centre for Evidence-Informed Policy and Practice in Education*: will develop a Cochrane Collaboration type database for education.
- *DfEE Research Programme*: investment in the Forum and Centre, and also in longitudinal studies such as teacher effectiveness and boys underachievement.

Important intellectual work has been taking place in education to support the 'what works' approach based on particular criticisms of educational research:

- *Users of research*: involvement by teachers in research is usually low, and peer review has a higher status than the needs and interests of users (Hargreaves, 1998).
- *Disciplinary diversity*: there is far too much irrelevant debate that does not serve the interests and needs of practitioners (Hargreaves, 1996).
- *Knowledge*: research is non-cumulative.
- *Impact*: teachers are more interested in what other teachers are doing that works than in research findings (Hargreaves, 1998).
- *Intellectualism*: research lacks objectivity, it is too ideological, and is politically biased (Tooley with Darby, 1998).
- *Organisation*: there are too many researchers divided across small institutions with no coherent approach (Hargreaves, 1998).

We must accept that as in all walks of life, including policy-making in government, bad behaviour can undermine the knowledge production process and, as Rudduck (1998) argues, while the internal debates have been important in enabling educational studies to develop 'the skirmishes ... irritated policy-makers' (p. 7). This enables us to see that knowledge production is not just about insular paradigm wars but is connected to structural and structuring interests. For example, it seems that randomised control trials (RCTs) have been used badly in the past and so might be used appropriately in the future. However, the power structures that contaminated the laboratory in the past remain today. It is also the case that RCTs have been used against particular social groups who are defined as not only being problems but actually being *the* problem because through social welfare programmes they keep taxes high. It seems that examining social interventions is less about what works in the interests of people and more about what is cheap, and this is connected to long-standing assumptions about human nature. Nevertheless, such positions need and demand an objective gloss and, so, particular intellectuals are able to use ontological and epistemological justifications to do particular ideological work. Willmott (1999a; 1999b) argues this about school effectiveness research in which contextual issues such as social class are treated as variables rather than a social and power relational experience, and so seeking to measure effectiveness in more and more sophisticated ways does not and cannot deal with issues of social justice.

Analysing social science research by using Bourdieu's tools means that achieving a better science is not just about scientists realising that methodological divisions are 'silly', but about how dialogue is central to democratic development. The emphasis on researchers providing the government with 'what works' could be about possible co-option, and the closing down of important places of dissent and critique (Bridges, 1998). As Hammersley (2000) argues, social science is relevant to our concerns about social and human action, but it may not be the particular political priorities of the government of the day. What is and is not worthy of research is a highly political decision, and needs to take place in a dialogic arena, otherwise governments can use rational value-for-money outcomes for irrational purposes, perhaps 'as a shield to defend itself against criticism, especially from the media' (ibid., p. 12). The argument in favour of diversity is also made by others who are concerned about the narrowness of the current agenda with too much emphasis on schooling and schools (Deem, 1996b; 1998; R. Murphy, 1998), and on technical competence that denies that all debates are intellectual ones (Beveridge, 1998).

The politics of epistemology can be taken a stage further by examining the claim that 'what works' is central to shifting interventions in people's lives from doing things because of tradition and/or personal preference towards using what is known to work. In the natural sciences this is based on cause and effect being close together and supports technological accuracy. Press a button and the machine does or does not work. Applicability of this to the organic world has been questioned by chaos theory in which interventions cannot be instrumentally controlled (Gunter, 1997). Applicability to the social world is equally problematic because 'what works' is essential frozen in time and space to be implemented in other contexts at other times. The knowledge claims of RCTs are based on the attempt to control chance through measurement and prediction. However, even if we take an ethical approach to research, is it possible to create a control group through randomisation when central to life is how we communicate about our experiences? In order to work, chance and choice have to be dichotomised, because randomising depends on chance but the lay person involved in the experiment may wish to exercise choice by using the drug rather than the placebo. Oakley (2000) is right to draw our attention to the importance of doing no harm in research, and it is possible to put in place mechanisms for ensuring this should not happen. However, what is and is not harmful is also a cultural, historical, social, economic and political construct, and there are those over time and even currently who could argue and provide evidence that learning will improve by corporal punishment. In the end corporal punishment was ended not because we had statistics to prove that it did not work, but because we had beliefs about how human beings, particularly in adult–child relationships, should behave towards each other. Issues around trust, like and respect cannot be beaten into us and neither can we necessarily be convinced by rational empirical evidence.

The problem lies with what we mean by evidence-*informed* practice, and how it could be seen to be positioning children and teachers as being in a deficit position. The child stops being a child and becomes a type within a generic category. Alternatively, it could be one piece of evidence that is used alongside others, in which case it is the judgement of the person or persons using it that comes into play. In this way, while having such data about 'what works' is helpful and illuminating in decision-making, there are other valid reasons for action and inaction such as resources, or a strong belief that something is a good/bad thing to do. In other words, interventions are part of a political process regarding what should and should not be funded, and what should and should not be done. People may be right or wrong in this, but the point is that social interactions are based on such contestation. History shows that even in totalitarian regimes, where the emphasis is more on management than political dialogue, dissent, albeit underground, continues.

What is useful and who is a user of research is, as Deem (1998) argues, a political construction. Twenty years ago gender research was not seen to be 'useful' and so teachers would not be encouraged to be involved in it, but now that boys are underachieving it has become central to institutional data collection and analysis. Consequently, 'it is rarely, if ever, possible to predict in advance whether any given research project will have utility to someone other than the researchers conducting it' (ibid., p. 176). It may be that we have to have a more sophisticated analysis of what 'using' actually means, and how we conceptualise the 'impact' of research on practice. Researchers are agreed that it takes time (Beveridge, 1998), or as Gipps (1998) states 'knowledge works its way into habits' (p. 73).

Hannon (1998) argues that the diffusion of research into practice is necessarily complex: 'teachers do not use research as a cookbook but as a resource in constructing their view of what is worth aiming for and likely ways to get it' (p. 151). Furthermore, he argues that much of the significant change in education such as site-based performance management has not been based on research evidence, and this has had repercussions on teachers as users of research because they are not allowed to show an intellectual disposition which might seek spaces to generate alternative insights and, because teachers are not trusted, their ability to read, listen, absorb and act on new ideas has been undermined. Teachers are intellectually debilitated through over-bureaucracy and the official denial of professional judgement within their practice. Attacking the perceived privileges of researchers in HEIs by arguing that teachers should be researchers is unhelpful and unproductive. Teachers-as-researchers is important, but they cannot or should not replace professional researchers who are currently located in HEIs. While there has been a growth in postgraduate research, and this work is seen to be valuable (Maguire and Ball, 1994), there is concern that the partnerships between practitioners and HEI researchers are being undermined (Heck, 1991). Professional training and experience as a researcher is important, and cannot be learned by teachers at the same time as doing the job of teaching or leading or managing (McIntyre, 1998). For teachers to engage in research enquiry within practice, as a medical team might do in an operating theatre, so that proposed interventions are articulated, judgements tested and actions observed then there is a need not just for resources to be better deployed, but for resources to be considerably enhanced.

In relation to working with 'users' of research there is no disagreement with this in principle and, as Rudduck (1998) and Deem (1998) have argued, teachers have a long tradition of being included in and leading research. Enhancing this involvement is very well supported but it is regarded as problematic given the range and diversity of users and the time and financial resources required to involve users in this way (Hegarty, 1998). Much of what is written about 'users' assumes that they are apolitical and more likely to be supportive of technical 'what works' solutions, but there is a strong tradition in both feminist and action research of working with practitioners based on clear and open values with a commitment to praxis.

In summary, any investigation into researching leaders and leadership in education needs to be located within the current politics of preferred research. This is shaping what is acceptable to policy-makers, and could possibly close down arenas for dialogue through which alternative approaches can be revealed and developed. We are currently going through an experiment in leadership in educational settings based on site-based performance management without the evidence from RCTs, and this could be because it is impossible scientifically and politically to undertake work that officially experiments on children and adults. Also the government might find out that constructing headteachers as leaders is not working in the ways they would like, and so they would lose the means by which accountability for the local implementation of policy can and should take place.

Knowledge workers in HEIs are well aware of their historical privileges and the power structures that have traditionally given them a loud voice in educational theory and practice. Change within and to this is not necessarily problematic, and an important case can be made about the democratising potential of intellectual work through dialogue within communities. However, challenges to elite power only becomes a problem when particular ways of knowing are used for political gain and through this alternatives are marginalised. Beneath the cloak of 'what works' there is a power struggle over making education match up with other powerful knowledge interests such as medicine. Murphy, R., (1998) argues that the disparity in the level of resources must mean that these fields will produce a higher quality of research, and he goes on to argue that we must also recognise that there is a lot of very poor medical research going on. Perhaps respectability for knowledge workers and knowledge production should come from knowledge that is generated within the struggle for democracy, and those in education and medicine are uniquely placed to lead this.

Instrumental leadership

Researching leadership located in the tradition of the natural sciences has a strong link with instrumental activity. Hall and Southworth (1997) show that from the 1970s and 1980s there has been a growth in the production of handbooks (e.g. Lyons, 1974) and the promotion of business and competency based work (e.g. Earley, 1992; Esp, 1993). Furthermore, they go on to show how work such as Torrington and Weightman's (1989) analysis led to prescriptions about school leadership in the 1980s that uncritically accepted business management solutions to organisational and leadership effectiveness (e.g. Peters and Waterman, 1982). The social science tradition evidenced in the work of Baron and Taylor (1969) became marginalised because within the climate of educational restructuring recipe-book models met the requirements of reformers who needed a particular conceptualisation of headteachers and their work in order to make required changes to the public sector.

The laboratory epistemology underpinning leadership research remains strong, and the researcher is presented as a neutral data gatherer and interpreter. The claims made about this type of work are based on the deconstruction of leadership activity into behavioural and task functions such as visioning, and decision-making, and using these variables to test connections with learning outcomes. Leithwood et al. (1999) used 20 out of 34 studies of transformational leadership (6 qualitative and 15 quantitative) to identify 13 different types of effects: 'effects on students, effects on perceptions of leaders, effects on behaviour of followers, effects on followers' psychological states and organisational-level effects' (p. 31). Leithwood et al. (1999) conclude that 'twenty studies provided evidence about the effects of transformational leadership on several different categories of outcomes' (p. 38). However, what is noted is that the effect on students currently remains unproven and it is possible that the impact is mediated through teachers. Nevertheless this does not prevent the authors from claiming that while there is no empirical evidence for this leadership model (or others) having a direct impact 'the demands on schools cannot await the outcome of such research' (ibid., p. 32).

This type of work has been criticised as it seems to be more about justifying a particular model of leadership than about seeking to understand how leadership is practised and understood within a dynamic context. Hallinger and Heck (1999) have reviewed 42 studies published during 1990–95, and come to similar conclusions regarding the complex nature of the impact of school leaders on outcomes: 'school leaders do not *make* effective schools' (p. 185). Furthermore, they go on to provide an agenda for dealing with the 'blind spots' in research:

- *Conceptual clarity*: to have clear understandings of what vision, mission, and goals mean, and the relationship between variables needs to be theorised and made explicit.
- *Leadership is distributed*: to move beyond the headteacher/principal as the focus of research so that other leaders and their leadership is made visible.
- *Learning organisation*: to move beyond the effectiveness framework so that the theory of the learning organisation is used to describe and understand leadership effects.

- *Cultural context*: to understand both the impact of local settings on the theory and practice of leadership and the impact on outcomes.

However, while this provides a useful and exciting agenda for many positivist researchers, it is still regarded as conceptually and empirically limited. What seems to distinguish this position is the extent to which the context in which leadership takes place is recognised and built into the research design. As Duke (1998) argues: 'separating leadership from context is analogous to identifying the food one wants for dinner while ignoring where it is to be consumed. Whether one chooses to eat a salad at a fast food restaurant or a country inn has a great bearing on the quality of the experience' (p. 166). The question raised from this is whether and how leadership impact on learning outcomes can be measured in isolation from the local setting. Lakomski (1999) argues that it is 'epistemologically unproductive' to continue with trying to measure if leaders make a difference because it is bad science: 'It may turn out to be the case that there is not one theory of leadership, but many, modular accounts' (p. 49).

Biographical leadership

Those who locate themselves in qualitative work not only raise concerns about the operational aspects of positivist approaches, but also take the position that personal accounts of leadership experience and perspectives about the job are vital if we are to shift the emphasis away from the 'characteristics of leadership' to the 'character of leaders' (Rayner and Ribbins, 1999, p. 3). The case has been made and continues to be made that we know very little about the work and lives of those who occupy leadership positions and, so, there is a need to develop ways of investigating this (Hall and Southworth, 1997; Gronn, 1996). Furthermore, Hall's (1997b) work on women headteachers leads her to argue that without this type of approach in researching women who have become headteachers and who were not 'masculine' then we will not be able to challenge 'theories associating management with masculinity' (p. 321). Seeking to use research to understand how women lead and engage with power issues within contextual settings is a feature both of historical work (Watts, 1998), and contemporary studies (Fennell, 1999).

Qualitative studies have grown in use, and claims are made from a range of researchers from around the world about the importance of research that captures the real-time activity of leadership in practice (e.g. Bezzina, 1998; Bogotch and Roy, 1997; Brown and Rutherford, 1998; Kasten and Ashbaugh, 1991). Work does vary depending on whether the approach is to focus on practice as a collective experience, e.g. the school as the unit of analysis, or whether the intention is to survey individuals to obtain and analyse their individual and/or collective stories. Work by Burgess (1983) is an example of the first type of study, and he used participant observation to focus on how the school worked and how people 'defined and redefined the situation in which they were located' (p. 4) (others include Ball, 1981; Best et al., 1983; Hargreaves, 1967; Lacey, 1970 and Richardson, 1973). Focusing on researching the individual has tended towards short-term encounters regarding the life and work of head-teachers (Hall, 1996; Tomlinson et al., 1999), or in exceptional projects a researcher has worked on the life of one person, for example, Gronn's (1999b) work on James Ralph Darling, Kyle's (1993) work on Cara David and Southworth's (1995a) case study of Ron Lacey.

Survey work based on qualitative interviews is widely used, and this tends to operate by the researcher approaching headteachers with a series of questions that theorise the stories that the individual wishes to tell. Hustler et al. (1995) are very much in the tradition outlined by Allen (1968) when he introduced and celebrated the edited collection as being the product of a conference dialogue between the 'campus and school yard' (p. xiii). Huster et al. (1995) provide an interactive process consist-ing of interviews, and the production and discussion of oral texts:

- *Heads above the parapet*: individual interviews with eight secondary headteachers.
- *Thrust and counter-thrust*: discussion of the interviews with the edu-cational commentators leading to new questions. Discussion transcript and questions sent to headteachers. Follow-up interviews with the headteachers.
- *Lines of enquiry – the commentators' personal perspectives*: eight essays written by the educational commentators.

The intention of the editors is that the debate will continue beyond what is recorded in the book, and they are aware that the process of 'debate at a distance' does have its problems, not least the lack of face-to-face contact, but they regard it as a 'practical compromise' given the demands on each of the research participants. A central feature of this work is not just the identification of contradictions in the professional lives of head-teachers, but also how debate can uncover the different layers making up the complexity of contradiction.

Ribbins, in collaboration with a number of co-researchers, has gathered data through face-to-face interviews (Ribbins and Marland, 1994; Pascal and Ribbins, 1998; Rayner and Ribbins, 1999; Ribbins, 1997a), and he argues that the agenda for the interview is 'more open and shared' (Ribbins, 1997b, p. 10) compared with the process described by the Mortimores (Mortimore and Mortimore, 1991a; 1991b). The place of the headteacher in this type of research does vary from the headteacher as 'incidental actor' through to being a 'co-researcher' in which the strengths of each position (headteacher and professor) are valued. Ribbins and Sherratt (1999) describe how this latter approach has been developing in the study of headship at Great Barr School in Birmingham. Sherratt argues that in being able to tell his story about 'the dilemmas of headship as these are experienced by heads themselves in situ' then he is able to contribute to an account in ways that are not always evident in research reports. He attributes objectivity to the co-researcher, and Ribbins makes the point that as a subjectivist he provides as good an account as he can, but it cannot be an absolute truth. He goes on to argue that in engaging in a dialogic process 'what is different about our research is that I believe that the account we can give together must be richer than any account I could possibly give on my own of your exercise of leadership at Great Barr' (Ribbins and Sherratt, 1999, pp. 192–3).

This emphasis on how meaning is developed and constructed enables a shift away from focusing on the abstractions of role and effectiveness to how a complex professional life unfolds. This has been particularly important in enabling researchers to reveal the realities of what it is to cope with changes such as site-based performance management and so invalidate the quick-fix handbooks. Southworth (1993) reports on work undertaken in two projects (a) the Primary School Staff Relationships project (PSSR) and (b) the Whole School Curriculum Development project (WSCD). The methodology used in these projects was based on observation and interviews, and so they were able to describe and report on what they saw validated through feedback and discussions with teachers and headteachers in the case study schools rather than produce abstractions of what ought to be. This grounded approach enables Southworth and his colleagues to capture the complexity of leadership and to argue that what we need are more descriptive accounts of headteachers at work. More recently, Southworth (1999a) describes how he interviewed ten primary headteachers who were experienced in the job, and so could give an account of pre- and post-site based restructuring from 1988. From this he was able to describe the continuities and changes in the experience of headship and theorise around issues such as accountability, and reveal the dilemmas in their work such as the tension between the management of the school and the professional leadership of teaching and learning.

Combining different methods from different positions has led Ribbins (1997b) to place interviewing and observation within a 'multi-perspective in action' (p. 10) where the researcher needs to develop a research design that gives access to a range of data that produces an 'enriched portrait of heads and of headship' (ibid.):

- Documentary evidence about the formal role of the head.
- Observation of the head and how s/he goes about their work.
- Discussion with the head about what they are doing and why.
- Discussion with others about what the head is doing and why.

Such an approach enables the interplay between what is said is done and what is experienced as being done. This could possibly uncover what Willower (1998) describes as a 'typical case being democratic values imposed by undemocratic, manipulative means' (p. 239). Day et al. (2000), in undertaking a study into headteacher effectiveness commissioned by the National Association of Head Teachers (NAHT), found that there was little research that gathered data from a range of interested and involved people 'about both the "production" and the "consumption" of leadership in schools'. They go on to argue that their use of multi-position research facilitates the traditional 'silent voices' in leadership research to be recognised through including children and parents (ibid., pp. 29–30).

Accounts generated from qualitative research are both exciting and problematic at the same time; exciting because they provide an account of practice that can contribute to debates about educational change, but problematic because we need to ask, whose account is it? For those who hide behind the detached objectivity of scientific approaches this type of work is inevitably ideological and flawed. For those who are disposed to understand rather than control experiences, the issue is not about taking a position (because we all do this) but in how best to make the intellectual struggle within research as clear and as transparent as possible. Qualitative researchers do not hide behind method, but problematise the inevitable problematics of method. For those who, like Hall (1996), are researchers outside the practice of headship, there are opportunities (not taken by all writers) to describe their research as 'watching from the wings' (p. 17 ff), and so raise questions about how they are located in the study and how their gaze upon practice can be described and given meaning. As Hall (1996) notes: 'I was thus a familiar stranger in the heads' worlds, continually juggling familiarity and strangeness, closeness and distance, in order to collect good-quality data' (p. 21). For Southworth (1995a) his motivations are based in his own professional experience as a headteacher, lecturer and researcher, and as such his habitus enables him to critically read research accounts in ways that show them to be a 'monocular view of the work' of headteachers. Being explicit about the resources used in an account, is the means through which the orientation of the researcher can be revealed and understood. In this way the dishonesty of sterile detachment through assumed disinterested self-positioning is avoided and, so, the research recipient has the opportunity to engage by overtly positioning themselves in the process.

Overall, what the range of qualitative work outlined above is seeking to do is to open up the complexities of the working lives of post-holders. Hall and Southworth (1997) show that this type of work also enables research to reveal the pluralism about what being a headteacher and headship are about. In particular we need to note how stories either in short-term or long-term case studies show how headteachers' work and their orientation to that work and what it means for their professional identity change from post to post, and within post over time. How this is revealed is central to debates in relation to the number and type of methods used, e.g. observations and/or interviews, as well as who is to be the focus of the research, e.g. the post-holder and/or those who experience their leadership such as other staff, children and parents. Furthermore the symmetry in the relationship between researcher and researched is a focus for current development in which accounts by role incumbents, often in conversation with or as co-researchers with field members in HEIs, are the product of a visible and open dialogue. This has the possibilities of seeing research as a collaborative struggle in which traditional positioning at the chalkface as opposed to the academy is broken down through the recognition of relevant skills from different professional trajectories.

Critical educational leadership

The level and type of theorisation before, within, and after the gathering of qualitative data varies from those who seek to ask a series of questions (e.g. Mortimore and Mortimore, 1991a; 1991b) through to policy sociologists who take a critical approach to issues of power and policy (Ball, 1990a; 1994b; Grace, 1995; Menter et al., 1997). Qualitative work lives in the life of the researcher and can be uncomfortable in the questions that are asked and the experiences that are revealed. Research enables questions to be asked of your own practice and how power structures can operate through the research process. This means that little is assumed about beliefs and activity, and such questioning enables all interests to be open to scrutiny. Social processes can be theorised in ways that connect the individual and their experiences with the structures that shape and control choice, and so there is an emancipatory goal in opening up covert technologies. There is little point in undertaking systemic reviews of research according to scientific quality measures regarding methodology and method because such measures can be implicated in the silencing of the voices to be heard.

Critical research enables us to see how and why experienced teachers are in receipt of systems that are more about domesticating the teacher into exisiting power structures than about enabling teachers to work in an emancipatory way with colleagues and students. The advanced skills teacher (AST) is good example of this, with Blackmore (1999) and Smyth and Shacklock (1998a) providing a detailed analysis of teacher experiences in Australia. The goal of AST was to enable experienced teachers with highly developed skills to be given status and financial reward, and recognition to be given to those for whom promotion into educational administration was not desirable. However, as Smyth and Shacklock (1998a) go on to show, teacher experiences of the AST scheme was an 'intensity-in-process' in which an exaggerated performativity was required, and this exhausted and undermined teachers, and so put many off. While on paper the scheme has rational and laudable aims, the actual expectations of the AST scheme varied from those who saw it as affirming their work to those who were encouraged to proactively demonstrate their leadership, and 'despite this putatively positive portrayal of AST teachers, many teachers, including potential and unsuccessful candidates, claimed that they saw little evidence of changed work habits, or demonstrable "advanced" skills, in their AST colleagues' (ibid., p. 158).

Even more significant are the cases of experienced and successful teachers (endorsed by colleagues, principals and the community) who failed to gain AST status. What seems to be the case, and this is complex, is that teachers did not have the correct type or amount of evidence (documentation collected over the years) and found the fabrication of themselves and their work to be unappetising. In other words, the AST process attracted those who had the habitus to position themselves in a particular way, and this enabled how teaching and learning are described and measured to shift more towards the value of abstract criteria and statements of competence. This changing of teachers' work and how they teach and talk about teaching enables policy intentions to be absorbed and realised and, as Smyth and Shacklock (1998a) go on to show, this is an exclusionary process. Alternative positions are marginalised and personal struggles are silenced; in particular, women may not have had rational and planned careers with hard and pure evidence of having made a difference, and 'the likelihood of these, and other forms of gender-bullying, or gender-exclusion, as work-site experience for promoted women in schools, may be a real deterrent for seeking higher-status positions in and beyond classroom teaching' (ibid., p. 191). It seems that the AST scheme is part of the discourse around what a school of the future is going to be, rather than a concern for the dispositions and experiences of those who are currently in schooling. It is a clear attempt to construct and image teachers in a particular way and concerns have been raised in the literature about long-serving and experienced teachers who are being sidelined as management systems such as appraisal operate more in favour of younger teachers (Menter et al., 1997). Performance systems, of which AST is an example, are based on assumptions about professional and personal dispositions that are uniform, universal and do not change over time.

This is important and well-trodden territory for those who take a critical approach to research in which social justice issues are central. Those who position themselves around this type of work are explicit about their position and the assumptions underpinning it. This is best explained by Griffiths (1998) who stresses the importance of *educational* research which is within an ethical framework and seeks 'personal and professional' improvement and, building on Carr, she argues that it is *for* education rather than *on* or *within*. However, the acknowledged contested nature of values through the interplay between agency and structure means that educational leadership is about power, and Corson (2000) gives us a glimpse of what this means in everyday practice through his reflections on what is and is not intended. He notes that 'often we are less able to treat people's interests fairly when the people we are dealing with are a little different from ourselves, in culture, language, or social class. Often too, we are less able to be fair when we deal with the interests of people who are not present at the time' (ibid., p. 94). In which case, we might add, how can we be certain when improvement has taken place and can it be inclusive?

Summary

Researching leaders and leadership in education is located in debates about the value and values of educational research, and as such we need to be mindful of political positioning that seeks to structure preferred ways of knowing. This does not discount those ways, but is concerned to ensure this is not lost through unreflexive ridicule and the impatience of having to be seen to act and act in particular ways. The irony is that Oakley's (2000) call for an end to the paradigm wars might exacerbate them because officially approved of knowledge production requires a particular and preferred type of intellectual work, and to do this an intellectual elite needs to be consecrated. Site-based performance management requires scientific-based research that concerns itself with headteachers as rational leaders who make a difference to learning outcomes, and this assumes that headteachers have to do the tasks and behave in ways that give the impression that they do make this type of difference. This excludes other models of headship and ways of working that might work and feel better but are not officially approved of. What is helpful is that, for the time being at least, headteacher and teacher participation in biographical and critically theorised work continues and is growing in its ability to speak with and to educationalists about matters that are increasingly becoming silenced.

The next chapter develops the argument further by focusing on theory and theorising because, as Skeggs (1997) argues, 'methodology is itself theory' (p. 17), and the decisions we make in the design and implementation of a research project are based on theories of power. We need to be honest about this otherwise our choices, based on overt or covert intellectual resources, could be a part of the structuring process that is disconnecting education from the struggle within and for democratic change.

5

Theory and Theorising

This chapter presents and analyses positions and positioning about how leadership has been and continues to be theorised. In many ways this is a continuation of the previous chapter, and the divide is more about organisational convenience than significant conceptual differences. The chapter begins with a review of the place and purpose of theory within educational studies, and I illustrate the current debate about leadership by means of a review of the intellectual origins, claims and critiques of transformational leadership. The current configuration of this model is based on overtly functionalist knowledge claims through: (a) locating leadership with holding a particular post; (b) focusing on the tasks and behaviours required to deliver outcomes; and, (c) locating the leader and the function of leadership within a unitary organisation. Alternative conceptions of power challenge this model by arguing that: (a) a leader may have contractual authority for being a leader, but they may not necessarily exercise leadership; (b) leadership is a relationship that all are capable of exercising; and, (c) leadership within education should be directly connected to the ongoing development of democracy.

Struggling for theory

Within educational studies theory and theorising is a place of struggle, not just between competing theories, but also in arguments about whether theory plays a role at all. The position that I take in this debate is that theory and theorising is central to intellectual work through 'challenging the irrationality of conventional thinking in order to make educational ideas and beliefs less dependent on myths, prejudices and ideological distortions that common sense fossilizes and preserves' (Carr and Hartnett, 1996, p. 3). However, the place of theory within educational studies has been seriously undermined in the 1990s, in contrast to the 1960s when the 'ologies' (psychology, sociology, history and philosophy) mattered and helped to support and develop educational practice.

Indeed, practitioners still gain inspiration and intellectual nourishment from this though having the time to be immersed in research and theory is regarded as problematic when it is often an incidental rather than integrated feature of practice (Marland, 1993; Williams, 1993).

Over the last 20 years, in policy terms, theory has been used pejoratively and characterised as 'useless' and 'trendy' (Goodson, 1997), and more recently the then Her Majesty's Chief Inspector (HMCI) Woodhead (2000) ridiculed academics for engaging in 'wacky theorising' (p. 13). Tooley's (with Darby, 1998) report about educational research raised concerns about the 'adulation of great thinkers' (p. 56) such as Bourdieu, Foucault, Lyotard and Vygotsky together with charges of bias and problematic methodologies. Replies to this have been numerous (e.g. Nash, 1999; Ozga, 2000), and I would agree with the latter in responding to Tooley's charge of partisanship: 'there is no neutral, Olympian space from which an unbiased, objective account of policy research can be given. We are all partisans but only some of us acknowledge it' (Ozga, 2000, p. 36).

In many ways the objectification of bias deflects attention away from the serious issue of how the politics of consent, assent and dissent, so essential to a democratic way of life, is in danger of being eclipsed by a research community that could become cut off from disciplinary knowledge (Bridges, 1998; Ranson, 1998). Furthermore, the current anti-intellectual climate threatens to eclipse the important and rich vein of collaborative work between researchers in schools and HEIs in which the practitioner is both positioned and enabled to position themselves as theoriser, and contributor to knowledge. This is evident in the growth of action and developmental research processes, and more recently through work with pupils and their contribution to school improvement (Rudduck et al., 1996a). The Cognitive Acceleration through Science Education (CASE) project is illustrative of how 'what works' in relation to pupil learning processes and outcomes, is based on the very theorists, such as Vygotsky, that are being ridiculed (McGuinness, 1999; Shayer, 1996; 2000).

Theory is not the concern of an elite caste who then hand it down to be applied, but is integral to learning activity and professional interaction. In this way, as Edwards (2000b) argues, we *engage* with theory and, while we may not give enough recognition to this or even declare it in public, it is still the case that theories and theorising are integral to our everyday practice. This opens up some important avenues for how we understand theories about and theorising within leadership, and in particular the different positions taken on how we might be users, abusers and generators of theory. Questions can be raised about how users of theory give weight to particular theories, how and why decisions about what is or is not useful are made and how theorising through and within empirical work develops new knowledge and understandings.

Certain work seems to capture the imagination of knowledge workers and has a long-term endurance in their work, and a good example of this is Hughes's (1985) dual role model regarding the headteacher as a chief executive and leading professional, and this continues to inform and support current analysis (Busher, 1997; Garrett, 1997). However, other theories seem to come and go, and I have argued that a particular weakness of the entrepreneurial trend within educational studies is the presentation of work that does not explain or problematise its intellectual heritage, or seek to make a contribution to the original discipline (Gunter, 1997). Members of the field of education management are concerned about a 'cherry-picking' approach towards theories and models in which some knowledge workers within that field seem to be positioning themselves as consumers and repackagers of concepts and models which are lifted from their epistemological foundations, 'neutralised', and relocated in other contexts (Gunter, 1999a).

Struggling with theory

Engaging theory and theorising with practice is essential to knowledge production within and about educational experiences, and positioning is central to this. Duke (1998) uses the metaphor of a parade and where you stand. Close to the route you will see the detail of faces and voice, but you may miss the patterns afforded by the bigger picture of the 'spectacle'. In contrast, a vantage point from a tall building means that you have 'more of a panoramic perspective, but at the cost of the highly personal drama played out at street level' (ibid., p. 165). There are some knowledge workers who seek to use theory and to theorise within and close to the empirical setting, and Southworth (1995a) is explicit about this: 'In much of my work on school leadership I have tried to chart the "theories" headteachers hold about their work ... I am deeply interested in headteachers' "folk theories" about school leadership' (p. 55). Others prefer to work on a much larger canvas and approach empirical work through theories that explain the connection between the individual and the contextual setting in which they are located, such as Blackmore's feminist analysis of leadership (1989; 1996; 1999). Midway between these are researchers who use theory to distance themselves from the empirical work to gain perspective but still wish to be closely connected to the data. A good example of this is Wallace and Hall's (1994) work on senior management teams and their use of a 'dual perspective' based on political and cultural concepts.

Building on this we can ask questions about the purpose of theory and what we want to use it for. Theories and theorising can do a number of things for us:

- *Description*: provide a language and a structure to describe what is happening.
- *Understanding*: provide conceptual tools to explain what and why something is or is not happening.
- *Improvement*: be normative by providing one or multiple ways in which

change can take place.
- *Politicisation*: be critical and emancipatory by providing the description, understanding and change imperative to enable radical changes to existing power structures.

As Ozga (2000) argues, theories are relevant intellectual resources but they 'are not all of the same size, weight, complexity or quality' (p. 43) and so the theory issue is far more complex than the list assumes. Theories and theorising have a number of purposes, from being a lens through which to look at practice, through to being a predictive model that can become prescriptive by determining what educational practitioners should do. There is a strong theme within educational studies regarding the importance of relevance, and what Hoyle (1986) calls theory for improvement or action. Action within the organisation can be pragmatic and/or justified as habit or common sense, though Bush (1995) argues against this by noting the limitations of the narrowness and context specific nature of experience alone. Eraut (1993) has focused on the interplay between theory and practice by bringing our attention to how knowledge and expertise can be understood. He argues that there is public knowledge that can be *propositional* (knowing that) and is gained from facts, theories and case studies. In contrast there is private knowledge that can be procedural (knowing how) and is often tacit, but can also be through the public domain in which access to theories and research can be personally absorbed and used. The connection with theories for understanding (Hoyle, 1986) such as those based on the social sciences is complex, and in approaching this I am well aware of how *critical* is used within and through theory. A critical description for one knowledge worker can be about the accuracy and clarity of what is presented, while for another it can be about using theories of power that challenge and question established assumptions about organisations and people within them.

Theorising power

The conceptualisation of practice as struggle means that power is both the object and subject as well as the means through which it is taking place and, as Ball (1987) argues, it is ideological as issues of values and rights are involved. Wallace and Hall (1994) see power as the ability to identify and draw on resources in order to 'intervene in events so as to alter their course' (p. 29). Interventions can be about goal-seeking through to resistance and blocking. Resources vary and include knowledge and skills through to the giving of rewards or sanctions, and can be deployed through the pursuit of interests in consensus and conflict situations. Power relations are structured, and privilege can be formalised through *authority* or the legitimacy that comes with appointment and a defined role within the division of labour. Influence is less formal and can involve manipulation, and the interplay of covert and overt interactions. Hoyle (1982, p. 87) refers to this as 'the domain of micropolitics' which is 'a dark side of organisational life' (Hoyle, 1999, p. 43), and it remains a neglected area of academic work because while we know of its importance it does not seem to be a respectable area of enquiry.

Research into teacher experiences of educational restructuring has renewed interest in how policy texts are received, interpreted and reworked (Bowe and Ball with Gold, 1992), and how the day-to-day realities of headship are not so much about charismatic visioning as about bargaining and negotiation (Eden, 1997; Gronn, 1996). A recent symposium on micropolitics in *School Leadership and Management* (vol. 19, no. 2) illustrates the enduring relevance of political literacy for educational practitioners. Central to practice are the 'two faces of micropolitics': first, the internal organisational or what Hoyle (1999) describes as *management* micropolitics and, second, *policy* micropolitics, and, building on Ball (1987), this defines the school as a site where external policy and social issues such as class, gender and race are played out. The interrelationship between the politics of the external and internal is where the day-to-day realities of leading and leadership are located, and how practitioners seek to position themselves to conform, resist or ritualise.

A deeper issue seems to be that the endurance of rational models means that it is the visible abstractions such as vision and mission that dominate writing and research about organisations and people's positioning within them because this can be described and simplified in order to meet the demand for measurable outputs. As a result we tend to focus on definitions of organisational production (e.g. monitoring and evaluation) rather than ask questions about how people experience organisational life, how talk is important in how work gets done (Gronn, 1983; 1993), and how power is exercised (Lukes, 1974). As Hodgkinson (1999) argues: 'despite the assumptions and presumptions of the textbooks, administrative reality is less a field of honour than a battleground of wills, a domain of confused, confusing and conflicting values' (p. 10). While a leader may have authority through their job description, the power relationship is one that is historically and culturally located and structured but, as Anderson (1996) argues, how culture is conceptualised and presented in the field glosses over dynamics. What this raises is whether theorising through and with culture is about enabling us to describe and explain the setting in which we work, or whether it is used to provide control strategies. Blackmore (1989) takes this a stage further, and shows that the failure to connect leadership with theories of power means that what is promoted as good practice is often unchallenged. For example, the current absorption of feminine ways of working into leadership strategies, active listening, emotional commitment to people and the job, and working collaboratively in teams, fails to connect with power issues that turn both women and men away from seeking promotion, or leads to resignation.

Blackmore (1999) has challenged privileging power structures and how current leadership theories and models sustain them, by arguing that there is a lot which does and should 'trouble women' in 'new hard times':

- *Women are absent from leadership positions*: while this is generally seen to be no longer acceptable the reasons given are usually that feminine ways of working will deliver efficiency and effectiveness. What is troublesome is that women's role in the workplace is connected to economic output rather than concerns about equity.
- *Women in leadership positions are disruptive*: this brings trouble as 'strong women are difficult and dangerous because they trouble dominant masculinities and modes of management by being different' (ibid., p. 3). Social justice issues are costly and interrupt the smooth management processes of problem-solving.
- *Women need to be troubled*: accepting that women are in deficit and need to be upgraded through training to take on the leadership role in newly restructured educational organisations is problematic and this should trouble women. In particular, we should not ignore 'both the differences amongst women and the difficult political context in which leading women now work' (ibid., p. 3).

Blackmore goes on to use research and theory to provide a feminist analysis of these issues, and in particular she focuses on how performativity is being experienced not as the presented neutral process but as a top-down technology. Consequently, the challenge for the field from this analysis is whether 'the focus upon leadership is itself the biggest barrier to gender equality' (ibid., p. 222). However, raising issues of gender and management is not easy, and Gold (1993) describes how she has met resistance to the issue. Hall (1999b) talks about how men and women researchers still 'remain at separate tables' regarding gender issues even though 'they are more likely nowadays to be consulting the same menu' (p. 164).

In summary, struggling for theory is very much about revealing the 'stupid theorists' (Inglis, 1985, p. 40) who avoid the problematic nature of practice, as well as providing alternative and challenging vistas from which to view and understand the world. Nevertheless, this is dangerous territory, because in struggling for theory, we are also struggling over it and how we seek to position ourselves. Ladwig (1996) warns us that this could be an 'academic delusion that our debates matter to anyone other than ourselves' (p. 10), but without this debate we are in danger of being in receipt of ways of working that will and do matter to all.

Transformational leadership

Theories of leadership for improvement and action are historically located, and have been laid and overlaid on top of each other.

Furthermore, as Fidler (1997) notes, the leadership imperative seems to come in waves, and when new challenges are presented there is an upsurge in interest. However, as the theories outlined in Figure 5.1 show, the enduring and stable feature is the agency of the leader, combined with the assumed control over both the self and others.

Theories	Leadership based on the following questions	Illustrative texts
Trait	What is leadership? Do I have the right qualities to be a leader?	Stogdill (1974)
Style	Do I know my preferred leadership style? Do I know how to obtain a balance between a concern for tasks and for people? Have I had the correct in-service training on the behaviours required to achieve the right style?	Blake and Mouton (1964)
Contingency	Have I reflected on the context that affects which leadership style is appropriate? Do I know how my subordinates will respond to particular styles?	Fiedler et al., (1977) Hersey and Blanchard (1982)
Transformational	Do I have a vision and a mission? Can I empower my followers to live the vision? How can I ensure my leadership has positive effects on production outcomes?	Burns (1978)

Figure 5.1 Theories of leadership

Transformational leadership has its origins in non-educational settings and Burns's (1978) work is celebrated for establishing leadership as a relationship based on an exchange between leaders and followers. Engagement between leaders and followers is a struggle that is controlled through transactional leadership, that is, negotiation, and the motivations and resources within it do not challenge but seek to satisfy. In contrast, transformational leadership is about building a unified common interest in which motivation is underpinned by 'attempts to elevate members' self-centred attitudes, values and beliefs to higher, altruistic attitudes, values and beliefs' (Starratt, 1999, p. 25). Those who inhabit leadership roles have particular attributes and behaviours (Beare et al, 1993; Diggins, 1997; Jenkins, 1997). The agency of the leader in exercising leadership has been categorised as the four Is :

- *Inspiration*: motivating the subordinate through charisma.
- *Individualism*: focusing on the individual needs of subordinates.

- *Intellectual stimulation*: influencing thinking and imagination of subordinates.
- *Idealised influence*: the communication and building of an emotional commitment to the vision (Gronn, 1996).

This can be illustrated by Figure 5.2 which is a summary of how leadership behaviour is categorised into generic and global dimensions that are action oriented and so lead to particular practices that in turn lead to positive outcomes.

Dimensions	Outcomes
Direction Setting • Building a shared vision. • Developing consensus about goals. • Creating high performance expectations.	Charismatic school leaders are: Highly respected. Trusted Symbolise success
Developing People • Providing individualised support. • Creating intellectual stimulation. • Modelling practices and values important for the school.	People are central to an organisation. Structures and tasks cannot be understood except through people.
Redesigning the Organisation • Culture building • Creating and maintaining shared decision-making structures and processes • Building relationships with the community	Collaboration is central to outcomes.

Figure 5.2   Transformational leadership (based on Leithwood et al., 1999)

Leithwood et al. (1999) conclude that the school organisation of the future is a 'high reliability learning community' (p. 223) which is based on a need to maintain the core purpose of learning combined with a need to deliver outcomes. High-reliability organisations are those such as air traffic control systems where goals must be achieved 'all of the time' (ibid., p. 213) otherwise there would be a public outcry over safety issues. It is argued that this type of 'perception-of-disaster pre-condition' (ibid., p. 213) thinking is becoming more accepted in relation to educational reforms because the failure to learn basic skills undermines the effectiveness of learning throughout the school system and, so, unemployability impacts on the economy. Consequently, Leithwood et al. (1999) argue that transformational leadership needs a broader and deeper approach, as illustrated in Figure 5.3:

Aspects of the model have been drawn upon and developed by other international writers:

- Visioning is an enduring feature in leadership models, e.g. Bhindi and Duignan (1997) see it as central to their arguments for 'authentic

Dimension	Outcomes
Problem-solving • Understanding the problem. • Solving the problem.	The following are effective: Guided practice in problem-solving. Encountering progressively complex problems. Knowledge acquisition about common problems. Guided reflection on problem solving processes.
Fostering Teacher Leadership • Nature and perceptions of teacher leadership.	Principal leadership is more influential than the leadership exercised by teachers overall. Principal leadership is greatest on school improvement planning, school structure and organisation, school mission and school culture. Teacher leadership greatest on school improvement planning, and, school structure and organization. Principals and teachers are expected to lead in different ways and have different types of impact on the school.
Building Teachers' Commitment to Change • Personal goals. • Capacity beliefs. • Context beliefs. • Emotional arousal process.	The following are strong influences on teacher commitment: The direction-setting dimensions of leadership. Building shared vision. Creating consensus about school goals. Demonstrating high performance expectations.
Creating the conditions for growth in teachers' professional knowledge and skill • Development of individual teachers' capacities	Symbolic features of transformational leadership do not make a direct contribution to school improvement and could be seen by teachers as trivial. Transaction or instrumental tasks can be used for transformational purposes.
Leadership for organizational learning • Team learning. • Whole school learning.	Leadership makes a difference to group and whole school learning. Leaders are able to control the opportunities for and the ways in which learning takes place, e.g. missions, cultures, structures and resources.
Maintaining the emotional balance • Preventing teacher stress and burnout.	Leadership is a factor in the creation and amelioration of teacher burnout. Leadership has an indirect impact on teacher burnout through the effect on organisational factors.

Figure 5.3   Developing transformational leadership (based on Leithwood et al., 1999)

leadership' built around 'trusting relationships', and Stålhammar (1994) makes a case for 'goal-oriented leadership' as the means through which vision can be created and achieved.

• Emotional commitment has been used by Klein and Dikert (1999) to argue that leadership is not technical but is artful and creative.
• The intelligences of leaders has been developed by Gardner (1998) in which leaders can display the talent to connect with followers by being 'able to tell a convincing story; and they can embody that story in their own daily lives' (p. 204).

- The agency and behaviour of the leader is located, for example, in the symbolic importance of talk and actions in leadership communication and relationships (Kelly and Bredeson, 1991) and in leadership competencies (Diggins, 1997).
- Cultural change through 'collaborative cultures' is the means through which the leader can empower and support learning amongst staff (Jenkins, 1997).

Bass (1985) has been important in developing a testable model of leadership (Leithwood et al., 1996), and in education important work has taken place in creating an evidence base regarding leadership effects in educational institutions (Caldwell, 1998; Geijsel et al., 1999; Hallinger and Heck, 1996a; 1996b; Leithwood et al., 1997; 1999). Leithwood et al. (1999, p. 38) show that the direct effect of leaders on 'student outcomes are modest but important' and this is related to levels of satisfaction with the leader. This model has been globalised across western-style democracies (e.g. Caldwell and Spinks, 1988; 1992; 1998), in which the role of the principal and teacher is being changed in ways that can be described as transformational leadership (Goldring, 1992; Hallinger, 1992). The claim made by those who position themselves around transformational leadership is that it is a theory that is comprehensive and fits with the restructuring context, and in particular is vital to the change process. Transformational leadership has been given official approval within government policy and the current training agenda, and in the Foreword to the propectus for the National College for School Leadership both Blair and Blunkett tell us that: 'Leadership and vision are crucial to raising standards and aspirations across the nation's schools' (DfEE, 1999, p. 2).

Educational transformational leadership

Transformational leadership and its variants have been and continue to be subjected to critique from a variety of different positions, not least the need to be aware of the historical and cultural settings into which globalised models are being imported. As Kam-Cheung (1997) reminds us, in Chinese history the group is more important than the individual leader. Critical evaluations focus on the power issues underpinning epistemological claims about leadership traits, behaviours and relationships, and argue that what is being presented as a new and innovative approach to school leadership clearly serves the old established purposes of centralised control and authority. Internationally, work by Bates (1989; 1993), Blackmore (1989; 1996; 1999) and Smyth (1989a; 1993; 1996; with Shacklock, 1998b) has been central to bringing together and presenting a critical position about the impact of mandated models of leadership on teaching and learning. Within the UK important work has been done regarding the historical roots and impact of official leadership models embedded within government policy and how these are promoted by particular knowledge workers (Ball, 1990b; 1995, Grace; 1995; Whitty et al., 1998).

Gronn (1996) argues that charismatic approaches to leadership are not new but can be traced back to Weber. This connection with the social sciences enables two important intellectual resources to be drawn on: first, the interplay between agency and structure enables us to reveal that it is not 'possible to reduce complex educational problems to administrative issues . . . soluble at the school level' (Angus, 1989, p. 63); and, second, there are, as Smyth (1989b) argues, alternatives to the 'behaviourist and functionalist views that have come to entrap those who live, work and conduct research on the area of educational leadership' (p. 4). This combination of problematising the taken for granted models of leadership with the development of alternatives is central to the debate, and a key point is that transformational leadership is not really transformational. It is argued that the current shaping of transformational leadership enables and supports existing power structures to be maintained and developed, and in particular it is a 'top-dog theory' that meets the needs of management (Ball, 1987; Watkins, 1989) or in Allix's (2000) terms 'implies a pattern of social relations structured not for education, but for *domination*' (p. 18). Foster (1989) argues that the authentic *transform*ational aspect has been stripped away and so it is less about social change and more about serving bureaucracy. The argument that culture can be managed and manipulated based on Deal and Kennedy's (1982) work is disputed, and in particular the point is made that culture is contested, particularly in professional and educational settings (Angus, 1996). As Blase and Anderson (1995) argue, managing the culture is about domination, and denies the heterogenous nature of the groups who are actually involved in the restructuring processes in education, and unless participants have a 'micropolitical literacy' (p. 137), or what Maxcy and Caldas (1991) describe as a 'critical imagination' (p. 48), then working together may be more about collusion than a democratic encounter over choices.

Leadership as a performance means that the links between leaders and education are cut, and so transformational leadership is more about leadership in educational settings than educational leadership. Angus (1989) argues that there is no evidence that entrepreneural traits such as vision and risk-taking bring educational success. Furthermore, Gronn (1996) argues that there is a strong romantic notion around transformational leadership in which 'significance is mostly attributed in the popular mind to the idea of a "leader" or "leadership" as *the* causal entity rendering ill-structured, complex problems meaningful and explicable' (pp. 11–12 original emphasis). The questioning of the knowledge claims underpinning the cause and effect connections between post-holders and learning outcomes is what Bates (1989) describes as a 'parody of natural science' (p. 133) because there is an attempt to exercise leadership as if it is in laboratory conditions so that if we create the right context then leadership practice can be replicated to good effect.

Gronn (1996) emphasises what he calls the 'barren models of follow-ership' (p. 12) because they give too much weight to agency of leader, and: 'leadership is seen as something performed by superior, better indi-viduals (invariably, ageing white males), rather than by groups, located in top positions, and as something done *to* or *for* other inferior, lesser people' (p. 12,). Furthermore, the hunt for positive leadership effects can actually disguise the negative ones, through 'an anodyne instilling in them of a disposition of learned helplessness,' (p. 11). Recently, Gronn (2000) has argued that leadership is distributed rather than concentrated, and this is based on the realities of the workplace in which people and the roles they perform interlock. This has a long tradition within the UK and international fields, and is located particularly in the humane tradition of Greenfield (Greenfield and Ribbins, 1993), and more recently Ball's (1987) and Hoyle's (1982; 1999) analysis of the macro and microp-olitics of organisational life. Research being done to collect the stories and professional experiences of headteachers illustrates the complex interplay between agency and structure, in which as Angus (1996) argues 'educa-tional participants are . . . social and political actors rather than occupants of organizational roles' (p. 990). The realities of working and living within power structures reveals the importance of human agency on the part of those meant to follow, and this exercise of leadership is being masked according to Blackmore (1989) by a 'gender blindness' in leadership models.

Transformational leadership is being buttressed by performance man-agement models that are concerned with simultaneously individualising and collectivising output production and measurements. This is illus-trated by the quality movement, and more recently re-engineering (Hammer, 1996) that puts the emphasis on the individual to proactively determine product standards, and consequently be a part of a collectiv-ity based on the same values and commitment to the product. In this way performance management has shifted from the leadership surveillance of work to the self-discipline of performativity (Ball, 1999). Consequently, while Beare et al. (1993) argue that transformational leadership requires both masculine and feminine approaches, and McCrea and Ehrich (1999) argue for a 'change of heart and consider or strengthen the place of a caring feminine heart in their daily interactions with others' (p. 431), the alternative position is that all this does is to use people's skills to enable organisational management to run smoothly rather than enable tradi-tional power structures to be transformed.

The alternative position is that leadership is not located with one person and ought not to be: 'leadership is and must be socially critical, it does not reside in an individual but in the relationship between indi-viduals, and it is oriented toward social vision and change, not simply, or only, organizational change' (Foster, 1989, p. 46). History has been con-structed and written in ways that present progress and grand events as the product of individual agency, when the reality is 'a conjunction of ideas where leadership is shared and transferred between leaders and followers, each only a temporary designation' (Foster, 1989, p. 49). In this way leadership is commonplace, and happens locally and incrementally, and is successful in bringing about transformations (Ryan, 1998). This approach requires teachers to be critical in ways that subordinated followership denies.

Transformational leadership operates on the basis that schools as organisations are real and are outcome orientated, and this underpins the power structure supporting the leader. However, as Smyth (1989c) argues, teachers talk together on their own terms, and so empowerment is about questioning the ownership of the problem and where the capacity lies to change the situation that created the problem. This position is based on the observation that teachers have been excluded from participating in educational restructuring except as objects to be reformed by the government, and to be led by their structural betters. Smyth et al. (1998) argue that teachers have a long history of providing and displaying leadership, but it is a leadership that involves a different type of transformational role: 'teacher leadership is, therefore, about teachers understanding the broader forces shaping their work, resisting domestication and not being dominated by outside authorities' (p. 99). Teachers who think, challenge and question both habits and reforms have a different engagement with pedagogy than the technical requirements of job descriptions and competency frameworks. It assumes that there is a human and political relationship between teacher and pupil, where pedagogy is a leadership relationship based on mutual learning and development. Smyth (1996) argues for the restoration of 'Educative Leadership' to self-managing schools in which the process by which the school and community is involved enables democratic and communal ways of working to educate all participants.

Summary

Positioning within and between fields over theories of and about leadership is concerned with power and the interplay between agency and structure. In reading about, listening to and practising leadership in education we need to ask questions about the theory being used and developed to make a case regarding a particular political position over values and ethics. Knowledge about the knowledge being presented, and a critical approach to the claims being made, enables us to be aware and potentially to seek liberation from the structures that structure who we are and what we can and cannot do. Those engaged in educational practice are made powerful and powerless by the theories and theorising that is or is not revealed.

Chapters 4 and 5 have provided a strategic overview of theorising research into and about educational leadership and leadership in educational settings. Now that this groundwork has been done I move into the theorising and research about particular aspects of educational leadership. Again choices have been made in order to illustrate what we do and do not know about leaders and leadership. Chapter 6 is concerned with where leaders come from and how they are prepared for their work. This leads on to three chapters (7, 8 and 9) which looks in detail at head-teachers and role incumbents such as senior managers, and middle managers, before going on to investigate teachers and students as leaders.

6

Preparing and Preparation

What we know from research and theorising about how people come to be and are prepared for leading and leadership is the focus of this chapter. I draw on knowledge about the personal and professional decisions made by individuals to move into and out of roles, together with work that looks at the contextual settings in which agency is exercised and structured. This work is located mainly in the humanist tradition based on biographies, though important critical work that seeks to connect agency with issues of social justice such as gender enables a rich understanding of the complexities of working lives.

Pathways and careers

Professional pathways have tended to be theorised through the identification and abstraction of phases or stages (Pascal and Ribbins, 1998; Rayner and Ribbins, 1999; Reeves et al., 1998; Weindling, 1999). Gronn's (1993; 1999b) work on Sir James Darling combined with a broader analysis of how leaders are 'made' (Gronn, 1999a) has led him to argue that there are four phases to what he describes as a 'leadership career':

1. *Formation*: socialisation and experiences from childhood to adulthood.
2. *Accession*: preparation and positioning to be a leader.
3. *Incumbency*: experience and maturity as a leader.
4. *Divestiture*: letting go from the leader role.

The background to this work is a commitment by Gronn to biographical methods and he argues in favour of conceptualising leadership pathways as a career, and in so doing states that this must: first, allow for those who have ambition and plan their career as well as those who experience serendipity; and, second, while there are some leaders who are able to reflect upon and be explicit about their career as it forms, it is more usual to consider career pathways in retrospect. While Gronn acknowledges the problematic nature of this, he does make a strong case for aspirants learning from the research evidence so that they can 'think strategically as regards themselves and their future careers' (1999a, p. 25). Gronn (1999a) argues that this career approach needs to be located within a historical, cultural and social setting which are not of the leader's choosing. In other words, we are born and raised in contexts at particular times that seek to determine and shape us and, so, our choices and actions need to be understood within this environment.

Hall (1996) builds on work from a range of settings, including education, to argue that the linear career model based on clear goals renders invisible the realities of women's lives. Evetts (1994) shows how career choices and experiences are located in personal lives, and she is particularly interested in the dilemmas regarding decisions to apply for a job and everything that goes with this, such as moving house and the impact on a partner and children. She develops and argues in favour of analysing these struggles as 'strategies' in order to avoid the dichotomy of structure and agency, and develops the following typology:

- *Single career*: one person seeks promotion.
   The one-person career strategy: unmarried.
   The two-person career strategy: married, but second person does not seek promotion.
- *Dual career*: both partners have sought and gained promotions.
   Postponement strategy: one partner waits while the other obtains promotion and then seeks promotion themselves.
   Modification strategy: one partner adapts their career to fit in with the promotions of the other partner.
   Balancing strategy: both partners simultaneously or alternatively gain promotion.
- *Marital breakdown*: when partnership strategies are unsuccessful (ibid., p. 53).

Hall uses Evetts's (1994) career typologies to show how at different stages in a professional life there are different pressures and opportunities to be handled. For example, she identifies that Heather and Vanessa experienced 'accommodation' where they combined work and family in ways that enabled them to take steps 'to avoid suggestions that they were doing either job less well'. They received support from heads who understood the dilemmas, and once they were headteachers they 'also tried to reproduce the support they had received as working mothers in their attitudes to colleagues with similar concerns, whether men or women' (pp. 49–50). What is interesting from Hall's (1996) research and analysis is how the struggle to position the self in a leadership role has strong connections to agency and 'self efficacy' (p. 61). Hall identifies a strong commitment to children running through the professional lives of the women heads, and how choices about moving job or seeking improved credentials are connected to a review of their own development and how it contributed to their professional skills. In this sense, if barriers to promotion were experienced by the women, they were able to overcome them and they were able to help others (both men and women) who followed on. Of course, what we do not know are the stories of the women (and the men) who were unable to overcome the barriers.

Biographies of headteacher career pathways have increased and it seems that we can only see the place of other post-holders and teachers through the lens of a total career. As yet there is no work on the pathways to middle management as a research enquiry in itself. While there is a growing body of work that theorises and describes the career history of headteachers, and there is evidence of differentiated experience in applications for and being successful in being appointed to headship, we do not know enough about those who apply and give up, or who do not apply at all. Much political post-holder succession is done in public and, so, politician watchers can often speculate on the 'best prime minister/president we never had', and while members of staff common rooms can engage in some of this, for an aspiring headteacher decisions not to apply or their failure to achieve an appointment does not receive this level of public scrutiny, and perhaps rightly so. However, research can and does open up our understanding of lost aspiring leaders, and those who may not aspire because of the power structures in which they live and work and, in particular, how the post of headship or subject leader as they see it being lived by role incumbents or described through policy texts puts them off. Furthermore, while we may wonder that school restructuring has led to questions about the future of the deputy head and what this means for recruitment to headship, perhaps in addition to asking questions about where do headteachers come from we should ask where do headteachers go to?

Working lives: choices and selection

Research into the process of headteacher selection shows the drive to make the process more systematic and transparent through the adoption of rational job and person specifications (Morgan et al., 1983; 1984). Kirkham (2000) argues that, while governing bodies have taken this on board, what applicants need to know are 'the particular conditions which prevail in the school itself' (p. 19). In this sense there remains the issue of the human engagement of whether the job 'feels' right and, in addition to this, Kirkham also notes that hunch and amateurism continues. It seems that what we really need to know more about are the working lives of those who are involved in the decisions, choices and events surrounding leadership formation and accession.

Data gathered through headteachers' stories about their professional lives shows diversity and that the pathways to headship are not uniform or predictable (Ouston, 1997). What seems to be a central feature within the 36 headteacher and senior executive/post-holder interviews gathered by Ribbins (Ribbins and Marland, 1994; Pascal and Ribbins, 1998; Rayner and Ribbins, 1999) is that within a career there is evidence of the complex interaction between agency and structure. Socialisation processes in the development and generation of habitus illustrate that the positioning and repositioning within the field of education from childhood through to senior manager incumbency in an educational institution is fluid, dynamic and, often, unstrategic. Ouston's (1997) analysis of headteacher biographies shows that there is no strong parental influence on the choice of career; attitudes to schooling varied, with a lack of a positive attitude to primary but a more positive one towards their secondary experiences; and only one of the interviewees left school to go into higher education with the intention of becoming a teacher. However, underpinning the interviews is a disposition towards people and the importance of positive and productive relationships, combined with experiences in other occupations that revealed their habitus towards and for teaching. Once in teaching the interviews show that the movement into senior management is connected with a disposition towards being the headteacher, and a realisation that this is where they wished to stake their professional capital. For example: Ashford (with Ribbins, 1998) tells us: 'I did not think of having my own school until I saw what Roy was doing. I liked it and I wanted to do it. I wanted to support and facilitate the work of other teachers as well as run my own classroom' (p. 55). Beeson (with Ribbins, 1998) recalls:

> 'The second head tried to persuade me to go for promotion a couple of times but I said I was happy where I was. But I began to feel she was making it difficult for me to do the things I wanted to do, and heard the odd comment that "well you haven't got the rank and authority to do that". On one such occasion I decided enough was enough'. (p. 76)

The preparation for this repositioning is connected to a number of experiences while in middle management and deputy roles, and research from the USA and Britain shows how principals/headteachers feel unprepared for the role (Daresh and Male, 2000). This is what Pascal and Ribbins (1998) call 'accession' (p. 20) in which the struggle regarding position and the accumulation of capital is central in 'the preparation and construction of oneself as a credible candidate for office and acquisition of a marketable performance routine to convince prospective talent-spotters and appointment panel members and selectors' (p. 20). Learning from other heads either positively or negatively seems to be important, as Clarke (1997) states: 'The head I worked with there has retired now but my time with him helped to clarify the sort of head I wasn't going to be' (p. 95). Positioning of the self in the right school is important, though this is not necessarily linear, and there is a lot of evidence about how headteachers have experienced being positioned by others (Reeves et al., 1998). David Davies in conversation with Peter Ribbins (Davies with Ribbins, 1998) tells the story of his applications for headship in which he applied for three headships. The first two he was told not to apply for by the LEA adviser but went ahead anyway, and the third he was told to apply for even though he was reluctant. He got the job.

What seems to be important is how networking, sponsorship and reputation management, through letting people know about vacancies and encouraging applications, is essential for a successful appointment. This tends to favour men more than women (Riley, 1998), and Evetts (1994) shows that there are 'differences in career identity, socialization and expectation (i.e. women teachers don't apply) and differences in gender discrimination (i.e. women candidates for headship posts are more of a risk)' (p. 39). Draper and McMichael (1998a) profile those who are *very likely to apply* for headship as people who have a strategic approach to their career with headship in their sights, feel that they are ready and are not put off by the demands of the job. They 'are men rather than women', 'are younger rather than older' and 'accept the loss of contact with children' (ibid., pp. 168–9). What is interesting here is that these characteristics of the 'typical applicant' are ones that could sustain barriers against both knowing and realising professional aspirations. These characteristics privilege traditional norms and exemplify the 'glass ceiling' (Davidson and Cooper, 1992; Hansard Society, 1990) and 'concrete ceiling' (Davidson, 1997) that limit professional opportunities in both the public and private sectors. Consequently, as Roach (1993) argues, as a women deputy head she is faced with adopting ways of understanding the world that do not fit with her habitus, and in making applications or discussing job descriptions, certain jobs are characterised as men's work or women's work in which, as Acker (1992) notes, there is a 'skill hierarchy' regarding what is and is not legitimately competent (p. 112). Abrol (with Ribbins, 1999) tells us: 'There is prejudice in our own community and the racialism is from the other side, it's three times the battle being a woman, an Asian woman in a male-dominated society and then in a racialist community' (p. 65).

How we explain those who do and do not break through is complex, though research does emphasise structural injustices in which existing power structures such as culture either discriminate against or put people off from seeking promotion (Al-Khalifa, 1989; Ozga, 1993). There is evidence that role models are important, though as Adler et al. (1993) note this is 'not enough to end a pattern of male and white dominance' (p. 24), and while women are able to acknowledge the positive influence of those who have supported and encouraged them, organisational networking and informal mentoring tends to favour men of a particular type: 'mentors tend to chose protégés who are like themselves, so men chose men' (p. 33). How people experience their lives, work and organisations is central to identity and the choices that are made regarding promotion and career. Acker (1992, pp. 252–3) identifies the features of a gendered organisation in which jobs remain 'gender patterned' through which men are advantaged, and symbolism creates a 'gendered persona' in which identity is shaped around what is and is not acceptable. How things are done within the organisation tends to be rational, efficient and effective, though this is usually presented as being gender neutral.

There is considerable evidence of what it means to be not accepted with the implications this has for leadership, and also of harassment against those who have broken through (Al-Khalifa, 1989; de Lyon, 1989). Nevertheless, research into experiences provides evidence about how people develop productive strategies to work through the barriers of stereotyping, and the isolation of being perhaps the only woman or the only black person at a management level or in an organisation (Walker, 1993). As Hall (1993; 1999b) argues we could be limiting opportunity by how we conceptualise leadership and management as masculine because once a women has broken through then they are doing the job: 'management can be defined in terms of how they are doing it, not according to a pre-determined model which they may or may not fit' (Hall, 1993, p. 37). Furthermore, it could be argued that conflating male with masculinity means losing opportunities to research and theorise about how men are put off applying or are uncomfortable in the roles that they are expected to perform. Reay and Ball (2000) argue that gender identity is much more fluid and contradictory than much of the writing and theorising about women managers suggests. Consequently, Blackmore (1999) argues in favour of a 'feminist postmasculinist politics of educational leadership' because it would 'recognize first and foremost the politics of difference; not a difference that dilutes into diversity in the negative, assimilationist sense, but one that values particular first order differences of gender, race, class, ethnicity and sexuality equally' (p. 218). In particular, she goes on to argue that there is a need to theorise in ways that engage both women and men with issues of power because 'institutions promise power, but such promises are illusory for most men' (p. 220).

James and Whiting (1998) have been working on the contexts in which both men and women as deputy headteachers decide whether to seek headship. This is particularly important at a time when the government is seeking to integrate teacher experiences of in-service training so that there is a pool of accredited potential heads to draw from, and at a time when there is a concern about job satisfaction (Mercer, 1997a; 1997b), and serving heads are leaving the profession early and posts remain unfilled (Dean, 2000b). James and Whiting (1998) found that deputy heads varied in their position or what they call their 'career anchorage' in regard to headship. Some are 'active aspirants' with applications in progress, and some see themselves as 'potential aspirants'. Others have experienced the process and are 'unpredictables' as they are unsure of future applications, and the 'unavailed aspirants' have tried it and will not apply again. Finally, there are the 'settlers' who have not and do not expect to apply (ibid., p. 356). What is interesting about this work is how the decision whether to aspire or to settle was made earlier rather than later in their senior management experiences. The survey work had some interesting things to say about gender in which women are more likely to be an 'aspirant' or a 'settler' rather than an applicant, though evidence from the interview data shows that both men and women provide similar family and personal reasons as to why they do not apply. The picture of headship that is acquired is one that deputy heads do not want: there are not enough resources to do the job, and public accountability is too risky.

The implications of research are that in seeking to theorise about the professional working lives in which teachers make decisions to seek promotion and headship, needs to take into account the agency of the individual, i.e. their beliefs, self-esteem and aspirations combined with the settings and power structures in which decisions and choices are played out over time. Post-holders still, by and large, come from the education profession, in spite of neo-liberal moves to open access to business managers, and so they enter and work within structures and cultures of requirements and expectations regarding what a leader and manager should be and how they should conduct themselves. The consequences of this are that we may not ask deeper questions about the power tied up in the cultures and structures that sustain the systemic logic of role incumbency, and the emphasis on how it is naturalised and integrated with personal and organisational progress. In this way our gaze may not fall on pupils and teachers exercising leadership through the pedagogic process, and they remain silenced through this (Blackmore, 1999). Clearly, research work is showing that the push-pull aspects of career create tensions and is often contradictory, though the identity of being and valuing being a teacher remains strong.

Leading and leadership over time

Being appointed to a particular post with a particular job description, does not, as I have already argued, automatically confirm the person as a leader or having the capacity to exercise leadership in a particular context at a particular time. We know that dysfunctional succession can contribute to school ineffectiveness (Fink, 1999) through not only what might be regarded as expected disruption, but also the unexpected impact of other changes that could take place. Furthermore, we need to take into account whether the accession is for an interim or permanent post and, as Ortiz and Kalbus (1998) show in their study of superintendent succession in the USA, there is little research into the experiences of those who take on an acting role.

Benaim and Humphreys (1997), in their study of novice headteachers, show that there are a number of issues around practice:

- *Complexity of the process*: the tension between demands for change and

the need for the new headteacher to integrate.
- *Challenges to be faced*: becoming resilient in handling comparisons with predecessors and questions about competence.
- *Display of change management abilities*: dealing with people and handling micropolitical activity in developmental processes.
- *First year of headship*: positioning of and by the headteacher that could lead to isolation and distance.
- *Occupational culture*: handling the quantitative and qualitative changes in headteacher responsibilities.

This type of work enables us to see that headship needs to be conceptualised in ways that provide an understanding of the dynamics, and Day and Bakioğlu (1996) provide a four-phased approach: initiation, development, autonomy and disenchantment. The interview data gathered illustrates the complexity underpinning headteacher experiences and how they are 'affected by life history, previous role preparation, inherited school culture, external environments and personal-belief factors, and their ability to manage stress' (ibid., p. 222). Work by Draper and McMichael (1998b) found that new headteachers experienced 'detachment gains' by throwing off the restrictions of being a deputy but also 'detachment losses' by leaving friendships behind. Also of significance are the 'attachment gains' of moving to a new school in which they could take charge and make things happen. However, for longer-serving headteachers there are issues around sustaining headship, and a central feature of Day and Bakioğlu's (1996) findings and analysis is the identification of the disenchantment phase and the consequences this has for educational development and improvement. They conclude that: 'the potential for learning and development among school headteachers declines after an initial surge over four years within the first eight years of headship' (ibid., p. 224), and so there is a need for 'intelligent planned support' (ibid.).

Draper and McMichael's (1996) research into the decision to take early retirement by headteachers shows the impact of additional pressures of doing the job and a reluctance to continue with the challenge of how best to work things through for the benefit of the school. Evetts's (1994) work shows that there are four types of head who did not express concern about their careers: those who are new in post, those with plans to retire, and those who still had challenges either inside or outside school. The main concerns came from male headteachers who Evetts (1994) identifies as being in mid-career where they had been appointed young (certainly younger than female headteachers) and faced the prospect of being in the same job until retirement. What is problematic for headteachers is that there is no career structure beyond their appointment, except perhaps to move to another headship. Mercer (1997a) concludes that there is a need to provide support for, and further research into, headteachers in 'mid-career' in order to 'prevent the haemorrhage of experienced headteachers' (p. 280). Evetts (1994) goes on to show how career structures are formed by the choices of those within a long-standing process and, as long as teachers seek and obtain promotion, this will remain the culture and structure of experiences and expectations.

Ribbins (1999; Pascal and Ribbins, 1998; Rayner and Ribbins, 1999) has built on this work into the stages of headship and argues that there is evidence of heads who experience a 'reinvention or rebirth, in which the incumbent moves on towards a newly created professional life, within a significantly different context and with newly created parameters' (Pascal and Ribbins, 1998, pp. 10–11). A career structure beyond headship has possibilities as heads may seek new challenges through work with the LEA, within an HEI, or a government agency such as working as an NPQH trainer and/or an OfSTED inspector and/or a performance threshold assessor. Increasingly, heads who have taken early retirement have the opportunity to move into the marketplace and work as consultants through contract and agency work. Nevertheless, how we understand work and lives is being challenged by the intervention of government policy into the headship of schools through the secondment of heads of successful schools to schools that are officially deemed to be failing or struggling. This is an aspect of headship that is unresearched, and we only become aware of it through dramatic cases (e.g. the Ridings School [Clark, 1998]). It is hard to see how the headteacher as celebrity superhead does and will fit into how we understand and theorise about professional lives. We do not know enough about who is chosen, why they are chosen, why headteachers respond to the invitation and what this means for their own professional experiences, and the impact on the schools where they have been moved/seconded from.

Learning, experience and support

Understanding how work is experienced and how professional learning takes place has been explored by Restine (1997) who argues that there is no automatic cause-and-effect connection between having experience and actually learning from it. Using the medical triage procedure as a metaphor for 'educational triage', the process of 'prioritizing, deciding and acting' enables the professional learning experience to be captured and understood. In particular the respondents talked about 'leading from beside and behind' rather than pulling or dragging people along from in front. Knowing where to focus is summed up in 'holding on and letting go' in which principals learned to challenge their established assumptions and so could let go of some ideas and put their energies into others (ibid., pp. 263–4). Overall, Restine (1997) concludes on the integrative nature of learning through practice with others who can support reflection on that practice. This work moves us forward by raising questions about appropriate preparation and training, the types of knowledge required and what types of provision are and should be made for educational professionals.

Research into newly appointed headteachers shows that practice is about developing a new identity and an understanding of the often contradictory cocktail of the expectations, realities and philosophies of headship. Southworth (1995b) argues that it is not so much that new headteachers face isolation, as they will have experienced this as classroom teachers, but that 'new headteachers have to come to terms with both feeling more alone and being more responsible. They are expected to make decisions and exercise authority and may have no one to turn to for advice, help or assistance' (ibid., p. 19). Work has been done on the importance of induction in which mentoring by a professional peer can play an important part in supporting the immediate taking-charge issues facing the new headteacher. While mentoring has become a systemic feature of initial teacher training, its place in supporting headteachers is known about but has not always been officially resourced and supported. Nevertheless research evidence from England and Wales (Bolam et al., 1995b; Bush and Coleman, 1995; Kirkham, 1995; Pocklington and Weindling, 1996; Southworth, 1995b) and internationally (Daresh, 1995; Playko, 1995; Walker et al., 1993) is clear about the benefits of mentoring and ongoing training.

What seems to matter most, and can raise concerns about mentoring, is establishing a professional relationship between the 'novice' and 'experienced' headteacher. If the wrong people are matched or if one becomes too dependent on the other then it can fail, and what is unclear so far in the writing is how mentors are accountable in ways other than ending the partnership. Central to this is an understanding by those who design the system and those who work within it of the power issues underpinning the relationship and how the purposes of mentoring are conceptualised and lived. Bolam et al. (1995b) report on an evaluation of a national pilot scheme for mentoring new headteachers in England and Wales, and find that, while the training had discouraged the mentors from 'offering solutions to the new head's problems', half of the mentors had done this and a large majority of headteachers and mentors said it was helpful. Integral to this is how the problem-solving approach enabled mutuality in which the mentor also gained because working with the new headteacher reduced their isolation and supported reflection on their own headship (Bolam et al., 1995b; Bush and Coleman, 1995; Playko, 1995). Training and matching is important as otherwise mentoring could become a co-option process into individualistic, and potentially conservative, ways of working (Walker et al., 1993). Mentoring could be a means through which accepted power structures go unchallenged, and Southworth (1995b) argues that while the process may support reflection he is not confident that it is enabling *critical reflection* in which headteachers are enabled to ask fundamental questions about how and why things are done.

Given the weight and significance of research findings about the benefits of formal mentoring and evidence about how heads build networks and seek informal support (Cole, 1996), it might be expected that government plans for the development of aspiring and new-to-post headteachers as leaders would adopt peer mentoring. Without specific funding mentoring practice will flounder as predicted by Pocklington and Weindling (1996). A lost opportunity has been the HEADLAMP programme in which new headteachers where given £2,500 to support their professional development during the first two years in post. Kirkham (1995) regrets that the scheme does not mention mentoring and without this component it will fail to support headteacher effectiveness. Similarly, headteacher appraisal has been underfunded, and any personal and professional gains have been overtaken by events in which OfSTED inspections, combined with current moves towards PRP and increased governor involvement, have put more emphasis on performance than on development (Healy, 1994).

Professional development and training

Currently, there is a strong emphasis on leadership preparation through formal professional development and training across the world. Coombe and White (1994) report on how the leadership skills of headteachers in African schools can be improved; Kitavi and Van der Westhuizen (1997) provide a case study of skill development for new-in-post principals in Kenya, and Sapra (1993) provides demanding training agenda for educational managers in India in order to meet the requirements and implications of reform. This type of work is important in enabling an understanding of how professional development in education is being worked through on the ground in particular national, cultural and political settings.

Historically the emphasis in education systems in North America, Europe, Australia and New Zealand has been on the *preparation* of professionals but, increasingly, the emphasis in England and Wales has been on the *training* for a particular post with the specific know-how and skills required to be a competent and accredited leader. In spite of attempts to do so, this is not settled, and contestation continues around the areas of purpose and provision. Work by J. Murphy (1998) is important in enabling us to see how in the longer-established tradition of principal preparation in the USA the purpose and nature of provision is economically, socially and historically located. There are periods of 'ferment' over the what, how and why of principal preparation and training, and this has more to say about the impact of enduring power structures than it does about any enduring truths.

Accounts by headteachers in England and Wales show a strongly individualistic approach and varied experience of being prepared. Ashdown (with Rayner, 1999), Davies (with Ribbins, 1998) and Morgan (with Rayner, 1999) note that no training was available when they were deputies, while Hinchliffe (with Ribbins, 1999) recalls attending but cannot remember much about a course. For Beeson (with Ribbins, 1998) the most important course she did was on counselling, as it supported her work with parents, while for Hyde (1997) the experience of going on a management of change course in industry had an impact on how she saw herself and work: 'after the course I realised I needed another challenge and that is why I applied for a headship' (p. 113). Ashdown (with Rayner, 1999) argues against long-term academic study in favour of experiential learning, while others demonstrate a strong commitment to long courses leading to specialised research dissertations (Abrol with Ribbins, 1999; Craig with Rayner, 1999; Gasper with Pascal, 1998; Matthew with Pascal, 1998). This research evidence enables us to see how particular headteachers have worked out an approach to their own development and how this connects to their disposition to learn. At the heart of these stories is the purpose of learning and whether it is instrumental or technical learning in which particular competences are identified and measured (Earley, 1993), through to learning that is about the philosophical and humanistic approaches to leadership (Greenfield and Ribbins, 1993; Hodgkinson, 1991). There is a concern to emphasise that learning is not just about capability but also capacity, and in particular the development of political literacy. This approach leads Ehrich (1997) to argue from an Australian perspective that 'while professional development tends to be seen as an instrument for enforcing education policies mandated by governments, the principal has a role to play in reclaiming the agenda and ensuring that it meets the needs of individual teachers and school – based needs' (p. 17).

There are two underlying issues here regarding what is to be learned and how adults in professional roles learn. What is clear from the literature is that the formal learning process has been subject to criticism across the world, and Johnson N., (1993) reports that in the USA, Canada, Britain and Australia there are concerns about the type and quality of leadership preparation courses (see also Bredeson, 1996). For example, Mulkeen and Cooper (1992) present their observations about the USA where knowledge claims are based on a science of organisational control underpinned by a technology of knowledge transmission. However, the preparation for leadership as an intellectual and practical process is increasingly being reported on, and HEIs are developing a range of ways to support learning:

- problem-based learning (Crowther and Limerick, 1998);
- experiential learning through fieldwork, simulations and the stories and experiences of practitioners (Johnson, N., 1993; Danzig, 1997; 1999);
- supporting partnership arrangements in the development of leadership centres (Harvey et al., 1999);
- evidencing through portfolio approaches to assessment (Wildy and Wallace, 1998).

Maxcy (1998) reports on how the move away from the uncritical adoption and transference of business models into education has enabled more socially critical work to be developed. This is in keeping with the growing pluralism in American society where traditional approaches to educational administration 'overlooked the ethnic, racial and religious, literary, sculptural, and configural nature of leading human enterprises' (ibid., p. 219). Maxcy (1998) presents an 'ethno-democratic school leadership' programme which 'means leading from a race/culture orientation with critical-mindedness and value-mindedness in the forefront' (p. 218). In this sense the abstract rights of democracy are challenged through the recognition of difference, and a case study of Hispanics is presented in which empowerment is a political process supported by 'dialogue and problem-posing' (ibid., p. 233). In this way, understanding the current and potential workings of a democratic way of life is developed through teaching in which participation and dialogue enables lives and cultures to be understood and recognised.

From the 1960s there was a rapid growth in the provision of postgraduate courses in educational administration (Hughes et al., 1981). There has always been a strong emphasis on creative ways of supporting the learning process (Taylor, 1973), and it has become an accepted feature of professional development that teachers and post-holders in schools undertake an award-bearing course such as a Master's degree (Creissen and Ellison, 1998). Recently the growth in the taught doctorate (EdD) provides opportunities to combine workplace learning with the development and practice of research literacy. However, what is evident when reviewing the field in the UK is the trend towards more competence and prescriptively determined learning, in which HEIs become the home for assessment centres where leadership skills are measured (Lyons et al., 1993). Earley (1993) charts the development of this through the use of 'occupational standards' which are associated with the Management Charter Initiative (MCI) and the School Management South (SMS). Earley (1993) presents the benefits and concerns about competences and this tends to be about the 'what works' issue rather than the impact they are having on identities and how this connects with the business management structures that sustain site-based performance management in education. Set into context, competences are a part of the science of effectiveness and improvement that is disconnected from pedagogic relationships. As Riley (1998) argues: 'competence is important but it is passion and commitment which will keep the attention focused on young people' (p. 150). Ouston (1993) argues that 'questions of value and philosophy are not addressed in the MCI/SMS approach' and she shows how what is meant by 'effectiveness' and 'competence' are not agreed (p. 213). Furthermore, she goes on to argue that who decides what is good practice is not just a matter for general universalistic descriptions (that can be interpreted as prescriptions), but is a matter for schools to work out themselves at local level.

In reviewing developments in North America and the UK, Hart (1999) argues that: 'the move to outcome-based standards versus course driven or curricular standards is one of the most prevalent changes in school leadership development' (p. 331). This is exemplified in the National Standards for both headteachers (TTA, 1998a) and subject leaders (TTA, 1998b). The *National Standards for Headteachers* are in five sections and present '82 criteria which a candidate has to meet and which the training and development needs to address' (Lodge, 1998, p. 350). These standards are the basis on which training and assessment of readiness for headship through the award of the NPQH takes place. While there have been a number of celebratory accounts of the NPQH technology (Collarbone, 1998; Creissen, 1997), the training and assessment has been reviewed following criticism from a wide range of researchers, practitioners and commentators (Bush, 1998; Gunter, 1999b; Riley, 1998). As Riley (1998) shows in her comparison with the standards produced by the Council of Chief School Officers in the USA, and the core job description for headship by the Flemish Ministry of Education, the emphasis in England is more on accountability and securing outcomes. Winkley (with Pascal, 1998) as a headteacher argues that it is possible to go through the training 'and still not be terribly good as a head' because much of the training is what can be learned very quickly. The most important aspects of headship are missing, such as the culture and values of the school and: 'these are really deep, philosophical questions that are both intellectually demanding, but also require you to think about yourself as a person.' (ibid., pp. 236–7).

The introduction of centrally determined and accredited training for those seeking to move into headship is an attempt to break with the past, and as Fidler (1998) states, 'there has been a conscious attempt not to use existing qualifications, structures or experiences as the backbone for the new initiative' (p. 314). Furthermore, the experiences of women into and within management programmes in developing innovative ways of learning have also been sidelined (e.g. Atchison, 1993; Harrison and Williams, 1993; Shipton and Tatton, 1989). It seems that locating development with individual educational professionals in partnership with unions, HEIs, LEAs and consultancies, is no longer regarded as appropriate. The marginalisation of HEIs is deliberate and part of a political concern to eradicate the humane and critical traditions of understanding experiences and meaning. What seems to have been problematic in the English setting has been the binary approach to theory and practice, in which debates have been framed around implementation of theory or its relevance and utility (Bolam, 1997). Consequently in evaluating the NPQH pilot the TTA makes the statement that 'in a small number of regions, some candidates expressed a concern that the training was too academic and theoretical' (TTA, 1997, p. 2). The lack of explanation of this statement suggests that the meaning is self-evident, and it is consistent with the current drive towards 'what works'.

This demonisation of theory does not take into account the work on how we understand professional knowledge and practice. Eraut (1993) distinguishes between knowledge that is procedural (knowing how) and propositional (knowing that). Green and Manera (1995) relate knowledge to position, and so those new in post have 'exploratory knowing' compared with the 'embedded knowing' of longer-in-post principals. Routine tasks are handled through 'experiential knowing', and challenge is coped with through 'efficient knowing' (ibid., p. 12). The realities of professional work are those of dilemma, contradiction and uncertainty, and so deliberation, so essential to achieving tasks and outcomes, is problematic. As Eraut (1993) argues: 'in most situations, there will not be a single correct answer, nor a guaranteed road to success' (p. 228). This is precisely the reason why, in Owens and Shakeshaft's (1992) view, organisation theory should be taught. They argue that educational administrators need to learn how to 'read' an organisation and so be able to make sense of it. Theory and theorising provide the language, concepts and method by which this can be done. This type of work has traditionally been the domain of the HEI knowledge worker, but increasingly their experience as researchers, consultants and writers has not been regarded as relevant to practitioners, and the fact that many in HEIs began their professional lives as teachers and managers is quietly forgotten. Consequently, NPQH trainers had to be trained and accredited without due regard to credentials and experience. Hall (1998) reminds us that, traditionally, management training has put more emphasis on the use of knowledge, and rather narrow scientific knowledge, than on the production of knowledge. She goes on to argue that postgraduate work such as taught doctorates have the potential to enable the educational professional to reposition themselves differently as both a user of intellectual resources and as a generator of work-based knowledge.

Summary

Asking questions about how a person becomes a head of subject, a senior teacher or a headteacher is a process in which the interplay between agency and structure is revealed. Individual professional and personal choices within the setting of partnerships and family are located in complex settings which are personal and institutional, local and global, historical and political. Research seems to be telling us that those who take on a leadership role (and their families) find themselves travelling a difficult but worthwhile journey. Increasingly, research and theory is asking questions about this journey and, while the emphasis is clearly on those who are structurally successful, work is revealing the experiences of those who decide not to make applications and those who find the system riddled with structural injustices. While we are increasing our knowledge of real lives and are able to theorise and use theories that connect agency with structure, the current official emphasis on training rather than professional learning is a backward step. In the drive to modernise schools, what we are told we know about leadership and what is worth knowing remains rooted in the science of rationality and the laboratory. This does an important job in shifting dispositions towards the identities that are allowed to be made public, as well as enabling preparation and on-the-job support to be done 'on the cheap'. However, humanist and critical knowledge workers remain because they continue to present compelling alternatives for those who are unconvinced about the science of institutional effectiveness.

The next three chapters take this forward by focusing on what we know about those who are at particular stages in their professional lives. I argue that the ongoing modernisation through site-based performance management is distorting the educational nature of professional work, and is undermining the opportunities for teachers and students to practise leadership within learning.

7

Headteachers and Principals

Finding out about the professional lives and work of principals and head-teachers is an international research phenomenon and in this chapter I present what we know about the work of principals/headteachers. I draw mainly on qualitative evidence that has been gathered from and about headteachers regarding experiences. I investigate critical approaches regarding how headship is being shaped and restructured in particular ways for particular purposes.

Headteachers and their work

Burgess (1984) argues that the lack of empirical work on headship has not stopped people writing about it. What work there is on headship tends to be about mainsteam secondary headteachers, and even less is known about primary and special education headteachers (Pascal and Ribbins, 1998; Rayner and Ribbins, 1999). Knowledge about other post-holders is also paltry as the role of the deputy headteacher is under-researched (Ribbins, 1997c) and in danger of being seen as a structural irrelevance through this neglect. Perhaps within this intellectual desert the particular work that stands out is Wallace and Hall's (1994) study of the senior management team, which confirmed the centrality of the head and the endurance of hierarchy but with the actuality and further potential of teamwork development through the building of a shared history. There are two integrated but often contradictory strands around traditional headship authority and the power structure that sustains it, and the collegiality that is central to successful professional allegiances and identities. This has been shown by Hughes (1985) in conceptualising heads as having a dual role: first, the headteacher as chief executive in the allocation of resources, and in presenting to governors and LEA evidence about academic achievement and, second, the headteacher as leading professional through teaching, the professional leadership of teachers, and working with pupils and parents. The two roles are interrelated and are context specific, and Grace (1995) has shown recent trends in the reworking of the headmaster tradition into the market and marketable chief executive headteacher, and how this has hindered the possibilities for the continued development of professional collegiality.

The version and model of the performing school that is structurally supported in the struggle over the development of schools, with its emphasis on strong leadership integrating teachers, pupils, parents and communities, is not an inevitability. Having a chief executive role is not necessarily incompatible with being a leading professional, though achieving the balance is a challenge, and requires all educational professionals to exercise professional courage in ways that could go against the current grain. However, the reworking of headship as executive leadership means that this model remains official good practice and is endorsed through government policy and interventions into the professional and personal lives of teachers. Nevertheless in the 1970s the emphasis was on challenging the traditional authoritarian approach because of the development of comprehensive schools and new responsibilities that meant: 'a head must delegate or disintegrate' (Watts, 1980, p. 293). In addition, the powers of the headteacher were increasingly seen as unacceptable to teachers and children.

Coulson (1980) writing in the 1970s notes the enduring features of primary headship: first, the emphasis on being the head *teacher* rather than an administrator, in which the head's educational philosophy underpins what and how things are done; second, seeking to influence children's learning both indirectly through teachers and directly by everyday and personal contact with the children; third, as a filter for external demands, the head protects the children and staff from changes and influences which could undermine the classroom. Coulson (1980) challenged the focus of attention on the headteacher as being both paternalistic and undermining of teacher professionalism, and shows the impossibility of one person being able to undertake the workload efficiently and effectively. He goes on to argue in favour of a management system that will enable collegiality to develop through policy-making groups being formed (this is what eventually is labelled 'teams'). This recognises that some teachers, in Hoyle's (1995) terms, are 'restricted' professionals while others are 'extended', and, therefore, staffing needs to be differentiated so that those who gain satisfaction from the classroom are not undermined, and those who wish to develop management and whole-school expertise are given such opportunities. This tension between the professional collegiality of all being teachers and the need to create a division of labour in order to get things done, becomes more complex when personal and professional models of headship are challenged through external policy demands on schools.

Increasingly from the 1980s the issue was not so much that the autocratic legacy of the headmaster tradition could be challenged by a more participative approach to pedagogy, but that management systems had

to be put in place in order for schools to be able to serve the requirements of external policy and political scrutiny. This can be illustrated by
Hall et al.'s (1986) ethnographic study of headteachers in which the orientation towards teaching and learning became increasingly challenged.
This research showed that the main features of a head's working day are
fragmented, cover a wide range of tasks and are 'people intensive' (ibid.,
p. 11). Furthermore, they note two important features of their data
gathered from studies of 15 headteachers: first, while managers in general
can spend at least 40 per cent of time in formal meetings, the work of
headteachers is more reactive and less strategic than this; and, second,
headteachers teach and hence, unlike managers, they continue to work
in the core business activity as well as oversee others' work. From the
data gathered by observing and interacting with four case study heads,
it is clear that they had explicit educational philosophies based on the
curriculum and displayed different dispositions towards, for example,
pupil grouping and equal opportunities. In this sense their professional
relationships with teachers were around pedagogy and the curriculum,
and their contact with pupils was within this setting, i.e. through the
teaching and learning process (including a figurehead role and assem-
blies), assessment and the pastoral process. What seems to be a vital
aspect of what heads do is around relationships, and Hall et al. (1986) go
on to argue that the four case study heads interacted with the staff around
'providing professional leadership' regarding teaching, pupil welfare,
performance and 'staff development' from selection through to
promotion (p. 71). Research from interviewing staff in the 15 schools
shows that what is valued is that the head is present in school and that
s/he is approachable. The authors go on to conclude that while there are
patterns underpinning headteacher practice rooted in educational philosophy, the variety of ways in which headship is practised, related to the
range of demands on them to make choices and decisions, was out of
step by the 1980s. In particular, the growing emphasis was on effective
headship through the creation of a differentiated management system of
new roles and delegation though management job descriptions. Models
of headship based on being immersed in school life through pedagogic
and curriculum issues, as well as the day-to-day ups and downs of the
unexpected, were no longer regarded as appropriate because the increasing demands of government policy meant that heads had to change how
they understood their own and other teachers' work.

This demand for a more rational management structure in schools is
connected to concerns about the role of the deputy head. Survey work by
Todd and Dennison (1980) showed that where larger secondary schools
had been developed there were multiple deputy head appointments, and
so the role was increasingly being defined and there was evidence in the
survey schools of emergent senior management teams. The emphasis on
the control by the headteacher via and through a proactive orientation to
the development and use of management systems is illustrated in the

growing number of texts at the time that sought to provide a managed approach to ensure that the head was in control (Barry and Tye, 1975). The use of instrumental models from the private sector became popular but were limited in their ability to describe and understand the educational work of headteachers, and the disconnection from a public sector value system meant that they where unable to support the drive towards developing more democratic models of headship and professional collegiality so essential to comprehensive schools. It seems that the drive towards modernisation was aimed at moving headteachers away from educational values and collegial processes towards the marketised performance that we have witnessed and experienced in the post-1988 period. Of particular interest is whether headteachers have been able to maintain the varied approach to their work based on educational philosophies and a commitment to the curriculum. Certainly the mandated model of headship as presented within current government documents does not see the headteacher as a head *teacher*, but as a leader and manager in an educational setting. The model presented is one of creating a unified system from the DfEE through to the home via the school, in which the headteacher seems to be a middle manager for the collecting of effectiveness data and the delivering of targets. Headship is being reworked around strategic business like models rather than leadership growing out of pedagogic expertise.

Getting underneath the imaging and language of current preferred leadership is difficult, as headteachers cannot be seen publicly to disagree or present alternative models. Nevertheless, research continues to show that the interplay between core values and personal models of headship and the internal and external demands of the job is central to how we need to understand the realities of headteachers' work. Work by Day et al. (2000) shows that headship is about tensions where heads may not be able to do much about the situation, but decisions based on the exercise of professional courage have to be made. Furthermore, dilemmas arise from how headteachers see their role and goals, and this is connected to how the purposes of education are played out. Trying to maintain a working consensus amongst professionals but dealing with issues of performance, keeping things going but also pushing for change, are all areas of possible trouble, and do deeply trouble headteachers. Scientific leadership has little relevance to this except that we need to acknowledge how it works to support government policy through making schools headteacher-proof by denying the realities of productive political activity. As I have argued, alternative epistemologies exist and this is what the next two sections deal with, which enables issues around the interplay of agency and structure to be investigated in more depth.

Talking headteachers

When heads talk about their work, and while it is a personal account and a contextualised account, there are interesting patterns. The habitus where headteachers are disposed towards children and their colleagues is a central feature of their stories and accounts. This should not be too surprising as much of the biographical and ethnographic data published in the 1990s is based on headteachers who were recruited to the profession and achieved their first headship prior to the legislation of site-based performance management. Furthermore, the struggle between individual habitus and the increasing structural straitjacketing observed by Hall et al. (1986) in the early 1980s continues today, with the realities of headship very much about relationships and trying to maintain educational values. However, there is self-reported evidence from the 1990s that the tasks of headship have changed beyond just the language of leadership and having a vision. 'There is not just more work to do, but there has been a qualitative shift in the type of responsibilities (Craig with Rayner, 1999; Marsh, 1997; Morgan with Rayner, 1999). This has challenged the dispositions of headteachers, and how particular individuals have responded does vary but there is evidence that transformational leadership is taking heads away from teaching and learning. As one headteacher states: 'there has been such a great increase in workload, and so many changes to manage, that I haven't been able to be as involved in teaching. It is fair to say I think that I am far more remote from the staff that at any time since I've been a headteacher' (Morgan with Rayner, 1999, p. 246).

The managerial division of labour seems to be a double-edged development. On the one hand it enables the work to be done but, on the other, it has distanced headteachers from teaching and made them managers of the conditions in which teaching takes place, such as the buildings and the budget. Delegation is a risky business at a time when headteachers can suffer a loss of livelihood through the consequences of failure or the politicking around what is regarded as failure (Hayes, 1995; Wallace and Hall, 1994; Wallace and Huckman, 1996). However, the importance attached to collegiality, delegation and role definition remains in the stories of headteachers and wider research surveys (Bell et al., 1996; McEwen and Salters, 1997). This is more than just the functional aspect of someone else taking responsibility for the job, but also has its roots in the importance of professional relationships. Whinn-Sladden (1997) talks about how a good deputy has to 'fit between the head and the staff and wear both hats with ease', and how this person has to be a good teacher in order to 'raise everybody else's expectations'. She goes on to say that: 'If you have a bad one you really are up against it but if you have a good one they are doing half the work for you' (Whinn-Sladden, 1997, p. 43). Brown (1997) talks about the importance of a 'no blame culture' and how people understand what this means for professional engagement: 'this policy is about commitment, rather than compliance, and about ensuring that individuals are aware that as long as they act in a proper and professional way in pursuing what are often risky ventures, they will not be "jumped upon" when things go wrong' (p. 149). What is particularly interesting here is that the professional and staff development features of staff–head interactions identified by Hall et al. (1986) remain central particularly because, as Mercer (1996) argues, headteachers are experiencing professional isolation as a result of educational restructuring.

Site-based performance management has led to increased status and powers of governing bodies in England and Wales. The relationship between the headteacher and governing body (particularly the chair) is seen to be crucial to effective education. As Whinn-Sladden states:

> I feel most responsibility to the governors. They in turn are taking on more and more responsibility because I am working with them both as individual governors and in groups on different aspects of the school and school development with a view to increasing their understanding of what we are doing and where we are going. (Whinn-Sladen, 1997, p. 52)

The boundary between the professional educator and the laity can be a place of conflicting expectations about role and tasks, and there is evidence of governors who are drawn from the business community who challenge and can go over the boundaries (Deem et al., 1995; Mahony et al., 1998). It is also of interest that, as Mahony et al. (1998) argue, headteacher political literacy and manipulation can be used to ensure that the governors provide a 'democratic alibi' for action (p. 123).

Heads are very much aware that society has changed with more demands on schools and especially within an increasingly litigious society (Gray, 1997), but at the same time there are strong cultural legacies in some communities where expectations of education and aspirations for life experiences remain low (Davies with Ribbins, 1998). Bates (1999) tells the story of being seconded to the headship of Lilian Baylis School in Lambeth with the brief to get the school out of special measures or it would face closure. The situation she found herself in is best described in her own words:

> Understandably morale amongst both staff and pupils was extremely low. The school had been publicly 'named and shamed'. The local press had not just been negative but at times vitriolic in its coverage of the fortunes of the school. Teachers had been told they were failing and pupils had internalised this message of failure and many pupils had developed poor self-images and low aspirations. The strength of feeling in the community about the school took me by surprise. They wanted it closed. Few believed that anything could be done to improve the school. Local people told gruesome stories of violence, pensioners afraid to walk the streets, gang robbery and intimidation. On my first excursion into the local community shortly after taking up my post I met a number of the local traders in Lambeth Walk. I introduced myself cheerfully as the new headteacher of Lilian Baylis. Several

looked horrified, others looked doubtful, looked sad, took my hand and said pityingly, 'You poor cow'. (ibid., p. 87)

Within a year the school was out of special measures, and 'named and acclaimed' (ibid., p. 94), through the establishment of positive educational and professional working relationships within school, and communicating this to the community. In this sense accountability is a complex and fuzzy concept, in which taking risks and making interventions in classrooms and the community is more about professional expertise based on pedagogy than it is about technicist development plans. Habitus leads headteachers to a knowledge and understanding that people disposed towards working with people encourages an emotional commitment to children in which there is creative risk-taking. Nevertheless the dilemmas created through the interplay of habitus and the structural context in which a headteacher is working can create what Barker (1999) describes as a 'double vision' (p. 73) where his commitment to comprehensive education and democracy has been challenged by the external demands for internal change that are disconnected from the achievements being made by pupils and teachers.

Headteachers talk a lot about being accountable to themselves, and this has its roots in their teacher backgrounds and their intrinsic commitment to teachers and children. Hyde (1997) talks about the importance of staff and children being able to trust her, and Matthew with Pascal (1998) is explicit about how children hold headteachers (and everyone else in school) endemically accountable through their experiences of teaching and learning. Nevertheless headteachers do vary in how they see their links with parents and the wider community. Hyde (1997) argues that she does not feel she can exercise a 'general social responsibility' (p. 119), while Searle (Hustler et al., 1995) sees his work as being directly connected to the community in which he is explicit about his radical approach as a socialist and as someone deeply involved in and commited to comprehensive schooling. This political role has supporters, and work in the USA by Laible and Harrington (1998) leads them to argue that administrators should have the courage and the capacity to 'stand for what is right for poor African-American and Mexican-American children, regardless of political consequences for themselves' (p. 118). Ashdown (with Rayner, 1999) argues that provision in special educational needs will only improve if parents and teachers mobilise themselves as a coherent interest group. McConnell (with Ribbins, 1998) echoes this by arguing that heads are people who are in a structurally powerful position: 'we are vociferous, we are capable of getting together, we are capable of organizing ourselves and because we care passionately about our children we will do it, and we will mobilize parents and parents are voters – they can hit politicians where it hurts most' (p. 169).

From published stories and accounts there is much evidence of headteachers describing their ability to exercise agency, i.e. to have a clear educational philosophy, and to make choices. As Michael Gasper (with Pascal, 1998) states: 'the heads I'd worked with knew what they were at, you might not have liked the way they went about it, it may even have been ridiculous in the funny sense of the term, but they knew what they wanted and how they were going to do it' (p. 121). Taking a philosophical position on educational issues is demonstrated through headteachers telling stories about their childhoods and how they learned about work and the importance of education, and have been influenced by experiences of injustice. Clarke (1997) talks about the negative effects of private education on his brothers, and the impact of failing the 11+ on one of them: 'I think I can trace the effects of that school experience throughout both my brothers' lives and as a result of all of this, I developed pretty strong views on education' (p. 93). Who headteachers are and their backgrounds is important, and this cannot be written out of the storying of their headship practice: 'Whatever your vision, it is finite: it's clouded by the baggage we all bring to it, by our characters, our ideas, the lot' (McConnell with Ribbins, 1998, p. 161). Furthermore, having integrity and the integration of the personal with the professional is seen as vital by headteachers, and Evans (with Ribbins, 1999) tells the story of being interviewed where he argues that it is essential not to give answers that the panel wants to hear but 'to be true to yourself' (p. 165).

A passion for the job and an emotional engagement with children and people seems to be central to positioning around values and the accession to a post that can make this even more explicit (Duffy, 1999). Davies (with Ribbins, 1998) describes what it feels like: 'I wouldn't do anything else. I thoroughly enjoy my job. We are very privileged to work with children' (p. 111). Furthermore, there is a deep intellectual commitment to headship that cannot be adequately summed by describing it as values. Elizabeth Duffy (1999) draws inspiration from Freire's (1996) work in order to argue that: 'teaching should be a creative, passionate profession, not a "delivery" of a common package of knowledge and skills by teachers who have been passed by, and/or been deformed by, the Teacher Training Agency's quality control bureau or who blindly follow the leader's vision' (p. 111). In the day-to-day realities of the job, it seems that this approach is evident in taking tough decisions in the interests of children's learning. Hyde (1997) tells the story of her response to technology being made compulsory. As the school was about to face an OfSTED inspection this limited the scope for interpretation and development in line with school curriculum policy and design. The decision was taken to change the curriculum at Key Stage 4 and in Hyde's words this was 'one of the worst decisions I have ever taken' because 'the girls have followed a Technology syllabus which I can only describe as absolute garbage' (ibid., p. 121). Headteachers talk about their deep commitment to children's learning and so in Davies's (with Ribbins, 1998) school the children are not prepared for SATs, but are educated in ways that still enable them to do well, but also have knowledge and skills that will take them beyond the test. Teaching and learning for all matters, and matters in a bigger sense than scientific measurement of achievement. Evans (with Ribbins, 1999) argues: 'I cannot think of anything I would rather do than be the head of a big comprehensive school. But it must be a true comprehensive which caters for everybody' (p. 184). Keeping the focus on teaching and learning has been difficult for headteachers as they have faced the demands of site-based performance management. Having a clear identity based on pedagogy means that the professional identity of headteachers can be protected. As Abrol (with Ribbins, 1999) states: 'you must be a leading professional not just a chief executive . . . you must consider LMS in terms of its implications for the curriculum, for school development, and for school improvement' (pp. 69–70).

What we know is that the lives of headteachers and principals are complex, and there is a strong interrelationship between formal work and their broader lives. To put it simplistically, heads and senior managers do not clock in and clock off, but their habitus is such that they are disposed to have their professional lives embodied to the extent that it is a core part of their identities. Partners, children and hobbies are important to headteachers and, as Evetts (1994) and Hall (1996) have shown, different emphasis is given at different times to the balance between school and personal lives, but a central feature within the habitus is the classroom and the commitment to the children they are working with and on behalf of. Humanistic approaches enable us to penetrate the interplay between what real people doing a job actually think, feel and bring to their work and the contextual setting in which it is happening. Critical approaches seek not only to describe and understand the contradictions but also to explain by conceptualising the link between agency and structure through theories of power. This is the focus of the next section.

Critical headship

A central theme of work in the last half century has been to show how accepted models of headship, mandated through government policy or sustained through the cultural and structural rituals and expectations, have been challenged through what we know about the realities of the job and hence new understandings of what headship is and what it ought to become. Radical practice has asked fundamental questions about power structures and cultural norms. For example, single role incumbency has been challenged, and Court (1998) reports on how two candidates for a principal's post in Aotearoa, New Zealand, successfully argued for and were appointed to a co-principalship in a primary school. Creative scholarship also asks important questions, and Davies (1995) not only reminds us that many schools are often headless because of events outside their control, but there may be other more democratically supportive ways in which role incumbents achieve and are accountable for their headship. Nevertheless, as this chapter shows, the traditional and official descriptions of headship remain and have been reworked into the headteacher of the twenty-first century, and this is in spite of important work that shows that headship is a struggle rather than a leadership blueprint. However, acknowledging this is not enough, and critical approaches theorise it so that agency and structure are interconnected through conceptualising power.

What is interesting in reading accounts of and by headteachers is the extent to which they are able to exercise agency and professional courage, and the extent to which they accept, go along with, or even collude with, the ways in which headship is being 'designed and driven by policy-makers (and) not by the practitioners' (Southworth, 1999b, p. 63). In post-compulsory education Jephcote et al. (1996) show how further education (FE) college principals have experienced a shift 'from a provider-led dependency culture to the culture of the business entrepreneur operating in a competitive market' (p. 46). Menter et al. (1997) report on a primary context where the descriptions of practice were based on traditional commitments to children and education, but activity showed an acceptance of managerialism. In this way agency operates at different levels related to the ethical commitments to pedagogy or to the self and family, and the differentiated levels of consciousness of the scope of current and planned changes. There is not just a struggle within headship over the functions, tasks and relationships involved, but also over how headship is being conceptualised and prescribed (Hall and Southworth, 1997).

Ball (1994b) argues that legislation has not created a clear and unambiguous model of leadership. While heads are being given new tasks to do and are expected to adopt particular ways of behaving, it is 'the change in relationships and in culture that is most significant in redefining heads' role and self-conception' (ibid., p. 101). Ball goes on to identify the contradictory situation in which relationships with governors, teachers and parents are an unsettled terrain where boundaries are tested and ways forward negotiated. How identities are known and understood is located in what Ball argues is a 'professional discourse' based on public sector values, and is evident in claims and practices around professional discretion. Site-based performance management is based on two, possibly irreconcilable, 'counter discourses': first, the privileging of entrepreneurial activity of leading the school in the marketplace; and, second, empowering people through extending community involvement in a school. What seems to matter is how these are played out in formal and informal encounters, and whether the headteacher as marketeer is actually enabling democratic development. As Ball argues there seems to be a philosophical and practical discrepancy between competition and inclusion within the community. At the heart of this work, based on qualitative interview evidence and vignettes, is how headteacher, teacher and governor dispositions and actions are represented. Ball (1994b) does not argue for a direct cause-and-effect connection in which new work equals new identity, but 'that the pressures and conditions of their work in these circumstances make certain leadership roles less easily obtainable and more risky than others' (p. 95).

How this is being played out in the lives of headteachers has been researched by Grace (1995) and he shows 'three broad ideal-type head-teacher responses to the changed culture of leadership in English schools' (p. 73):

- *Headteacher-managers*: endorse site-based management and believe in its importance for improving teacher and pupil performance.
- *Headteacher-professionals*: put the emphasis on collegial relationships and attempt to work through the reforms in ways that do not distance themselves from pedagogy.
- *Headteacher-resistors*: a small group who sought union leadership on defending schools from the imposed curriculum and assessment changes.

Gender seems to be a feature here as Grace (1995) states that the first category is mainly male, while in the second group women heads expressed concerns about the potential separation of headteacher from staff and pupils. Researching women who have broken through the glass ceiling and how they interpret and practise leading is very recent, and Yeatman (1990) is explicit about women as femocrats who are privileged in the labour market but are connected to economically disadvantaged women through their joint location within patriarchal structures and cultures. Nevertheless femocrats are in receipt of technocrat models of leadership, but in resisting this they may weaken their privileged position and, so, could undermine their radical orientation.

Hall's (1996) analysis of women headteachers shows that they demon-strated agency and were in control of gender as a feature of their practice and identity. In particular, Hall (1996) argues that all of the women in her sample fitted the Grace (1995) 'headteacher-manager category' in which: 'they demonstrated the possibility of playing the game but according to their rules which are not always the same as the other players . . . we are observing a dance floor on which women are suggesting new steps to men and women partners, whom they are leading, not following' (p. 193). Hall argues that these women headteachers are 'educational entrepre-neurs' who are concerned to ensure that the school survives in a quasi-market, and at the same time resist external demands and reforms that would undermine a professional commitment to pedagogy. Nevertheless as Hall (1999a; 1999b) and other commentators have noted (Reay and Ball, 2000) there is a dilemma here in terms of how headteachers position themselves within the field of practice and are able to ask questions about the relationship with the field of power. How and whether headteachers can and should challenge the policy prescriptions that are reworking their identities and silencing alternative ways of working is the central dilemma. Furthermore, Reay and Ball, (2000) ask us to consider that not only is the fact that women are holding power 'extraordinary . . . in a British labour market' (p. 147), but that those women will usually adopt male ways of working in order to be regarded as authentic leaders and will have usually got there through the auspices of a male mentor. Consequently, we need ways of researching gender (and age, disability, race, and sexuality) that do not essentialise gender with a clear emancipatory agenda in which women's ways of working are opposed to masculine management, but instead enable gender, age, disability, race and sexuality to be visible in how we describe and understand how headteachers live within, relate and seek to work through dilemmas in complex settings.

Summary

Headship is an ongoing experience of contradiction and dilemma, and for those whom headteachers interrelate with. Heads have talked about the tensions between the control imperative, and the professional and human disposition to want to work with and through people (Day et al. 2000; Dempster and Mahony, 1998; Møller, 1997; Wildy and Dimmock, 1993). Researchers who are interested in leadership effects of headteachers and principals emphasise that context does need to be taken into account; as Hallinger and Heck (1996b) state: 'the principal's role is best conceived as part of a web of environmental, personal, and in-school relationships that combine to influence organizational outcomes' (p. 6) (see also Glover et al., 1996a; 1996b). Headship is not necessarily leadership because holding a post does not necessarily imbue the person with the capabilities and capacities for leadership, though the merging of headship and leadership is enabling reform to take place as both are power structures that can be made to fit with each other. As Webb and Vulliamy (1996) show 'curriculum leadership and teaching skills seem set to continue to be pushed further and further down headteachers' list of priorities' (p. 312). What needs to be said is that there is resistance to the consequences of stripping away of education from heads who exercise leadership through the endurance of educational values and an orientation towards children as learners. However, how long this can continue is difficult to assess.

While the professional hierarchical separation of headteachers from teachers is an enduring feature of English schooling, and is reinforced by salary differentials, this is being overlaid by a performance management leader and follower divide (Grace, 1995; Raab et al., 1997; Whitty et al., 1998). As Macbeath et al. (1996) show, the divide between headteacher and staff in Denmark is small, though new legislation which seeks to 'emphasise the distinctiveness of their role . . . (will) . . . in the view of the headteachers . . . open up a distance between them and their staff' (pp. 235–6). This divide is serious because it is not only structurally privileging a group of former 'full-time' teachers but is creating a whole strata of work that is no longer allowed to be the concern of those who remain teachers. For teachers to penetrate this growing divide, they have to play the managerial language and data game through performance management self-auditing and evidencing of competence. Teachers have to turn their backs on teaching as a conceptually informed practice integrated with learning, to a regime of numbers and graphs designed to tell them what does and does not work.

The next two chapters show that the drive to position headteachers as leaders and managers of a system rather than learning is having a detrimental impact on the identity and work of role incumbents in senior and middle management, teachers and students.

8

Teachers in the Middle

This chapter draws on current research that defines teachers who have job descriptions in addition to pedagogic responsibilities as middle or senior managers. There has always been a hierarchy between the head-teacher and teacher, and so the 'middle' is itself stratified according to tasks, status and pay. Site-based performance management is relabelling roles as team leaders and restructuring salary differentials around audited and measurable school outcomes. The type of questions that I ask cluster around the following: first, who are middle and senior managers, and what work do they do? Second, how are these post-holders experiencing their work, how are they seeking to position them-selves and how are they being positioned?

Middle managers

Middle management is a label that is used to position teachers with a subject/department and/or pastoral responsibility within an educational organisation. A teacher who has a responsibility allowance together with a specified job description outlining duties in addition to a classroom teacher is located as 'middle' within the hierarchy. Where the boundary lies with senior management can be contoured differently, and can be according to position on the pay scale through to how the senior man-agement team or leadership group membership is constituted. However, as Bennett (1995) has shown there is some resistance to both the label and the positioning from within the profession, particularly within the primary school where the organising of learning is based on horizontal collaborative and co-operative networks. In the secondary context a head of department is regarded as central to the control function: 'secondary schools are more likely to be places of dispute and argument than places of consensus, and individuals are needed who can undertake the respon-sibility of trying to weld together the often disparate and disputing sub-units into a coherent whole' (p. 104). Nevertheless, the complexity of teachers' work means that activity may not always be organised into a sub-unit such as a department, but may entail whole-school co-ordination such as pastoral work (heads of year, heads of house, director of sixth form), and the role of the SENCO, literacy and numeracy co-ordinators. In this sense it could be argued that the label of middle manager is inappropriate because it seeks to represent diverse work according to a unified structural dimension, and furthermore, by seeking to modernise teaching through the adoption of non-educational ways of working, such as line management, it challenges and undermines professional cultures. What is interesting about accounts of subject leadership/middle management in the post-1988 period is a lack of recognition of the curriculum and organisational structure as an arena of struggle, particularly regarding how important questions can and need to be raised about why learning is organised around the subject discipline and which subjects are considered to be legitimate (Ribbins, 1985). Consequently, while our knowledge of middle management has grown rapidly, the particular gaze has been more on role and function and less about knowledge power structures.

The general consensus is that located within the current form of site-based performance management the middle manager, such as a head of department in a secondary school, is 'pivotal' (Gold, 1998, p. xiii), though work by Turner and Bolam (1998) suggests that the role is better explained through contingency theory than by rational instrumental approaches. Internationally there are reports of varied practice, and Brauner (1997) shows how in Israeli secondary schools the head of department has no involvement in management, and this contrasts with the Singapore system where the role is very clearly defined (Guat Tin and Lee Hean, 1997). It seems that while the literature is clear that the department is an important means to school improvement (Brown and Rutherford, 1999; Leask and Terrell, 1997; TTA, 1998b), this is not always borne out in practice (Creemers, 1997; Witziers et al., 1999).

There is a strong emphasis on normative accounts in which both senior and middle managers can recognise and put in place a more effective middle management system (Blandford, 1997; Briggs, 1997; Field et al., 2000; Gold, 1998; Kemp and Nathan, 1989). However, within the literature there is also evidence of alternatives to the department and, in the immediate aftermath of the 1988 Education Reform Act, Earley and Fletcher-Campbell (1989) note that innovative approaches to school structures could be halted as a result of the National Curriculum. Evidence from Australia (Weldon, 1997) shows the importance of shared leadership with active teacher participation in the development of teaching and learning, rather than centralising tasks and responsibilities on a leader. Consistent with this approach is the prediction that research into learning combined with advances in information and communication technology means that schools will need to be structured differently (Stoll and Fink, 1996).

The positioning of the teacher into middle management roles can be traced back in recent times to the Burnham Committee award of additional payments to heads of department (Poster, 1976; Ribbins, 1985), and the development of comprehensive education in which larger schools required the establishment of a structure that in Spooner's (1989) view began as a pragmatic response to teacher shortage and became the means by which children were cared for in very large schools. However, an outcome of the introduction of site-based performance management means that middle management is becoming less concerned with child welfare and more a means through which accountability is achieved. In this way middle management is a creation of external policy and how senior managers require systems and structures that will secure implementation, rather than the product of how teachers seek to organise learning. Line management requires simplified responsibility and accountability structures, and is the means through which performance management is normalised. The growth in qualitative research studies is revealing the complexity of the positioning of the middle manager, and this goes beyond the performing of a role or the operationalisation of a job description, to understanding the location and exercise of power.

Working in the middle

Like studies into senior managers, the contextualised nature of the work and identity of middle managers is evident in research undertaken so far. Glover et al. (1998) argue that their research shows how the focus of the work of the middle manager is different for a head of a large department compared with those leading small departments who do not see themselves as managers but as teachers with additional administrative duties to perform. Furthermore, single-subject departments mean that the middle manager has a shared disciplinary identity and expertise with his/her colleagues compared with a head of a large faculty who is disconnected from this knowledge base. Turner (1996) identifies that while heads of department are concerned to lead a team of teachers, the size and working practices does depend on school architecture. Whether a department has a base (such as the science prep room) and the distance between the base/classrooms and central facilities such as a staffroom does impact on group identity and cohesion.

Research by Earley and Fletcher-Campbell (1989) uncovered the busyness of middle management work, and how they did not have the time to undertake reflective thinking and planning (and they found that senior managers experienced less of a 'treadmill' as they moved further up the hierarchy). Typical of middle management work is a long day, in which it is never completed: 'a faculty head remarked that his job was like "juggling lots of balls in the air at the same time". Middle managers often listed the things that were waiting to be done' (ibid., p. 27). More recent work by Busher and Harris (1999) acknowledges the endurance of complexities, ambiguities and tensions of being a teacher in the middle, and go on to provide a used description of the dimensions of this work:

- A bridging or brokering function between policies from senior staff and implementation in the classroom.
- Fostering collegiality and group identity.
- Improving staff and student performance by monitoring actual outcomes in line with required outcomes.
- Representative and networking role with external bodies.

We do not have biographical and narrative evidence about teachers as post-holders in the way that Ribbins, in collaboration with others (Ribbins and Marland, 1994; Pascal and Ribbins, 1998; Rayner and Ribbins, 1999; Ribbins, 1997a), has gathered about headteachers. Instead teachers working in the middle have come under the gaze of those interested in school improvement and effectiveness, and hence work has been more quantitative than qualitative and has tended to focus on performance management than on pedagogy. For Earley and Fletcher-Campbell (1989) the effective performance of middle managers is crucial to teaching and learning, and underpinning this is their capacity for leadership through a strategic approach to how time is deployed and the role understood. This type of work has been built on in the 1990s through school effectiveness research (Sammons, 1999; Sammons et al., 1997), though Harris et al. (1995) have argued that it is only recently that the researcher's gaze has shifted downwards from whole-school effectiveness to departments. Sammons et al. (1996b) report on a project that shows differences between departments within the same school, and so, while overall the school may be seen to be academically effective, it could be that one department is doing better than another in terms of pupil outcomes. Furthermore, they found evidence of some subjects that vary from year to year (e.g. French), and vary in how they approached particular student groups (e.g. gender, ethnicity and attainment at entry to the school). This type of work illustrates the importance of middle managers in how school effectiveness research is designed and conducted, especially when, as Brown and Rutherford (1999) note, there is evidence from research of middle management performing well in spite of the ineffectiveness of the senior management team (SMT). Busher and Harris (1999) reinforce this by arguing that 'UK research suggests that subject leaders can make a difference to departmental performance in much the same way as headteachers contribute to overall school performance' (p. 306).

Harris et al. (1995) have identified the characteristics of effective departments and these include management and pedagogic processes such as collegiality, clearly understood routines and a pupil centred ethos. They go on to argue that there is a need for more research into the weighing of the factors as some may be more important than others. Furthermore, the point is made that there is a need to contextualise the research and ask questions about the impact of the subject department in relation to the socio-economic location in which schooling is taking place. Witziers et al. (1999) report on research that shows differences between subjects with a tendency to value collaboration by language teachers compared with mathematics and history. However, they do go on to show that there is variation within the same subject between schools, and research highlights that there are whole-school factors that have an impact such as how much importance is attached to joint planning by senior management. Variability of performance amongst departments within the same school illustrates the complexity of what Sammons (1999) regards as 'cross-level relationships' (p. 250) between the school, the department and the classroom. The quality of teaching is important but on its own it does not lead to school effectiveness and so there are important effects at the departmental level.

The abstraction of the characteristics of effective departments connects with the positioning of the teacher as the performer of a leadership and management role. Consequently, there is a strong emphasis on the need to ensure that the role is clearly defined, understood, monitored and evaluated. This is not a new issue, and Earley and Fletcher-Campbell (1989) argued that taking on the responsibility for the performance management of a team, through, for example, classroom monitoring and departmental review, is essential but not widely understood. A decade later, Glover et al. (1998) found that middle managers tend to 'see their work as a large number of unconnected duties required by the administrative machine of the school' (p. 281) rather than having a highly developed sense of a role. This is confirmed by Harris's (1998) study of less effective departments where she found that weak leadership (either laissez-faire or authoritarian styles) led to more emphasis on routine than on teaching and learning.

There has been an attempt to settle the relationship between leadership, teaching and learning through the TTA *National Standards for Subject Leaders* (TTA, 1998b) in which the official model of leadership is transformational and is consistent with the *National Standards for Headteachers* (TTA, 1998a). This transference of business models into education that attempt to unify the structure and culture is illustrated in much of the literature with an emphasis on vision and quality systems (Blandford, 1997). Consequently, the role of the post-holder is to monitor and evaluate the quality of teaching and learning through classroom observation and the gathering of statistical evidence about learning outcomes. It seems that the preferred role of the senior manager is to oversee and ensure that policies are implemented and, if necessary, to make interventions into an ineffective department by using resources (including time) to enable teachers to focus on pedagogy combined with active surveillance by attendance at departmental meetings and checking that administration is taking place. However, while this type of activity is seen as focusing on appropriate roles, research into the day-to-day work of middle managers suggests that they exist as 'performers' as a result of internal responses to external change rather than through the requirements of their subject discipline or to facilitate pedagogy. As I have argued in previous chapters, site-based performance management has shifted the responsibility for the funding of education and the achievement of higher standards to the school, and this shifting down the line to the school has resulted in the shifting down the line within the school. In this way shared leadership is functionally downwards, it is about getting teaching and learning done, measured and made visible in externally determined ways (Grace, 1995). While skirmishes may take place over rooming and timetabling, such mundane matters need to be smoothed over so that there is no disruption to institutional goals.

Positioning in relation to professional judgement over subject discipline and pedagogic issues remains underdeveloped in current preferred models of managing in the middle. While Gold (1998) identifies the importance of promotion-bearing credentials based on subject expertise, she shows the integrationist aspect of the head of department within the accountability structures in which the department delivers institutional goals. However, the capacity to resist this is also evident within research that connects role to teacher identities (Bennett, 1995; Leask and Terrell, 1997) and habitus. Historically, teachers position themselves and are positioned as teachers through their subject discipline and/or pedagogic skills. Gold (1998) argues that 'in practice Heads of Department are promoted to the post because they know a lot about learning and teaching their subject' (p. 90), this is both essential for credibility and for educational leadership of learners, learning and pedagogy. Learning and using the required management and leadership skills is not enough because there is a tension between the department as a sub-unit of statistical aggregation of effectiveness fitting in with the school as a strategic unit of aggregation. Teacher identity with their discipline through subject associations and their intellectual positioning regarding knowledge claims is potentially disruptive to the smooth process of integrating teachers and whole-school policies. Why should an individual teacher teach their subject in the same way as other teachers in the building? Such a question can only be debated and resolved through questions around epistemology and professional practice, and it is unlikely to be accepted on the basis of the importance of an integrated approach of 'all singing from the same hymn sheet'. Bennett (1995) shows there are different conceptualisations about the nature and purpose of teaching: a craft, an art, a profession, a labour process that has implications for management, and this is illustrated in Figure 8.1.

The preferred way of teaching by current government agencies is for it to be a labour process or at best a craft, and any subject leader trying to impose this onto teachers who see their work as a profession or an art will be in difficulty. This opens up the possibility that bottom up creativity is stifled through the strategic monitoring of the delivery of

Teaching	Implications for leadership and management
Labour: 'following set plans and procedures . . . teaching as labour sees the teacher as a production line worker in a traditional, machine-based factory, and assumes that effective practice which will produce the desired results if adhered to can be concretely determined and specified' (p. 47).	To plan for and to control the teacher through predetermined standards about teaching and its outcomes.
Craft: 'is a repertoire of skills and techniques which make teachers basically competent to operate independently on predetermined tasks. It assumes that general rules can be developed and that knowledge of these and of the techniques will produce the required results' (p. 48).	To plan for, organise, and co-ordinate the work of the teacher. Checking results and if they are not good enough then the teaching methods are supervised.
Profession: the teacher exercises judgement rooted in theory and technical skill: 'teaching as a profession requires the teacher to go beyond the exercise of craft skills to diagnose problems, evaluate possible responses and adopt a chosen course of action' (p. 48).	Teachers self-manage and are supported by administration that provides resources and technical support. Performance and standards are through peer review.
Art: 'rules and procedures give way to intuition, creativity, improvisation and expressiveness. The teacher as artist, then, has to rely on personal insight as well as theoretically grounded knowledge, and therefore requires considerable autonomy and discretion in order to function effectively' (p. 48).	Teachers are encouraged by leadership and are supported by administration that provides resources and technical support. Performance and standards are through peer review.

Figure 8.1 The relationship between teaching, leadership and management (based on Bennett, 1995)

outcomes, and through the development of a culture in which teachers face assimiliation. There is a strong theme within the literature regarding the reluctance of subject leaders to observe and monitor teaching; this is seen as an abdication of role, and alternative explanations provided by Bennett's (1995) analysis are missing. For example, it could be argued that authentic professional autonomy is the means through which the teacher engages in practice as a pedagogic relationship central to effect learning, and a resistance to external monitoring is not so much a product of producer capture of the classroom but a recognition that monitoring is less about improving learning and more about organisational control. Furthermore, struggle is often characterised as rivalry and conflict rather than teachers working their way through philosophical and values-based issues about the subject discipline and learning. To try to eradicate or

fence in dialogue can be seen as an attempt to close down the department as an alternative site for the creative generation of alternative
visions to that put forward by the headteacher and senior management.
This is illustrated by Glover et al. (1998) who conclude that: 'the essential
feature of "middleness" appears to be that the subject leaders and others
are translators and mediators rather than originators of the policy and
culture of the school' (p. 286). This is problematic for subject and team
leaders, and how they come to terms with challenges to their identities
in which they may have to exercise management functions that oppose
pedagogy rather than support and develop it.

There is evidence from research of tensions between SMT and teachers
in the middle (Harris et al., 1995), and the latter are not always disposed
to contribute to strategic policy processes (Brown and Rutherford, 1998;
Glover et al., 1998; 1999). Evidence from Glover et al. (1999) shows how
the introduction of faculty heads leading a team of subject leaders in
secondary schools created a powerful group who allied with senior
managers, and this positioned subject leaders as lacking the necessary
understanding of whole-school requirements to shift from schemes of
work and making lists of things to do towards the monitoring and evaluation of teaching. Overall, this raises issues that are difficult to dissect,
and are being worked through at local level in different ways. It seems
that the expectation to perform a preferred role is that the post-holder
must see the work of their subject area within the context of the whole-
school, but this could be interpreted as senior managers expecting middle
managers to carry their burden of public accountability rather than
debate and discuss the process of pupil learning across the school. In their
study of senior management teams Wallace and Hall (1994) found that
'the hierarchical organisation of the schools meant that SMT members
were empowered to monitor the work of other staff, but not the other
way round. The potential therefore arose for a sense of distance between
the SMT and other staff' (p. 187). It is the drawing of boundaries and the
degrees of permeability that are crucial here, because by creating an arena
for debate and discussion the SMT needed privacy and, consequently,
they were unable to demonstrate responsiveness and that they had
listened. Furthermore, they were unable publicly to model the type of
consensus building culture that they wanted to see in departments.

It also seems that the same degree of privacy to questions and to
engage in dialogue is not afforded middle managers in their work with
teams of teachers. Work by Gleeson and Shain (1999b) in FE has found
that middle managers feel squeezed between senior managers and
lecturers, and within the context of severe financial difficulties they talk
from a position of 'double identities' (p. 470), of being a teacher with a
huge contact commitment together with the pressures from above for
economy and effectiveness. Restructuring in FE has led to the prospect
of facing redundancy or new contracts and, hence, the emotional side to
work, family and livelihood are interwoven into how work is understood

and practised. Gleeson and Shain (1999b) categorise FE middle managers' responses to change as:

- *Willing compliance*: an internalised commitment to the organisation and its corporate image through behaviour, language and dress.
- *Unwilling compliance*: displaying anger, frustration and bitterness about how FE lecturers have been treated, and how they as individuals have experienced changes in their status and role.
- *Strategic compliance*: pragmatically responding to the tensions between professional habitus and managerial demands.

Strategic compliers are the largest group identified, and their struggle within and through practice is based on strong historical and cultural legacies combined with a shrewd understanding of the realities of the new context for their work. Even though they are excluded from knowing the rationale for decisions, they need to know how to read 'the signs and signals which connect the top to the bottom of the organisation' (ibid., p. 485) and, so, they are able to manoeuvre rather than be allied with one section. This micropolitical approach is essential in enabling practitioners who live and work in historically informed cultures in order to filter, make sense of and have an impact on which versions of the performing school are being played out at local level. Informal connections, networks, agreements and bargains can be invisible. Possibilities do remain for middle managers to use informal channels and the grapevine for influencing decisions. Yet, resistance and challenge may still be public, and Brown and Rutherford (1998) give an example of how a head of department argued against a headteacher's position in favour of a licensed teacher by making the case that this undermined teacher professionalism. The head of department was able on this occasion to command the support of other colleagues, but how long such a resource-driven development can be resisted in public and in schools with a budgetary deficit is difficult to say. The drive for organisational integration and consensus can mean the stage management of meetings, and while there are forums to have input into strategic policy through being consulted this can be seen to be highly ritualistic.

Deputies and senior managers

'Senior management' is a term that has come to be used to encompass those teachers who have posts that have a whole institutional focus, e.g. budget, professional development, assessment. It is usual that senior managers will work together in a senior management team which as Wallace and Hall (1994) show is 'the brainchild of the headteachers' (p. 185), and so it is a very much a top-down creation. It could be that the SMT includes those in middle management roles, especially in primary schools where the demarcation is less clear through the adoption of multiple roles (Wallace and Huckman, 1996). In secondary schools a more inclusive approach might be taken with SMT being defined as a *school management team*.

Historically senior managers (i.e. those taking on work that could be done at headteacher level) have grown in importance as the division of labour within schools has become more sophisticated in order to discharge legal and professional responsibilities. Terminology has and continues to be struggled over with posts such as assistant and associate headteacher being used (Jayne, 1996). Comprehensive education was an important impetus to the growth in leadership and management (Grace, 1995), and it is generally regarded that site-based performance management has had a huge impact on the type and structural location of senior post-holders (Vulliamy and Webb, 1995). Since 1993 governors have had more discretion in the structure of senior posts (DfE, 1993) and research has identified the reduction in deputy posts and the restructuring of schools as leaner and flatter systems, often based on reasons of economy rather than organisational effectiveness (Snell, 1999).

Putting the spotlight on senior managers enables the positioning of the deputy to be made visible, and it could be argued that this post is historically and currently one that is in search of a clearly defined role. The conceptualisation of a deputy as standing in for the headteacher in their absence is clear. However, what this actually means in practice is not always transparent. Furthermore, as most headteachers are not absent for long, deputies seek a role that has integrity, coherence and purpose in its own right, which may or may not be preparation for headship in the longer term. Connected to this is the argument that the lack of a clear role definition for the headteacher is central to the ambiguities of senior management roles (Todd and Dennison, 1980), though whether this has been clarified or exacerbated by recent policy changes has yet to be uncovered.

Finding out about deputies is not easy as each writer is clear that they have been underresearched (Hughes and James, 1999), and as Ribbins (1997c) states: 'headteachers are interesting: deputy headteachers, it seems, are not' (p. 295). Our understanding of how deputies are experiencing their work comes from interview and questionnaire surveys that are effective in gathering attitudes and reported understanding of experiences. Furthermore, there has been important work (Wallace and Hall, 1994) that has used a range of methods such as interviews and observations, and Hall (1997a) notes the importance this has for professional learning: 'our observations were less comfortable for them and based on what we saw not just on what they said' (p. 329). What we do not have are recent biographical and longitudinal work about how deputies actually experience their work in real time in the way that work by Richardson (1973) and Nias (1987) has provided us with a rich and deep insight into how senior managers interrelate. While this would further enable habitus to be revealed through the everyday practices of leadership relationships and experiences, there is a growing amount of both quantitative and qualitative evidence that enables the experience of work to begin to be charted and understood.

The work that deputies do is inevitably and demandingly varied, and Garrett and McGeachie's (1999) research found a total of 52 different roles in the primary context that they categorised into:

- class teacher;
- co-ordinating;
- ensuring quality;
- external relations;
- general administration;
- professional development;
- strategic overview;
- school ethos;
- working with people.

While these are not listed in order, the central importance of classroom practice and the absorption of subject leadership responsibilities are key findings. It seems that the deputy job description is a place where professional and executive functions struggle for primacy, and it could be that the executive function is more about day-to-day management than about development. Harvey (1994) shows how deputy principals in Western Australia are dissatisfied with a role that is out of step with site-based management, and where the emphasis is on the traditions of administration and routine rather than on strategic and creative ways in which their ideas can contribute to moving the school forward. It seems that this is a role that in the restructuring process has been neglected as deputies are absorbed into senior management teams in which the traditional headteacher role could be further privileged. Furthermore, deputies have been put in the ambiguous position of moving work down the line but also absorbing or retaining work that cannot be delegated because of resource constraints. Research shows that time made available for discussion and planning is central to the role a deputy is able to play, and this is connected to resource deployment and the size of the school (Garrett and McGeachie, 1999), in which not only the deputy but also the headteacher can have substantial classroom responsibilities (Jayne, 1996).

It seems that deputies are positioned in their work by the headteacher, as Southworth (1995a) states: 'Deputies cannot be assistant heads ... unless their headteachers facilitate such a partnership' (p. 141). This is endorsed by Ribbins (1997c) who, building on Burnham, shows that historically 'the role of the deputy has depended crucially upon how the role of the head is interpreted and on what headteachers wish to make of the position of their principal subordinate' (p. 296). Hughes and James (1999) note the work of Mortimore et al. (1988) who argue that deputies are important in the effectiveness of junior schools, but also draw on the work of Nias (1987) to show that the head was always 'the boss' (Mortimer et al., 1988, pp. 85–6). In this sense the roles are different, and Hughes and James (1999) note the impact of personal factors, including expertise, as well as situational factors such as the school context, that affect how a role is defined and played out. However, Hughes and James (1999) are able to identify the factors that make a successful head–deputy relationship:

- A shared understanding of role and position in which the deputy role is subordinate and limited in comparison to the headteacher.
- Trust and respect in order to maintain confidentiality.
- Shared values and beliefs about education in order to promote them in school and achieve educational outcomes.
- A mutual 'willingness to talk' and air views rather than avoid difficult issues.
- Loyalty and support in which the headteacher took the final decision and carried the ultimate responsibility, but that the views and contribution of the deputy both in private and public is important to carrying through successful policy development and implementation.

In a primary school there is usually never more than one deputy, and so the opportunities for a strong partnership are greater than in a secondary school where there can be more than one deputy, and if not, there is a large senior management team who have taken on work that previously might have been classified as deputy work. Ribbins (1997c) uses Richardson's (1973) study of Nailsea School to show how in a secondary context the role and work of the deputy can be 'strait-jacketed' into particular types of work, which can be gender stereotyped as 'the administrator' and 'the carer' (p. 298). Ribbins (1997c) then goes on to explore how his work in collaboration with other colleagues in interviewing heads reveals experiences of deputy headship from the standpoint of headship. He begins his analysis with the overarching view that: 'surprisingly few of the 34 headteachers ... recalled their experience of deputy headship with affection and several retain negative views of the role' (p. 300). Nevertheless, the relationship with the head is a key influence regarding the experiences of having been a deputy; Michael Gasper (with Pascal, 1998) tells us that 'I worked for somebody who viewed her role as head as being to train me for headship' (p. 301), while Helen Hyde (1997) states that 'I did not get on very well with my head and only stayed four years' (p. 302).

Deputy–headteacher relationship is the space where it can all go right or wrong. Personality, events, rivalries, and bad behaviour can all conspire to make the deputy's day and work an unrewarding experience. It is how deputies learn about the headteacher that they do or do not want to be. Deputies are and can be just that, but the challenge for career deputies is that restructuring is rapidly displacing their primacy. Deputies are struggling for a role and distinction at a time of teams. Teams keep deputies in the middle as new career structures will enable those 'below' deputy to undertake NPQH training and leap over them into headteacher positions. They aspire to or undertake work that headteachers previously did, while watching their own work pass down the line (if there are the resources to do this). For deputies who aspire to headship they face continued integration into the headship of their boss, and must publicly support and extend this headship, but at the same time they have to break free to develop their status as a headteacher in waiting.

Senior management teams

The positioning and repositioning of the headteacher–deputy(ies) roles and relationships needs to be seen within the context of the growth of a larger team of senior managers within school. As the policies based on the Green Paper (DfEE, 1998) begin to work their way through the school system, the creation of a leadership team will be overlaid on top of the ways of working that have been adopted over time. Detailed and comprehensive work has been undertaken into the workings of senior management teams in primary (Wallace and Huckman, 1996) and secondary (Hall and Wallace, 1996; Wallace and Hall, 1994) schools. It is not possible here to give a comprehensive overview of this work except to recognise that there are a number of themes that need to be noted, not least the one that has already been raised earlier in this chapter about the relationship between the senior management team and what Wallace and Huckman (1996) describe as the 'credibility gap' (p. 311) between those making the decisions and those in receipt of them. The theme that has been implied but has not so far been given space in the discussion is what it means to divide the labour and the implications this has for accountability, especially since as Thomas (1997) argues schools will 'sink or swim by the effectiveness of their teams' (p. 332).

There is more to effective team working than synergy and getting on with each other, as there are issues around power and process, or what Hall and Wallace (1996) regard as 'high gain, high strain' (p. 297) in which the benefits of working as a team outweigh the barriers. However, there are cases where it can and does go seriously wrong, as Evans (1998) shows in her work on Rockville County Primary School where the headteacher and senior management team lacked credibility amongst the staff. Nevertheless, as we know from research into site-based performance management, headteachers have been more privileged by the reforms than teachers, but the feeling of being personally responsible has also intensified (Whitty et al., 1998) and, so, having a senior management team has been important in sharing the burden but it does not remove the public accountability for school effectiveness that is on the shoulders of headteachers. Consequently, researchers have raised the point that, while senior management teams are important, the delegation of decisions has to be tempered by a headteacher's ultimate accountability, in which case it may not be possible for a headteacher to hand over responsibility in ways that professional expertise, both current and to be developed, may demand. As Wallace and Huckman (1996) argue this could disempower the head because: 'there is no guarantee that other staff will then act within the bounds acceptable to the head and he or she – not they – is ultimately accountable for their efforts' (p. 321). Following on from this it is clear that team work has to evolve and take into account the people involved, and the historical and contemporary setting in which work is being undertaken and roles are being played out. This analysis effectively links the impact of site-based performance management laid on top of historical legacies of headship to the growth of managerialism and per-formativity. The abstracted performance indicators of examination outputs require role clarity and a division of labour based on the require-ments of organisational or unitary performance. What research is telling us is that this is in tension with the professional habitus of senior post-holders, at least for the time being. However, dialogue within senior man-agement teams may increasingly be less about values, pedagogy and children's needs, and more about information management, spin and damage control.

Summary

Research and theorising about leadership roles in the middle and towards the top illustrate that there is a tension between the drive for internal and external performance and professional ways of understanding teaching and learning. What is problematic is that much of what is written is highly normative and is about determining roles and work in ways that are consistent with educational restructuring. It is a pity that a range of voices is often not only silent, but also sometimes ridiculed as claims by subject leaders to be busy is often shown in a negative light rather than the fact that they may be overworked. We need to know more about how work is assigned, divided up, approved and disapproved of, so that habitus can be revealed and understood through the struggle over position and positioning. Important work is taking place that seeks to understand the situation in which post-holders are struggling over their identity, but more ethnographic studies are needed so that we can better understand these professional lives on their own terms rather than as a stage in a total career experience. Ribbins (1985), from the vantage point of the mid-1980s, asks whether schools are overmanaged and, so, teachers spend more time out of the classroom than in it. This question remains relevant today as we need to ask what role incumbency is for? Is it to support teaching, learning and student welfare, or to operate in ways that are approved of by external agencies and provide the data essential for external accountability? Schools must be led and managed, and much of this will be contingent on teaching and learning, i.e. the budget is more about the arrangements to support teaching and learning than about pedagogic issues of what is effective teaching and learning. However, it seems that role incumbency is more about this type of work than it is about expertise in educational issues, and hence budgets could come to determine what is good teaching and learning through value-for-money measurements. If we are to retain educational leadership, then our gaze needs to fall on teaching and learning where leadership is integral to activity.

In the next chapter I move this forward by focusing on teachers and students and how they are working for a learning space as a more productive alternative to their current position as followers.

9

Teachers and Students

From this stage in presenting struggles within leadership, I now move into work that demonstrates and illuminates the teacher–student relationship as the place where we need to refocus our attention. This is a different type of leadership to the one that the policy context is presenting, and it is a different type of teacher–student relationship to the one required to enable PRP to operate. As Sergiovanni (1998) argues the drive to improve student performance has led to:

- *Bureaucratic leadership*: focus on mandated outcomes through monitoring and evaluation.
- *Visionary leadership*: focus on motivating people with the change imperative.
- *Entrepreneurial leadership*: focus on competition within the marketplace.

These leadership strategies are central to current officially approved approaches to leadership which are placing educational professionals and students in a contradictory position. There are positions within school effectiveness, school improvement and education management that endorse these strategies. These positions tend not to take on board Sergiovanni's (1998) alternative strategy for pedagogical leadership: 'that invests in capacity building by developing social and academic capital for students and intellectual and professional capital for teachers' (p. 38). Those who have adopted a school improvement position do acknowledge the importance of pedagogy, but do not tend to see encounters between teachers and students as emancipatory in which learning is about collective knowledge generation (Fielding, 2001). This radical position is occupied by those who are socially critical and who not only challenge official models but put forward an alternative conceptualisation of leadership as being based on teacher–teacher, teacher–student, student– student and teacher–student–community relationships.

Empowerment

Teachers and students are currently being positioned by the 'aerosol' words (Smyth and Shacklock, 1998a, p. 81) of empowerment, collegiality, collaboration and participation, and spraying them around has devalued the potential meaning that we could draw from them. In particular, these words have been used to cynically manipulate what traditionally has been called goodwill, or 'discretionary commitment' (Hargreaves, 1998, p. 315) in which the teacher will work beyond contractual requirements. Understanding the emotions of teaching is critical (Golby, 1996; Nias, 1996) and teachers have gone above and beyond the call of duty to implement site-based performance management without damaging students. The costs have been borne by teachers and their families. The intensification of work, the blurring of home and school for the location of work, combined with the guilt of not doing anything properly, has led to feelings of despair at how external demands are undermining re-lationships (Hargreaves, 1994; Helsby, 1999). While there are important opportunities for teachers currently to develop and make visible their pedagogic skills through working with other teachers, these will remain highly problematic as long as they are about sustaining rather than chal-lenging existing power structures. As Nias (1996) argues, teacher emotion: 'is not an indulgence; it is a professional necessity. Without feeling, with the freedom to "face themselves", to be whole persons in the classroom, they implode, explode – or walk away' (p. 305). The neo-liberal version of the performing school requires teachers and students to be followers, but to feel good about it and, hence, research that is concerned to further this identity presents the language of functional leadership and the processes that it captures as unproblematic. Consequently empowerment is given and received, collegiality and col-laboration are interchangeable and are concerned with teachers working together to achieve learning outcomes, and participation is about working in teams. Here I would like to connect with, but not labour, the points I have already made regarding the illusory and delusory nature of the knowledge claims underpinning these ways of working (Gunter, 1997); suffice to say that they are one of the means through which the obsessive control of teachers and students continues.

Empowerment is directly connected to teacher effectiveness as it is argued that a teacher who is able to 'design and control their educational services free from a subordinating school administration are more effective than teachers who feel alienated and powerless' (Johnson and Short, 1998, p. 156). However, achieving this is not just about whether teachers are trained to do the designing and controlling, but whether teacher and student empowerment is connected to broader structures such as the public or private sectors. As Fielding (1996) argues empow-erment is not a process but is 'a struggle in difficult and often hostile contexts' (p. 406). Brundrett (1998) shows that collegiality has a high profile in the literature but it is normative, and is more about how we want to work, rather than what we actually do. What seems to be missing in much of the writing about collegiality is how it is conceptualised as an 'it': as complete, packaged and capable of being implemented. As such, cause-and-effect connections are impossible, and the failure of collegiality to be realised enables teacher and student work to become the site where surveillance and oppression operate.

Spaulding (1997) has undertaken research into teacher experiences of principals' work and found that only 12 out of 81 could describe it as democratic, and she goes on to show how much principal behaviour has negative consequences for teachers and teaching. A focus on teacher participation yields some important evidence for Spaulding (1997) as teachers are in receipt of decisions and also talk about 'pseudo-participation' where views are sought as a ritual rather than a sincere attempt to listen and take note. Teachers go through the motions and comply because they need the job, and feel that 'principals don't give them enough credit to make good choices and are too afraid that their own special interests won't be served' (ibid., p. 43). How headteachers or prinicipals interpret teacher engagement is central to this type of work, because as Hayes (1996) building on Gaziel and Weiss argues, misunderstandings can develop because some staff are 'internals' who see themselves as directly involved in all events, while others are 'externals' who see the outside world as determining their work. Central to this is where teachers regard their priorities as being, and Hayes (1996) goes on to show that teachers will always prioritise the classroom and may discount participation in areas that do not seem to be directly connected. Like Spaulding (1997), Hayes (1996) also found that teachers did not like to face ambiguous and unnecessary participation opportunities, and so there is a need to differentiate and be explicit about the type and level of consultation. This gives due recognition to teacher participation in how the rules of the game are worked through and agreed, though the tension between individual teacher development and school improvement has increasingly been resolved in favour of the latter (Bennett, 1999; Cutler and Waine, 2000). In particular, development planning enables the school as an organisation to be created and sustained, and because of its technical and accountability requirements it is unable to be developed in ways that could embrace the teacher's capacity to engage in educational leadership. Research by Broadhead et al. (1996) shows that teacher involvement is mainly in the early stages of decision-making, and reports on the benefits of planning emphasise managerial rather than child-centred practice (Cuckle et al., 1998). It seems that development planning is more about allocating tasks and responsibility than it is about asking questions about how and why things are what they are, and how they have come to be so.

Our understanding of how teachers position themselves in their work is through ethnographic case studies in which the complexity of interaction can be asked about, observed and revealed. Nias's (1988) work with primary teachers provides a very rich understanding of how identity and work are shaped through internal and external reference groups. Internal groups are pupils, and other members of staff, while external groups can vary from being elected as a local councillor through to working with other teachers and tutors on a postgraduate course. Reference groups are where we go to seek mutuality in discussing ideas and interests, and are used as power bases to promote or defend activity. For example, teachers can use pupils as a means of defending their practice, teacher commitment can be affected negatively or positively by the groupings around them, and teachers can seek out other groups external to the school such as in HEI as a means of supporting and developing their ideas. Habitus is central here to how the disposition towards and within teaching is embodied, but is also revealed through positioning with groups and by positioning others as being outside the boundaries. However, as Nias (1988) shows, reference groups can be positive in how values and meaning making take place with others, and this is essential because teaching can be individual and individualising work. The realities of practice are that collegiality is fluid and is being struggled over in the day-to-day work of teachers and students, and what is problematic and needs our attention is that the struggle is being contained within the school as a unitary organisation rather than connected to the broader debates about society and governance.

As Hargreaves (1995) has shown, much is claimed about collaboration and how it can enable personal and organisational gains from improving personal confidence and knowledge, through to the efficient and effective delivery of outcomes. While much writing on collaboration sanctifies working together, Hargreaves (1994) reminds us that there are historical and cultural patterns that can be highly structured through working groups that he calls 'balkanized cultures' (p. 213). However, changing these ways of working through teamwork may not achieve what is intended because it is about securing teacher compliance through ritualising working together rather than creating the space to challenge practice. Consequently, collegiality can become contrived as it is 'regulated', 'complusory', 'implementation-oriented', 'fixed in time and space' and 'predictable' (Hargreaves, 1994, pp. 195–6), and this is disconnected from how people work together and certainly how professionals need to work together in a post-industrial world. What underpins how we understand people in organisations is our approach to participation and how this connects with power structures. Bottery (1992) argues that the case for participation made around issues of decision-making effectiveness and the facilitation of positive working relationships is flawed, and this leads him to question the power structures underpinning the view that 'teachers have no rights to participation, only the opportunity if their employers feel it is in their (employers') interests' (p. 173). He goes on to argue that authentic teacher participation is based on:

- *The educational process:* teaching is a two-way process and so teachers (and pupils) are involved in decisions, and an ethical commitment to this can extend participation.
- *Teachers and pupils are people:* if we begin with human beings then management becomes a social and political process rather than techniques and tasks.
- *The needs of citizenship:* teachers as well as pupils need to, and be seen to, contribute and practise community involvement, not just for themselves but also for pupils.

Voice is problematic as it connects with capability and capacity. Some voices are louder than others, and in the publishing business such as the production of this book the author's voice is the loudest and controls selection and choice. Goodson (1995) alerts us to how voice has become increasingly an issue at a time when teachers are being restructured into technicist schooling. Consequently, teachers are team-talking more and being funded by government to undertake action research but this could be silencing their capacity to ask deeper and challenging questions. Capability can be trained, but capacity comes from political awareness and confidence that it is acceptable to speak and to speak loudly.

Work on pupil voice shows that the headmaster tradition located in the teacher by proxy does not support authentic learning. Children will no longer be in receipt of top-down power systems and sit quietly, and Fielding (1999a) shows how 'work within the field is now beginning to encounter students expressing doubts about the genuineness of their school's interest in their progress and well-being as persons, as distinct from their contributions to their school's league table position' (p. 286). Teaching is a relationship in which a condition for learning (e.g. a working consensus) is connected to both the personality of the teacher (e.g. humour) and pedagogy (i.e. the teacher creates and sustains interesting work and works hard on their behalf) (Wallace, 1996a). Consequently, as Wallace (1996b) goes on to show, engagement with tasks can be about compliance that is different from learning. For learning to take place there is a need for 'meaning making' in which children will 'make sense of their learning on their own terms' but also value and take on board how teachers put learning into its broader context (ibid., p. 65). This leads Rudduck et al. (1996b) to conclude that, while pupil voice does not lead to new and dramatic insights into learning and the purpose of schooling, it does enable us to see how childhood has traditionally been conceptualised in a way that undermines their contribution. Currently, children do not have rights and duties, and so are unable to be citizens and, consequently, their contribution to education is to be educated and trained. However, Rudduck et al. (1996b) argue that 'this traditional exclusion of young people from the consultative processes, this bracketing out of their voice, is founded upon an outdated view of childhood which fails to acknowledge children's capacity to reflect on issues affecting their lives' (p. 172). Given the slow pace of reform to the English constitution, children are the subjects of subjects and all that the market has done is to mutate this by creating children as stakeholders in product development and purchase. Research by Dempster and Logan (1998) in Australia confirms student concerns about the lack of leadership opportunities. Rudduck et al. (1996b) go on to show from their data gathered with children that there are 'six principles which make a significant difference to learning', which interact as a 'conditions of learning frame', and these are: 'respect for pupils', 'fairness to all pupils', 'autonomy', 'intellectual challenge', 'social support' and 'security' (pp. 173–4).

This analysis provides us with the opportunity to ask questions regarding how teachers and students are being positioned within schools and society as a whole, and whether there are alternative positions that require our attention. Furthermore, MacBeath et al. (1998) ask us to think about who learners are, and the development of multi-age classrooms in enabling the drive towards lifelong learning. If the challenge for schools and schooling is 'flexible and differentiated learning' (ibid., p. 25) taking account of prior learning and using credit transfer, then we might ask how teachers, students and communities will be enabled to participate in the dialogue about the restructuring of the curriculum.

Radicalising collegiality

Conceptualising teachers and students as leaders, and pedagogy as a leadership process, is not new but, as Crowther (1997) argues, both the theory and practice of educational administration has not engaged with this. In particular, Smyth et al. (1998) argue that teachers have not been involved in how site-based performance management has been conceptualised and, consequently, this will fail. Such an approach to teachers signals important messages and has implications for society and the political system in how people beyond the school learn about whether they, outside of positional authority, have the capability, capacity and entitlement to engage in leadership (Crowther, 1997).

One particular approach to understanding teachers and students as leaders is to make the case that they can display or even exceed the same traits and behaviours as those who are in hierarchical roles. There is a requirement that this should be so as otherwise we might wonder how students obtain employment or places on courses, or where future role incumbents in educational organisations come from. However, conceptualising teachers as conforming to the accepted models of leadership is more about assimilation into a preferred teacher ripe for promotion than it is about how teachers undertake their work and identify with it. It could be that teachers are engaging in work that is outside what a traditional post-holder is allowed to do given their integration into the management system. We know, for example, how student empowerment in regard of being able to participate in classroom and school activity can be limited by unreflexive pedagogy. Mewborn (1999) reminds us of how interaction within the classroom can be structured in such a way as to enable participation. The simple matter of 'wait time' can help to facilitate student–teacher interaction so that we shift from the average time of 0.9 seconds to 4–5 seconds and, so, give all students time to think, construct an answer and build confidence. This reinforces the arguments made by Joyce et al. (1997) that the most important activity in learning is that of the student, and it is 'the teacher's responsibility to provide the conditions that will increase the probability of student learning' (p. 134). In this way answers are not right or wrong but are about enabling cognitive and affective approaches to learning to be developed. We might ask: where is the wait time for teachers, and how are they enabled to think and construct innovative and challenging responses to current educational issues?

Knowledge of learning and how this connects to student experiences in the classroom is helpful but this should not stop here. I would want to turn the issue on its head and ask why cannot a teacher be a leader and exercise leadership on his/her own terms? Why cannot a teacher have a vision and mission for his/her classroom, and have his/her own development agenda? This is particularly the case as expertise in pedagogy should first be based on disciplinary excellence, i.e. the teaching of history rather than teaching as just a generic skill. In the current policy context it seems that teachers cannot be allowed to exercise leadership in this way as it would disrupt the power structures that are historically and socially located, and consequently teachers are unable to support pupils as leader learners. When teachers have done this it has been characterised as progressive and labelled as ineffective. It seems that teacher excellence has to be publicly measured so that it is acclaimed or shamed as a means through which teachers become dependent on post-holder disciplining and, so, are integrated into the performance accountability structure. Governors, headteachers, senior and middle managers cannot take the risk of teacher leadership as particular learning outcomes dominate the purpose of schooling, and so the noose is tightened with teacher 'Oscars' being used to consecrate those who conform.

Understanding this is relevant not just to those who are training to be a teacher or in their first post, but also in how the image of teaching and being a teacher connects with broader communities that are the places where future teachers are being developed or diverted away. The role of mentoring in pre-service training and in the induction of a newly qualified teacher is widely recognised as an important professional process (Barnett, 1995; Bolam et al., 1995a; Booth, 1993; Cross, 1995; Hutchinson, 1994; Martin, 1994; Simco, 1995). Mentoring can be a power relationship in which the mentee is enabled to survive the stresses of immersion, combined with being in receipt of knowledge and a way of working that is a combination of official craft-based constructions of what a good teacher is. This is made even more complex when the employment context of temporary contracts, no or little reduced teaching load, and the diversion of resources away from releasing the mentor for classroom observation, all combine to restrict professional interactions (Bolam et al., 1995a). Mentoring is seen as vital to enabling 'expertise' (Hutchinson, 1994, p. 304) and 'critical reflection' (Simco, 1995, p. 271) to develop, and this has the potential for revitalising the experienced teacher as mentor in the support and training they receive. In addition to this, mentoring as a leadership relationship has further potential, and Cochran-Smith and Paris (1995) argue for an alternative approach in which the mentor and mentee see their work as a 'shared activity' in which they 'work together to understand teaching, learning and schooling' (p. 189). This requires a critical evaluation of existing knowledge that is brought to the process, particularly by the mentor who is often chosen because of 'good practice'. Furthermore, questions need to be raised about the systems into which the mentee is being inducted, such as the school, and the standards that are set by government agencies.

There is a different type of teacher reflection to that designed to discipline work. As Hursh (1995) argues, teaching and education are highly political and, so, reflection needs to engage with how 'the organization of the school and the curriculum content and practices are outcomes of contested political goals' (p. 109). We cannot accept power structures as givens otherwise change cannot take place, and Crowther (1997) has researched the work of 15 'unsung heroes' (13 teachers and 2 para-professionals), such as the teacher who worked on breaking down cross-cultural boundaries prior to his pupils transferring to secondary school by arranging for them to live with the Aborginal community for a week in the final term at primary school. Crowther (1997) goes on to show that teachers insist that they are teachers rather than leaders and managers. Consequently, by focusing on work that is contingent on the classroom and calling it leadership and management, rather than on work that is integral to the classroom, the field has failed to develop teacher leadership. While some writers on leadership and management have focused on the school as an organisation and have tried to rework the connection with the community as marketing, Crowther's (1997) work shows a much deeper and educative connection between teachers' work and communities in which confronting barriers is about a 'process of culture struggle, consciousness-raising and emancipation' (p. 14). Such a political role may have been hidden in the marketing spin of brochures, but it has preoccupied teachers who are concerned to work with children as learners rather than consumers. Crowther (1997, p. 15) concludes that: 'teacher leadership is essentially an ethical stance' in which teachers are working for 'a better world' that is not just about the here and now, but about longer-term gains. This could be seen to be naive, and so Smyth et al. (1998) ask if it is possible to pull off and sustain such ways of working at a time when the design of work denies teacher and student opportunities to participate? While teachers may not have fully developed ways of practising teaching as a leadership relationship, and may even have bought into the competency agenda, this does not mean that dialogue should not take place. Smyth et al. (1998) go on to argue that central to teacher learning and their leadership is that they should not be 'fearful of "confronting strangeness" ' (p. 99) so that they can engage in intellectual work and ask questions that challenge what we do and why we do it, and why we do it repeatedly. Smyth et al. (1998) provide a case study of a school where dialogue about teaching and learning is ongoing and central, where people feel safe to challenge ideas and where teaching as a political process is accepted. Consequently, it is still possible for teachers to create the spaces and places where their leadership can be exercised and valued in debates about teaching and learning. This shifts the focus away from teachers resisting externally imposed change to establishing ways of working that enable external demands to be included in the discussion but do not override or subvert what teachers are doing and want to do.

Teachers and students engaging in authentic intellectual work has underpinned much of what I have been arguing so far, and work that facilitates this is socially critical because it connects teaching and learning with the communities (both national and local) that teachers and students are a part of (Smyth, 1993). Fielding (1999b) argues in favour of a 'radical collegiality' (p. 16) over that of collaboration which is defined as an individualising process based on the seeking and receiving of resources. In contrast, collegiality is 'overridingly communal in form and in substance' (p. 17) and it is radical when located in 'educational practice intentionally and demonstrably linked to the furtherance of democracy' (ibid., pp. 17–18). Consequently, collaboration and collegiality cannot be used interchangeably, and neither can collegiality be used to apply to teachers who are collaborating in teams. Rather, as Fielding (1999b) argues, there is a need to recognise 'inclusive collegiality' between students and teachers in which equality and difference are central. The emphasis is less on the delivery of outcomes and more on dialogue through which learning is about exploration and unpredictability. What does this mean for teachers? It could lead to a misinterpretation of teachers abdicating their expertise and training, and it could be the focus of neo-liberal attacks on teachers for failing to discipline children in ways that will prepare them for their place in the world. However, as Fielding (1999b) goes on to argue, working in a democratic way does not mean that teachers cannot engage in educative leadership both in the classroom and in the community. It does mean that teachers are central to creating learning as a dialogic struggle in which teachers also learn from students, parents and the community, and such learning is to be encouraged particularly because it is essential to the development of democracy. Furthermore, he goes on to show how radical collegiality is central to both teacher and student learning, in which students are not just sources of attitudinal data through completing questionnaires, but are actively involved in researching and feeding back pedagogic experiences with teachers (Fielding, 2001). The conditions for student voice are just as problematic as those for teacher voice, as it could be interpreted, on the one hand, as noise and, on the other, as a direct challenge to existing power structures. It could also be exploitative in how students are drawn into a way of working that retains an essentially disciplinary process rather than one that challenges how their identity has traditionally been constructed.

Teachers and students have both been undermined by the positioning of students as consumers, but both have a mutual interest in asking questions about who is currently representing their interests in this way, and why (Fielding, 2001; Yeatman, 1994). Action research is seen as an important way in which teachers can become more empowered in their work, and ongoing critical discussion about purposes and values supports its development. McTaggart's (1990; 1991) work is important here in the analysis of how western social science research is received and engaged with in Aboriginal communities. Knowledge developed as objective and universal could be seen to be about the assimilation of people into 'superior' ways of working, living and knowing. However, action research is not a neutral technical tool or process, but is value laden and highly political. Action research could be the means through which colonisation takes place, or alternatively it could be values informed in which purpose, knowledge and research tools are subjected to questions around praxis and the development of 'Aboriginal pedagogies consistent with their own communities' aspirations and forms of life' (McTaggart, 1990, p. 213). This work is important in how it alerts us to identities, and how those in receipt of problem-solving agendas may be the victims of power systems that could rob them of what they value, and so classrooms are important places in which control over identities can and should be questioned.

How we see the power relationship in the pedagogic process can be the same as that evident in the headmaster tradition so well explained by Grace (1995). If organisational leadership is top-down, and this mirrors and helps sustain the structures within society, then teaching and learning is justified as a power-over activity. Currently this is being reinvigorated through both the purpose of the National Curriculum in order to standardise learning (Martin Hughes, 1997) and the means through which it has been created, and so Ball (1994b) is justified in calling it 'the curriculum of the dead' (p. 28 ff). It is dead in terms of the implications for pedagogy as well as being the product of a time long gone in which humanistic approaches to how we arrange our decision-making and law were still heretical. There is a long and respected intellectual history here, and Corson (2000) reminds us of the work of Freire (1972) as being important in enabling interests to be recognised. While talking about democracy and education is not currently a capital offence, it is still difficult to talk about it in ways that are not open to interpretation as undermining those who have their careers and interests tied up in the current structural arrangements.

Distributing leadership

It seems from the argument so far that governors, headteachers, senior managers, middle managers, teachers, students, parents and wider communities are in a contradictory position. On the one hand the historical legacy of schools and schooling means that the neo-liberal version of the performing school is in the ascendant. It is simple and less complex to go along with the current manifestation of the headmaster tradition in which increasing demands for accountability have been handled through the extension of the market. On the other hand the democratic version of the performing school will not go away, and education as a field where there are positions other than those officially recognised means that alternative ways of working are alive. Leadership is being worked out and through at local level, and it is also the case that the realities of work mean that there is often no time to reflect on the implications of action and inaction except when something goes seriously wrong. After all, even if a practitioner spends all weekend engaging in externally demanded paperwork, come Monday morning children have to be taught and colleagues have to be worked with. This is why conceptualising and realising leadership as a relationship rather than a function and series of approved behaviours is necessary, not least because teachers have a history of practising it.

Research has already shown that the division of labour in schools has been the product of an increasingly complex schooling system with the post-1944 education structure unevenly overlaid by comprehensive education, and then various forms of site-based performance management. However, what is also the case is that opportunities to lead have traditionally been in the gift of the headteacher as a 'leader of leaders' (Day, 1995, p. 126) and, so, how the distribution of work has been conceptualised has been on the premise of avoiding potential headteacher overload. Increasingly the neo-Taylorist approach to getting new tasks done efficiently and effectively has been given a new-wave gloss in which delegation is the means through which individuals in teams can learn and develop. It could be that the restructuring of leaner flatter systems now means that we are all managers and leaders but, as evidence from education shows, this is a cheaper way to get the same amount or even more work done (Fergusson, 1994; Menter et al., 1997).

Sharing or distributing leadership has another understanding and has less to do with managerial efficiency and more to do with educational leadership working within and developing a democracy. Work by Moos and Dempster (1998) in comparing leadership in Danish, English, Queensland (Australia) and Scottish schools leads them to conclude that there is a demand from teachers and students to shift away from bureaucratic or position-holding leadership to a more distributed leadership. However, they are also aware that while democratic ways of working between parents and the school are more deeply embedded in Denmark than the other countries in their project, there is a need to move in this direction. Apple and Beane (1999), present real-life stories that illustrate what we might see when we experience a democratic school. They argue that in presenting the dilemmas, courage and beliefs in working with children and their communities they are not 'dewy-eyed romantics' and are explicit about the unresolved challenges for teachers and pupils (Apple and Beane, 1999, p. 120).

How we move this agenda forward is, as has already been noted, problematic given the historical legacies that we are located within. We need the means by which everyday educational practice can be understood and developed differently, and it needs to be able to connect to and problematise macro and micro policy-making. By far the most important contribution made to enable us to do this is Gronn's (2000) work on distributive leadership in which he draws on socio-cultural activity theory that has its roots in Marxist philosophy. This is an international field in which knowledge workers both chart their intellectual heritage and are developing activity theory within a range of empirical settings (Engeström et al., 1999; at www.edu.bham.ac.uk/SAT). Engeström (at www.helsinki.fi/~jengestr/activity/1.htm; 1987; 1999a; 2000; 2001) presents the following model of an activity system and this is illustrated in Figure 9.1:

What Engeström does is to represent the complexity of activity, including patterns of power, processes, and meaning-making, and locates them historically and socially. For those looking for a rational approach Engeström's theorising could suggest, in diagrammatic form, a neat and tidy solution, but this would be a misunderstanding as it is an intellectual practical approach to analysing activity as a continuous process of

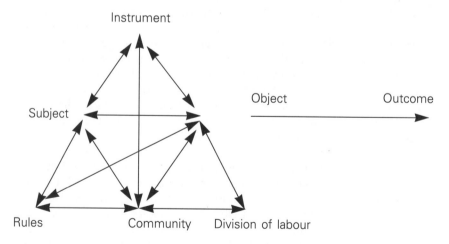

Figure 9.1 The structure of a human activity system (Engeström, 1987)

conflict and development. There are no linear cause-and-effect assumptions, but instead we can gain an understanding of the dynamics:

- *Subject*: can be an individual or a collective.
- *Object*: is the orientation of the action being undertaken by the subject.
- *Instrument*: stands for the artefacts or tools, and includes symbols and language.
- *Rules*: is the way actions are structured and which are often historically located.
- *Community*: stands for the setting in which activity and action takes place.
- *Division of labour*: how activity is divided into separate actions, undertaken by individual(s) in co-ordination with others.
- *Outcome*: is the consequence of the activity and action.

When an individual (subject) takes action in an activity system (e.g. a school) in order to achieve a purpose (object) (e.g. learning outcome) this is mediated through one or more of the other points, and so the relationship could be: subject–instrument–object, in which what is done and how it is done is mediated through tools and signs (e.g. timetable, textbooks, video, computer and behaviour policy) regarding what is and is not appropriate learning. The teacher and children working together create meaning about their work, and this is located in a complex process in which the division of labour, historical expectation and the school's goals all interact.

The particular contribution of socio-cultural psychology developed by Vygotsky and his followers is that activity is both socially and historically located. Much has been made of Vygotsky's (1978) zone of proximal development (ZPD) even though he himself did not emphasise it. Its attraction is in how learning is located in the past and the future, and how we can be supported in this learning. The ZPD is 'defined as the gap between a child's actual performance and the level achievable with the help of an adult or a competent peer' (Ryle, 1999, p. 412), and so the student–educator relationship is central in supporting learning. Developing our understanding of the dynamics in this relationship requires us to consider what it means to think and do in ways that are beyond simplistic interpretations of the teacher supporting learning, but to see how we can 'reveal the essentially socially mediated nature of human learning' (Tolman, 1999, p. 75). Leont'ev's (1981) contribution (colleague and disciple of Vygotsky), through his development of Vygotsky's ideas into activity theory, is to enable us to understand the dynamics of activity and action, and he does this through a metaphor of a hunt. He shows that an activity is the hunt in which a person is part of a collective process to seek food, while the action, such as hiding in an ambush, is what we do as part of that process. Engeström and Miettinen (1999) argue that this work is significant in enabling a division of labour between 'collective activity and individual action' (p. 4). If we conceptualise the school as an activity system then what is currently defined and promoted as effective leadership is highly simplistic in its failure to engage with the meaning and reality of action.

For Gronn (2000), socio-cultural activity theory enables the agency–structure divide in leadership to be handled through the recognition of 'conjoint agency'. In particular, the overemphasis on the agency of the transformational leader is overcome by the realisation that labour is actually and necessarily distributed. This enables Gronn (2000) to take our thinking on leadership theory and practice further because the focus on activity and action enables the messiness of human interactions with all their pleasures and frustrations to be centre stage. An activity system can enable a focus on teacher–student interaction in the classroom through to macro policy-making about the classroom, and enables mediation to be described and understood as something other than the blockage preventing the accurate measurement of leadership effects making a difference to student outcomes. Rather the complexities of how meaning is given to and within the division of labour, and how this is played out within a historical and socio-cultural setting, provides a more epistemologically productive way of how we seek to understand schools and actions that take place within them.

The relationship between the activity system and the external world also needs to be considered, otherwise what we may be encountering is just another more sophisticated version of systems theory. We know that systems theory has been very popular across a range of fields in enabling the realities of work to be described and understood, but it has also been used to support the growth of managerialism through its emphasis on the unitary organisation in the rational and linear processing of inputs into outputs (Gunter, 1997). Furthermore, while the relationship between the organisation and the environment is recognised as being potentially unstable, the solutions put forward have been about the seeking of equilibrium through marketing and consumer determined relationships. What is missing from much of the use of systems theory is a theory of power in which enduring historical, economic, political and social structures have impacted on the input–process–output–feedback loop. Activity theory has the potential to move us forward here through the interrelationship and interdependency of: instrument, rules, community and division of labour. In particular, we need to ask questions about how one activity system connects with another, and for Engeström (2000) this is at the forefront of current development for the next stage of theorising and empirical work. He summarises this development around five principles:

- *Collective*: an activity system can only be understood when seen in context of other activity systems.

- *Multi-voicedness*: there are different voices in an activity system, and the collective perspective shows this to be multiplied.
- *Historicity*: activity is embedded and shaped through time.
- *Contradictions*: there are tensions within and between activity systems that cause disturbances.
- *Expansive transformations*: contradictions lead to questioning and a consideration of alternatives.

The importance of this analysis for learning is reinforced by Engeström's use of activity theory work on health care in Finland. Instead of treatment being based on a single diagnosis and supported by separate medical professionals, the emphasis was shifted towards boundary crossing in which all those involved with the child with multiple illnesses move away from role position towards the provision of co-ordinated treatment and a co-operative care plan. This takes us into areas of professional learning and Engeström has drawn on Bateson's (1972) theory of learning:

- *Learning I*: contextual conditioning of right and wrong answers, e.g. rote learning;
- *Learning II*: learning of rules and right-wrong behaviour within the context, e.g. what the teacher expects from the pupil;
- *Learning III*: questioning of the context, rules and behaviours, and the development of alternatives.

Learning I and II can be observed happening together, and Learning II can create a 'double bind' in which contradictions can lead to Learning III. Engeström takes inspiration from this as he sees Learning III as supporting 'expansive learning' as a 'construction and resolution of successively evolving tensions or contradictions in a complex system' (Engeström, 1999b, p. 384). The potential for how we conceptualise knowledge is enormous, because through the study of the ZPD there is huge potential for recognising how within learning transactions 'the exchange of funds of knowledge' takes place (Moll and Greenberg, 1990, p. 344). How do we enable knowledge to be exchanged and why do we maintain the social, political and institutional structures that facilitate such exchanges? Edwards (2000a) builds on this by using Bereiter to ask questions about teachers' work and the:

> concern with how teachers assist children to engage as both users and producers of knowledge in preparation for their roles in the new knowledge economy. Teachers who are in a position to engage learners as users and producers of knowledge also need to be able to position themselves in a similar relationship with their own professional knowledge. But it isn't always easy to reposition oneself within an established system of professional practices bound by local histories and affordances. (p. 17)

Edwards (2000a) was discussing teachers' professional development through research networks and argues that the crossing of the boundaries between schools and networks is both risky and exciting, but teachers working in partnership with HEIs can, through such boundary crossing, challenge received identities.

These analyses connect with the field of power, and it is in this area that activity theory has further development opportunities. This opens up possibilities for rethinking organisations, and perhaps to get in touch with a rich intellectual history regarding how organisations have been conceptually worked and reworked. Such an approach enables Gronn (2000) to argue that what is so far missing from activity theory is a more explicit theory of power that will enable the source of the dynamics to be revealed. In particular Gronn (2000) is concerned with a lack of clarity about: 'what provides an activity system with its dynamism, nor what happens in the case of more open-ended, less well defined and new activities for which actions are less clearly culturally circumscribed and well defined' (p. 329). Theorising about power enables us to engage in discussions about influence, authority, dependency, manipulation, resistance, support, interests and legitimacy, and these have significance for Engeström's five summarising principles (see above) in which, for example, 'expansive learning' is located in structures that can privilege and deprivilege. There are issues of social injustice and exclusion that undermine individual and collective opportunities to engage in activity and the disposition to take or not take action. Gronn (2000) asks us to think about, for example, 'emergence influence' where in taking action one subject may become more influential than another 'due to current, previous, imagined or reputed performance' and this may have an impact on expectations about future activity (p. 331). This is where Bourdieu's work moves us forward, as his thinking tools of habitus and field enable us to see how dispositions to seek, to have, to use, to give and to attribute influence, are revealed through the contest over position and positioning. Activity is a competitive arena in which we need to ask: what structures the structures, and how are structures structured by this structuring? In this way power is not so much distributed or concentrated, more a struggle for distinction.

What more might this theorising do for us? The danger is that the drive for improvement and effectiveness could mean that activity theory is cherry-picked as a means of providing more sophisticated ringbinders and ticklists so that normative control mechanisms designed to regulate activity can be continued. Yeatman (1994) (see Chapter 2) would agree that claims for universal rights that bring about uniform and dramatic emancipation are no longer relevant, particularly for communities who have not benefited from exclusion legitimised by so-called democracies. Yeatman's arguments for communities struggling about and through tough issues as 'little polities' is helpful here, as activity theory has the potential to support how we describe and understand engagement by and representations of and within communities. In this way Bourdieu's concern to relate practice to and within power structures enables us to ask questions that not only describe our situation, but the contradictions of everyday life can be explored for what Connell (1983) describes as the 'possibilities' for action and by understanding the 'traps' that can limit action because assumptions are made about power and the ability to act.

The possibilities lie in the distinctiveness of education and the re-lationships that are formed and revealed within teaching and learning. The evidence presented in this chapter makes a clear case that the posi-tioning of teachers and students as technical knowledge workers is not working and is undermining a moral commitment essential to authentic social interactions. Furthermore, teachers and students are continuing to find spaces where they can intellectually breathe in a learning relation-ship as the users and producers of knowledge, as the CASE (Cognitive Acceleration through Science Education) project shows (McGregor and Gunter, 2001). Though it is disappointing that the longer that perfor-mance-driven restructuring excludes teachers and students then the space may be found through internal and external exiting (e.g. early retirement for teachers, and truanting for children). The traps could be in trying to bring about democratic educational change in one-to-one encounters, or the classroom, or the staffroom, in a field of power that is able to control and finance undemocratic prescriptions that have an educational gloss. This is where the debate has always been located and, although we are aware that our work is dominated by the field of power, investigating the interplay of agency and structure enables us to keep revealing that domination. In this way we can look for spaces where we can create and sustain alternative agendas, and respect differences rather than mandate difference.

Summary

This chapter has been concerned with *educational* leadership and this has deep professional and intellectual roots in educational studies. However, there are very powerful interests that are able to position and label this approach in ways that can ridicule and distort the value system under-pinning it. Research into theory and practice shows that teachers, including those with formal leadership roles, are unhappy with their lot and that this is not a temporary blip until they see sense. Such disposi-tions are based on deeply held values that are connected with their pro-fessional humanity rather than an eccentric conservatism. Research also shows that teachers have different expectations and satisfactions from work (Jones, 1990), and find it difficult to articulate their worries and dissent about how macro policy changes are being engaged with and worked through in school (Menter et al., 1997). This leaves us with a potentially depressing situation and Halpin (2001) asks questions about how might the sense of hopelessness be handled. The hopeful disposition is central to effective pedagogy and, as Halpin (2001) argues, there is evidence that teachers can work successfully with children whose very lives lack optimism. This could explain why even in schools found to be 'failing' there can still be officially successful pedagogy, and it could be that there is unofficially successful work going on which is unrecognised by the requirements of quality assessments, or by its very nature is and will remain private. Halpin (2001) asks us to think about creating and using utopias as a means by which we move from, why does it have to be like this? to, why can't it be like . . . ? This enables those involved in the teaching and learning process to approach the politics about the future in a way that has the capacity to put *transform* back into transformational leadership. Instead of trying to achieve a hegemonic vision for a school as a unitary organisation, we perhaps should focus on the pluralism of interests, because one person's utopia is another person's dystopia. Consequently, teaching and learning is the space where positions are taken around hope, self-belief and confidence, and it is perhaps through teachers and students engaging in a leadership relationship that competing stories of how reality is understood and could be different, can take place.

What we need is less emphasis on restructuring hierarchical leadership and more courage to enable teachers and students with managers to work on developing learning processes and the contextual settings in which they are located. Such an approach would politicise schools around pedagogy rather than around glossy manifestos, and it would also mean that the relationship between schools and HEIs might be based more on knowledge creation than on current imposed trends towards contractualism.

This challenges how we understand and practise accountability and it draws me into debates about professionals and professionalism in the final chapter of the book.

10

Teachers as Professionals

Researching and theorising within educational settings has revealed that positioning and being positioned as a leader, and engaging in the practice of leading and leadership, is a place of contextualised struggle. We can take heart from this because, while policy texts are seeking to settle the terrain, there are other experiences, stories and lives to be recognised and heard. Such alternatives are evident in the everyday practice of educationalists combined with research that seeks to understand, explain and theorise this context, and works to support development around education as being central to democratic governance.

The real lives of heads, senior and middle managers, teachers, students, parents and governors is one of negotiation, conflict and compromise, that is ultimately about power and their place within it. For those of us who are involved in research work with communities inside and outside schools, we need to ask questions about our position in relation to knowledge claims and methodologies. This invalidates claims of leadership as a paradigm shift because it enables us to question the elitist approaches to researching and theorising about schools and schooling as a hard and pure science as the means by which the neo-liberal version of the performing school takes hold. Instead, we need theories of knowledge production that illuminate what it means and feels like to work for the truth, and are located in dialogue and activity within democratic improvement. This connects directly with the nature of intellectual work: is the current policy context providing us with a leadership imperative to make it work or does it provide us with the setting in which we can understand and support how such policy is being worked through on the ground? Such a dichotomy could be unfair, and so perhaps we should see the issues around matters of purpose and in whose interests is all the busyness on the leadership terrain for. This is a highly political issue and we cannot claim to be neutral as our theories and methods are connected to positions about the interplay between agency and structure.

This is a matter of values and I have argued that as practitioners, researchers and theorisers we need to be open, as the consequences of conscious or unconscious deceit are huge. Making work transparent is not easy, and I cannot claim to have done it well, but the dialogue that I have tried to continue and support here is important for its own sake and not just because it might lead to clarity. My own position is that if we are sincere in our interest to improve and develop learning then we need to shift our gaze towards teacher and student activity and actions. In Luntley's (2000) words we have got to 'stop pussy-footing around' and show that the classroom is not a mechanistic 'black box' and, instead, put the teacher–pupil relationship at the centre of learning (p. 3). We need to exercise the professional courage to tell parents and the community what we do, how we do it and why we do it well, otherwise education will be mutated into a transmission and measuring process. As Smyth (1995) argues: 'we need to be clearer about what we regard as being educationally important because unless we can do that as educators, then our capacity to win the hearts and minds of the general community will be a hopeless one' (p. 174). This final chapter is about our capacity to do this by relating the previous debates about educational leaders and leadership to changing conceptions and notions of educational professionalism. I bring together important themes within the book, such as accountabilities, power and values, and I argue for conceptually informed practice that embraces a radical professionality.

Professionals and accountability

Professions, professionals and professionality are under pressure not just in education but across the public and private sectors. An important question about changes to teachers' work seems to be whether taking on business management tasks, roles and identities is a deprofessionalising and/or reprofessionalising process. Certainly Hughes (1985) identified the dilemma for headteachers in the relationship between a professional and chief executive role and, in the years following, this has become relevant for all members of the school community in how teacher identities have been challenged regarding pastoral care in tension with the growing requirement to be performance managed. It is also being extended to students who are increasingly to be monitored and measured rather than challenged, cared for and supported in their learning.

Ferlie et al. (1996) have shown that public sector workers operate with 'multiple senses of accountability which often co-exist in a confusing manner' (p. 202). Accountabilities can be understood in a number of ways as illustrated in Figure 10.1.

In education the endurance and current dominance of the neo-liberal version of the performing school has challenged the legitimacy of particular accountabilities and promoted others. Boyd's (1999) warning seems to be coming true: 'if we do not take the lead in developing sophis-

Accountabilities	Description
Bureaucratic	Public administration model: secured through cabinet government, ministerial accountability and anonymity of civil service.
Peer	Professional model: based on being a representative of a particular occupational group.
Organisational	Technical model: based on the identification of priorities, setting targets, planning and deployment of resources, e.g. staff, monitoring, data gathering about performance, and evaluation.
Democratic	Participatory democracy: extension of consultative processes within communities in the determination and delivery of services.
Market	Consumer choice model: the marketplace secures accountability through purchasing power.
Self	Individual model: importance of conscience and an inherent sense of quality that sustains an ethical commitment to doing a good job.

Figure 10.1 Accountabilities (based on Ferlie et al., 1996; Kogan 1988; Macpherson 1996)

ticated accountability and productivity measures, others with less sophistication will impose simplistic measures upon us' (p. 293). Organisational accountability combined with the market is a powerful means through which the process and focus of relationships is being reworked. The 'crisis' in education has been defined and landscaped in such a way that it is axiomatic that professional identity needs to be modernised if restructuring is to be successful (Nixon, 1995).

A problematic feature is the place of human beings in the process and, so, self-accountability is about preparing to be performance managed based on followership and HRM practices. In this way education is being ontologically and epistemologically purged, as particular forms of knowledge are privileged in ways that characterise dialogic intellectual work as being disruptive and irrelevant. Accountabilities upwards and downwards as part of a system of checks and balances through elected representatives and permanent civil servants has been ridiculed and reformed through the introduction of organisational accountability in government agencies rather than through the development of participatory democracy. Despite lip-service towards more community-based politics through site-based performance management, the dominance of organisational and market forms of accountability means that, as Menter et al. (1997) argue, school governing bodies 'demonstrate many of the features of quangos' (p. 94). It seems, as Ranson (2000) argues, that 'democracy has been at a distance from the communities it was created to serve' (p. 266) but the weaknesses in the system do not mean that the development of a democratic capacity is unwelcome. There is evidence from learning cities, such as Birmingham, of a 'search for new ways of strengthening local democracy to make it more responsive to the changing needs of communities and to strive to involve them in the processes of economic and social regeneration' (ibid., p. 273). The failure from neo-liberals to support the development of participatory governance within our communities does not connect with what research is telling us about what people want in those communities. Radnor et al. (1997) have found that headteachers and governors prefer 'forms of account-ability to be expressed through democratic participation rather than con-sumerist models of choice and market' (p. 221). Accountability is a two-way process, and government agencies also need not just to be attentive towards but also to listen to and respect those who are expected to make education work and work better.

Professions and professionalism

Central to the struggle to shift accountabilities in support of the neo-liberal version of the performing school is the development of a form of teacher professionalism that fits in with and facilitates an organisational and market orientation. Being a professional is traditionally conceptualised around particular traits that are a precondition and are evident in profes-sional behaviour (Bottery, 1998; Downie, 1990). While making a living is essential, and elite professionals are well paid, it is the intrinsic reward of working with people and providing a service that is more important than the extrinsic reward of financial gain. Consequently, the ethical commit-ment to clients, altruism and self-sacrifice have all been used to describe professional behaviour. A profession is therefore an identifiable group of professionals and is connected to both the abstracting of behaviours, which is what makes one profession distinctive from or similar to another, and the power systems that control membership inclusion and exclusion. Self-regulation and autonomy, particularly from the state and the government of the day, is essential in enabling professionalism to be exercised without political interest and favour. However, what is problematic is that the process of professionalisation is not a linear and smooth path, and this leads Etzioni (1969) to argue that teachers (like the police and nurses) are semi-professionals because they do not match up to the established pro-fessions such as doctors and lawyers. In this form of analysis teachers are in a deficit position through being compared and measured against the structural and structuring position of other occupational groups. Conse-quently, while doctors and lawyers have traditionally sought a dominant position from which to speak out on matters related to collective or national interests, such as ethics and justice, teachers have tended to do this through trade union activity. The dilemma for educationalists is whether they should struggle to be given parity of esteem and privilege with other 'pro-fessions' or whether there is an alternative claim for distinctiveness. Clearly, not everyone in education accepted the 'professional' label, but at the same time the claim for professional status has been used in political contests over education and employment issues. Professional behaviour has traditionally been based on stereotypes in which issues of gender, age, sexuality and race have not been acknowledged as having an impact on identity (Blackmore, 1999). In addition, much discussion remains unhistorical because of a failure to acknowledge that 'what is recognized as a profession in one place and time is not accepted in another' (McCulloch et al., 2000, p. 6).

Debating the meaning of profession and professional behaviour has a long and contested history in relation to education (Busher and Saran, 1995a) but, as Hargreaves and Goodson (1996) argue, previous resistance to professional status from government and business is currently being reversed in Australia, Canada and the USA, as there is a new interest in modernising the teacher. Claims about reprofessionalisation are based on the opportunities that can be realised through the growth of new types of work for those who are able to achieve management and leadership positions combined with increased participation in whole-school policy-making for the vast majority who will continue to be classroom teachers. Teachers are reprofessionalised through becoming what Hoyle (1995, p. 60; see also Constable, 1995) defines as 'extended professionals' through their increased orientation towards their clients (Figure 10.2).

In practical terms the reprofessionalised teacher participates in teams and, through being involved in whole-school development planning, new skills are developed (Busher and Saran, 1995b). Hoyle (1995) recognises the gains and losses in this process, and in particular the benefit to consumers of teachers no longer being able to avoid accountability for 'incompetence, inefficiency, treating clients with disdain and detachment and so forth' (p. 69). Certainly, as a new generation of teachers is trained and inducted this extended professionalism becomes the norm and, so, expectations regarding how work is controlled may shift (Foreman, 1995). Nevertheless, as McCulloch et al. (2000) show, 'myth' and 'memory' endure amongst a range of positions regarding teachers and their work, and this makes how we see the impact of restructuring as problematic because the legacies of professionalism are deep within our professional biographies.

From	To
Profession	Professional
Knowledge	Skill
Education	Training
Effectiveness	Efficiency
Conception	Delivery
Status	Contract
Clients	Consumers
Influence	Compliance
Responsibility	Accountability
Leadership	Management

Figure 10.2 Trends in the teaching profession (Hoyle, 1995, p. 60)

The tensions are evident in how educationalists are finding it difficult to conceptualise who they are and how to undertake their work because the exercise of professional judgement and their expertise regarding standards connected to broader community aims is being disciplined through the workings of site-based and government-directed policies and mandates. Teachers are facing the rhetoric of being 'modernised' in ways that they as teachers must meet the challenge of change (alone?) but, as Merson (2000) argues, the Green Paper (DfEE, 1998) draws on the Taylorist traditions of scientific management. Information and communications technology is presented as 'enhancing and liberating' (Merson, 2000, p. 167) but in reality may turn out to undermine social engagement and just be a more sophisticated means of monitoring and controlling. The problems of the education system have been laid at the door of teachers while their capacity for finding solutions has been taken away. The rhetoric has been of empowerment, participation and teams, but the reality is that teachers have had to continue to do what they have always done – be empowered to do what they have been told to do. What is particularly interesting about empowerment is how restructuring has led to teachers (often without additional payment or non-contact time) being given additional responsibilities. Menter et al. (1997) describe how teachers in the primary context felt initially disposed to new challenges and roles, but increasingly talked about the dilemmas of the work they now had to do compared with how they preferred to work with children. The irony is not lost that they have been sold new responsibilities as being a means of enhanced professionalisation but, at the same time, they are losing the capacity to exercise professional judgement. A continuation of this is how teachers are being exhorted to work together to solve problems, and yet they have been systematically excluded from the policy-making processes designed to identify and solve those problems. Helsby (1999) reminds us that context is important here in how teachers in the USA have experienced a more inclusive approach to educational restructuring, and we need to be mindful of this when considering the importability of leadership theories and research methodologies developed in this particular setting.

Claims can be made about deprofessionalism and how this is central to the restructuring of the public sector in which areas of perceived privilege have been brought under the control of transparent accountability systems and competency-based regulation (Jones and Moore, 1993). In order to be efficient, effective and economic in the provision of services the professional monopoly has had to be broken so that work leads to directly observable outcomes and is good value for money. Working on behalf of the community is no longer valid in the sense of esoteric claims about service and loyalty, but must be based on consumer choice principles in which labour and expertise will be bought if it meets the requirements of the purchaser. This attack on the moral capacities of professional work is the means through which labour can become more flexible, as the discretion about what work is and how it is to be done can be replaced by the effective and efficient deployment of time and skills (Quicke, 2000). This leads Ozga (1995) to make the point that professionalism is not so much about traits and qualities but how professionals serve the needs of the state and capitalism. In this way professionalism is a 'form of occupational control ... [used] ... in the management of the teaching labour force' (ibid., p. 32), and so what might be regarded as reprofessionalisation is the means through which the control of teachers (i.e the eradication of militancy) is currently being constructed and implemented. Ozga (1995) argues that professionalism has been replaced by site-based managerialism as the means by which teachers and their work are controlled through surveillance structures. While the contradictions in professionalism enabled teachers to use its features as the means through which to resist interference in their work, managerialism denies collective action through its individualising and performance-orientated agenda (Ozga, 1995). This is a labour process approach to teaching and has led to analysis suggesting that teachers are being proletarianised (Ozga and Lawn, 1988), not in the sense of fully becoming factory workers, but that teachers' work takes on some of the features of this type of work (Smyth et al., 2000). In particular, the separation of design from implementation combined with work intensification is seen to be the main impact on teachers' work, and for teachers working in a failing school then the very survival of the learning process, as well as their livelihoods, is at stake.

It seems that powerful deprofessionalising and reprofessionalising forces are working alongside each other, and in such ways that it may not be possible to distinguish them in abstract form though the impact can be seen through research that seeks to capture and theorise professional lived experiences (Shain and Gleeson, 1999). The implications for educational leadership are clear as the modernisation of teachers is about stripping away epistemological and subject discipline connections and replacing them with generic skills as the means by which the technology of transformation can take place. However, as we have seen, the evidence of an educative leadership habitus within teaching and learning is strong, and it does not easily sit with the reprofessionalising agenda of follower status for teachers and students. As Nixon and Ranson (1997) argue while the traditional 'agreements' within pedagogy are breaking down, it remains to be seen whether and how the new working consensus in the classroom and the community takes into account participation and difference.

Radicalising professionality

Moving forward from this position is not easy but it is essential if professional confidence and self-belief are to be built and rebuilt in classrooms (Helsby, 1999; McCulloch et al., 2000). Professionality is, according to Foreman (1995), concerned with teachers' work – what they do, why they do it and how they do it – and this is tied up with issues around meaning and the self: perceptions and feelings, not just skills and knowledge. This use of professionality is more than a language device and 'the shift ... is away from "professionalism" as the ideology of service and specialist expertise; away from "professionalisation" where the status of the occupation is at stake; and towards "professionality" which focuses on the quality of practice in contexts that require radically altered relations of power and control' (Nixon et al., 1997, p. 12).

Radical professionality requires 'radical collegiality' (Fielding, 1999b) and this needs us to build trust in ways that a disposition towards caring is not reworked into a competency but is central to what it feels like to want to work with people and enable learning. In a secular and material age this seems to be sentimental, but it has always been central to those who want to work with people as people rather than as customers. Caring transcends the factory system of clocking in and clocking off, and the workaholic entrepreneurial cultures where everyone is induced to stay longer and longer in the office on the grounds that it shows commitment and dedication. It is about old-fashioned altruism of putting yourself out in a big way by ensuring learning is planned through to more mundane and often invisible matters such as chatting in the corridor (Smyth et al., 2000).

As I have shown, those who research professional lives through qualitative approaches such as life stories and biographical portrayals combined with critical theorising are able to capture what it feels like and means to be a headteacher, subject leader, teacher or student, and this challenges the smooth, neat and tidy, managerial approaches to professionalism because it has the potential to enable the individual and collective to position themselves rather than be positioned. This approach allows us to consider how we begin to know the dispositions of teachers and students, not as a generic set of behaviours, but in Bourdieu's (1990) terms as socialised and socialising agents. Furthermore, this can reveal a radical professionality because a learning relationship with students means that teachers are automatically and currently engaged within power structures that position children, families and communities in advantaged and/or disadvantaged ways. When teachers (and students, headteachers, governors, parents and post-holders) engage in talk with another human then this is a dialogue which, as Smyth (1998) argues, is political and ideological: 'they are seeking to be heard, represented and have their perspectives and work recognised' (p. 340). Teachers know every day that their ability to make a difference is encouraged and tempered by the conditions in which learning takes place and, while classroom conditions might be improved through site-based performance management, the school as an organisation is not necessarily orientated towards the communities it is located within except as a market through which the school can directly and indirectly select appropriate students and parents. While teachers would agree that learning does extend beyond the classroom, and that schools should be 'hubs' (Bentley, 1998, p. 179) at the centre of a learning network, the challenges this has for how public sector education is currently being restructured are huge. Bentley (2000) argues that: 'the challenge is to create complex systems of learning which can combine formal and informal resources around the needs and abilities of individual learners' (p. 361). However, radical professionality is not just about supporting learning in this way but is also a concern with the power structures that limit and hinder learning, and so teachers need governments to have a commitment to equity, and this is what makes systems of learning complex and arenas of struggle.

Radical professionality opens up possibilities in which the realities of work as a teacher are communicated as people who are experts in pedagogy and their particular discipline. This is not easy because parents as private and public sector workers are objectified by managerialism as well, and hence radical professionality has an educative role in which teachers within communities can explore the power structures in which they are working. This is a different kind of relationship to the one that can be described around the binary divide of the professional and non-professional, and instead has the potential to recognise 'voice' rather than just give a 'choice' (Nixon and Ranson, 1997, p. 212). The challenge is further stretched because the values position is one that has been severely undermined within the Thatcherite and New Labour polity because it is about a public good based on education for all, as a means of developing and supporting democracy, irrespective of their ability to pay for it (Grace, 1989). This returns us back to the purposes of schools and schooling, and I am not so naive to think that in promoting this position it will eclipse the market-orientated work of others who seek to change education according to material values. Cultural barriers or what Ranson (2000) identifies as 'the denial of recognition', and socio-economic barriers or 'the inequality of distribution' (p. 265) limit voice in the ways that also limit choice, as research into markets has shown (Gewirtz et al., 1995). However, this book has made a contribution by revealing that there is evidence of the democratic project alive and well in classrooms and communities, and my disposition for doing this is based on its absence from much of what is mandated as ways in which educationalists in their communities should and must work.

Bottery's (1996; 1998; Bottery and Wright, 1996) work has been important in enabling us to think about how we respond to the undermining of professionals and their work in ways that take cognisance of criticisms of education that need to be listened and responded to. Bottery (1998) argues that we need to review practice and connect professional work to:

- *Resources:* financial affordability and restraints of the organisation and the economy.

- *Culture:* changes in society requires a political role in presenting and struggling for their contribution to meeting client needs.
- *Epistemology:* in which expertise is conceptualised around supporting learning rather than transmitting knowledge or providing cures.

This leads Bottery (1998) to argue in favour of an 'ecological appreciation of practice' in which ethics are concerned to reflect the complexity of professionality: 'one which ensures that they as individuals and as a profession are aware of developments within their society and are able to locate their practice within a wider picture of social and political issues' (p. 170). This allows autonomy to be realised in ways that the mythology of 'professional autonomy' used to demean teachers denies because, as Strain (1995) argues, autonomy is not a privilege but an essential requirement of teaching and learning as a relationship. In this way radical professionality occurs through working both publicly and privately with learners so that 'agreed social learning objectives may be achieved so that the integrity, freedom and potentiality of the individual learner can be protected, sustained and realised' (ibid., p. 55). Conceptualising professionality within an activity system takes this forward because it provides us with a way of describing and understanding the teacher–learner relationship in which the focus is on the learner's agency (see Chapter 9). By locating activity within a theory of power we are able to see how this is not static but a territory that is constantly being striven over, and we need to be alerted to the means by which professionality is both a structuring and structured process. Consequently, the newly formed General Teaching Council is not so much an institution through which teachers should claim that they have at last achieved one of the key features of a profession, but instead is a space where dialogue can be inclusive of teachers.

Much of the education policy of the last decade, most notably PRP (DfEE, 1998), has been introduced without full consultation, and in policy terms it could be argued that we are beyond leadership and are now moving directly into performativity. The mandated models of school leadership, as we have seen, are not about educational leadership but about enabling the headteacher to be a middle manager to both implement and be accountable for centrally directed policy. Senior and middle managers, teachers, students, governors, parents and communities exist to deliver and be accountable for statistical learning outcomes and the learning conditions in which this takes place. While there is an attempt to close down the spaces for intellectual work, professional courage is still possible and, so, radical collegiality is not just about challenging current policy prescriptions head on, but also about continuing to exercising professional courage at local level. Nixon (1995) reports on research across 15 secondary schools that shows how each is grappling with its educational purpose, but how there are common themes:

- The centrality of student learning within all the schools.
- Student self-determination and responsibility for their own learning.
- Supportive relationships between everyone as essential for learning.
- Breadth of achievement across all student activities.

Nixon goes on to argue that while this approach is not based on direct opposition or the development of an alternative form of schooling, it is based on a 'refusal' because 'it challenges the assumption that teaching can somehow be separated out into a series of technical operations. In so doing, it affirms those values that help define and shape teaching as a profession' (ibid., p. 222). This connects with forms of accountability located within pluralist communities, or what Macpherson (1999) refers to as communitarian and local, as opposed to centrist and managerial. In this way legitimacy is contested in an 'educative accountability' (p. 274) process where aims and evaluation are based on negotiation and agreement rather than the importation of frameworks and criteria. Work in Tasmania shows how stakeholders articulated 'governance values' (p. 279) regarding how school policy-making is conducted in a local and unique context, but also avoids isolation through how this activity is located and connected through vertical and horizontal 'governance re-lationships' (p. 279). This suggests that empowerment is a far more complex process than that presented to us in mainstream leadership models, and, as Clarke and Stewart (1992) argue, there needs to be a multi-stranded approach in which the requirements of customer, citizen and community are taken into account and the dilemmas involved are thought through: one person's empowerment can be another's disem-powerment. For example, parents have been technically empowered from 1988 through the local ballot for a school to opt-out of LEA control into grant maintained status, and equally so through the mandate of the New Labour government from 1997 in which these schools were brought back under LEA control as Foundation Schools. How parents on each occasion saw and weighed losses and gains in these ballots would be difficult to disentangle from other issues, but what is certain is that claims and counter-claims regarding empowerment can be made. Similarly, edu-cationalists and communities were sold site-based performance manage-ment on the grounds that it would enable more participation to identify and meet local needs, and yet local priorities have had to take a back seat while centrally determined agendas have been implemented.

Conceptually informed practice

While our attention may be attracted towards the new settlement being achieved through the modernisation process, it does not take long to realise that this is not new and neither is it settled. It seems that in the last 30 years we have moved from structure to culture to performativity. The shift from structure to culture (Stoll and Fink, 1996) enables us to think about the values underpinning what we do and how we might want to do it better. The shift to performativity enables the self to be integrated with the national political goals through regulated institutional systems. All three could enable leadership as behaviours and functions to be conceptualised and promoted, and a consistent factor in popular leadership models has been the control imperative. However, there is work that presents leadership as a relationship and is located in pedagogy. I have connected it with activity that is not just about action, but is about knowing and understanding the power structures that structure activity and are structured by activity. This connects teachers and students in the classroom with the communities within which they live and learn, and I have put a spotlight on radical professionality which is concerned with the struggle over knowledge claims and the capacity to be users and producers of knowledge. This requires us to develop knowledge in ways that makes 'what works' a conceptually informed practice, in which action is theory informed and informs theory, and is context informed and informs the context. As Atkinson (2000) argues, teachers base their work on theories; they may not be appropriate, but we cannot deny their existence. Furthermore, we cannot enable a critical approach to theory by just stripping it out of pre- and in-service professional development courses, because this just ensures that theory continues to be used and can be used unreflexively. The CASE project is illustrative of how theories of cognition such as Piaget and Vygotsky are enabling teachers to gain control over their work and to re-culture activity around teaching and learning: 'as one teacher said about their own school: "pedagogy is no longer a swear word in the staff room" ' (Gunter et al., 2001).

This is an inclusive approach as the intellectual work required needs us to build on (and, in some cases, rebuild) enduring and existing partnerships and relationships between educationalists in all sectors of education. The implications of this are that we will need to stop focusing just on the school as a unit of aggregation for measuring learning outcomes and start focusing on pedagogy as lived relationships that may not have temporal boundaries. The challenge in taking this position is that it questions those who have been positioned and advantaged through the neo-liberal restructuring, though there is evidence of resistance, refusal and opposition to managerialism through the continuation and development of radical professionality. Education is still a place and a space where you can be interested and have interests, and empowerment comes from realising this and from knowing that this is a legitimate place to be.

Continuing the intellectual journey

This book is a contribution to productively destabilising the current restructuring settlement by reasserting the importance of intellectual and critical debate for its own sake, as well as for practice. As I have illustrated in the resources I have drawn on, I am not alone in this work and in doing this I am not just opposing in a negative sense, but engaging with ways of doing and thinking that are there in our everyday lives and practice but may not be realised in official texts and leadership models. The Green Paper *teachers: meeting the challenge of change* (DfEE, 1998) is a dystopia as it paints a picture of teaching and learning that does not connect with the realities of lived, researched and theorised experiences, and neither does the vision match how educationalists in their *professional judgement* want to work with each other and with children. Such an analysis is the product of thinking with and theorising through the use of Bourdieu's theory of practice, and this leads us to ask questions about the challenges facing educational studies: what have we gained and what have we lost (Grenfell, 1996)?

The relevance of Bourdieu's work for this study of leadership in education is in its capacity to support and question thinking about the power structures in which we are all located. Engaging with our identities and work is not easy, and Bourdieu enables us to see this by how he develops his ideas through research over time and in a range of fields. Concerns about his writing style have led Bourdieu (1990) to argue that we must beware of common-sense explanations, and that 'the strategy of abandoning the rigour of technical vocabulary in favour of an easy and readable style . . . [is] dangerous' (p. 52). The reasons given are twofold: first, it encourages conservative thinking and supports the status quo because simple explanations enable the assertion that 'everything is just fine as it is'; and, second, if we provide simple explanations then it will encourage us to think that the issues are simple and, so, we will be open to manipulation. This enables us to move beyond the labelling of performance management and leadership, and ask why are these labels being developed, who by and what for? What are the issues underpinning the work and identities that such labels are meant to represent? Such questions mean that we have gained intellectually and practically because theory and practice are not dichotomised through the application of theory to practice, but instead theory is within practice, and practice is within theory.

Consequently, the challenge for those involved in leadership studies is to shift the emphasis away from the current policy imperative for *what works* to *what is it like to work* in education. Integral to this is the case I have made for conceptually informed practice based on a radical professionality and located in the ongoing struggle for learning. This has implications for intellectual work and, if radical professionality is to be worked for in schools, then it also needs to be the case in higher education. This requires an honesty that means that researchers cannot hide behind claims of detached objectivity because theory and research are inevitably political and are implicated within competing versions of the performing school. There are silences in work, positions move, are static and come into and out of view, and we need to question this if we are to be able to engage in 'argument and refutation' in intellectual life as opposed to the 'denunciation and slander' evident in mainstream politics (Bourdieu, 1998, pp. 8–9).

Radical professionality assumes teachers and students are critical intellectuals, and this enables those located in HEIs to recapture their intellectual purpose at a time when their work is being economised. The strengths of Bourdieu's analysis is in asking questions that keep open intellectual spaces. A leadership watcher might ask: what intellectual position am I taking in the field? How does that position relate to the positions taken by others in the field? How does that position relate to economic, political and cultural structures or fields? However, Bourdieu is not helpful when it comes to asking how this work is to be paid for or for employment security (Swartz, 1997). In this way thinking with Bourdieu could be pessimistic as it enables us to know the questions and the problematic nature of investigating them, but may not help us to get out of this trap (Connell, 1983). Bourdieu (1999) has shed light on this through his work on social suffering in which he argues that by making lived experiences visible and theorising the connections with the power structures that 'make life painful, even unliveable', then this is liberating for those who had thought it was all their fault. Furthermore, while fundamental change is difficult, non-interference is unacceptable: 'contrary to appearances, this observation is not cause for despair: what the social world has done, it can, armed with this knowledge, undo' (ibid., p. 629). In other words, teachers are not the problem in education, and the problems within education can be engaged with in ways that are inclusive. Possibilities do exist in how we seek to present ourselves and argue for the importance of intellectual work, and being an intellectual in education is something to be proud of. Speaking about issues that matter to us in our work is not provider capture but is integral to enabling us not just to be in receipt of a problem but to ask: whose problem is it and who is defining it as a problem?

The strength of Bourdieu's work is in enabling those interested in educational leadership to understand the problematic nature of the positions within a dysfunctional structured and structuring context. The relationship between the field of power and intellectual work is complex, and we can see how many field watchers seek to dominate through the manufacture of leadership products, but remain dominated. While others are seeking to open up alternative ways of working connected to the real-time and lived realities of teaching and learning, and are searching for ways of working in local communities that will allow questions of dominance and domination to be revealed, we must ask questions not only about the places where research and theory goes, but also the places that are actively avoided or remain undiscovered and underdeveloped. Is this a pragmatic response to a context in which certain places are not approved of, or is it a political position concerned to make a case for how we conceptualise the purposes of education?

Researching this further is the next stage in my intellectual project, and again I extend the invitation to others to comment and contribute to it. I intend to take this forward in two ways: first, through continuing my work on the intellectual history of leadership studies through the life histories and professional biographies of those who have been involved in knowledge production. This absence in this book is significant, not least in the claim to be using Bourdieu's theory of practice, that has been developed within empirical research and not at a desk. Questions need to be asked about how individual and networked location(s), identity(ies) and positioning(s) reveal habitus and the development of field (s). I have begun to do this (Gunter, 1999a; 1999c), but I intend to build on it to capture the life histories of knowledge workers so that we can explore our intellectual heritage and its connections with current and future knowledge production.

A second part of my project is to work on leadership as a pedagogic relationship and activity. This will enable the work begun on conceptually informed practice to be explored further through the ongoing exploration of radical professionality as inclusive of senior and middle managers, teachers, students, governors, parents and communities. Of particular interest here is activity as political struggle in which we need to engage in theory and research about the interplay between agency and structure, how power structures structure agency and how agency structures structures. Opening this up will enable us to capture and analyse activity, but will also reflexively develop agendas for the future we are struggling over. In this way, instead of change being a party political project designed to keep us so busy that we cannot think, change is a contested area of dialogue about development.

Of course, in putting forward these two projects and in silencing other potential developments, I am staking a claim for distinction and significance. In exercising this agency I am entering the field and playing the game, as Grenfell and James (with Hodkinson, Reay and Robbins, 1998) argue 'everything is up for grabs. It appears as if everyone is free to play, everything is negotiable' (p. 25). However, I am also mindful of this trap, and hence my invitation is to those of us who have an interest in and are interested in leadership to talk about what Bourdieu regards as an 'illusion of freedom'. Bourdieu (1990) argues that the importance of sociology is in enabling freedom from an 'illusion of freedom' because of its role in understanding the relationship between the 'instruments of knowledge of the instruments of knowledge' (p. 16). He argues: 'and so, paradoxically, sociology frees us by freeing us from the illusion of freedom, or, more exactly, from the misplaced belief in illusory freedoms. Freedom is not something given: it is something you conquer – collectively' (ibid., p. 15).

Bibliography

Abrol, S. with Ribbins, P. (1999) 'Pursuing equal opportunities: a passion for service, sharing and sacrifice', in Rayner, S. and Ribbins, P. (eds), *Headteachers and Leadership in Special Education*. London: Cassell.

Acker, J. (1992) 'Gendering organizational theory', in Mills, A.J. and Tancred, P. (eds), *Gendering Organizational Analysis*. Newbury Park, CA: Sage.

Adler, S., Laney, J. and Packer, J. (1993) *Managing Women*. Buckingham: Open University Press.

Al-Khalifa, E. (1989) 'Management by halves: women teachers and school management', in de Lyon, H. and Widdowson Migniuolo, F. (eds), *Women Teachers*. Milton Keynes: Open University Press.

Allen, B. (ed.) (1968) *Headship in the 1970s*. Oxford: Blackwell.

Allix, N.M. (2000) 'Transformational leadership: democratic or despotic', *Educational Management and Administration*, vol. 28, no. 1, pp. 7–20.

Alvesson, M. and Willmott, H. (1996) *Making Sense of Management: A Critical Introduction*. London: Sage.

Anderson, G.L. (1996) 'The cultural politics of schools: implications for leadership', in Leithwood, K., Chapman, J., Corson, D., Hallinger, P. and Hart, A. (eds), *International Handbook of Educational Leadership and Administration Part 2*. Dordrecht: Kluwer Academic.

Angus, L. (1989) ' "New" leadership and the possibility of educational reform', in Smyth, J. (ed.), *Critical Perspectives on Educational Leadership*. London: Falmer Press.

Angus, L. (1994) 'Sociological analysis and education management: the social context of the self-managing school', *British Journal of Sociology of Education*, vol. 15, no. 1, pp. 79–91.

Angus, L. (1996) 'Cultural dynamics and organizational analysis: leadership, administration and the management of meaning in schools', in Leithwood, K., Chapman, J., Corson, D., Hallinger, P. and Hart, A. (eds), *International Handbook of Educational Leadership and Administration Part 2*. Dordrecht: Kluwer Academic.

Apple, M.W. (1998) 'How the conservative restoration is justified: leadership and subordination in educational policy', *International Journal of Leadership in Education*, vol. 1, no. 1, pp. 3–17.

Apple, M.W. and Beane, J.A. (eds), (1999) *Democratic Schools: Lessons from the Chalk Face*. Buckingham: Open University Press.

Ashdown, R. with Rayner, S. (1999) 'Facilitating teachers and enabling learning: the leadership task in a special school', in Rayner, S. and Ribbins, P. (eds), *Headteachers and Leadership in Special Education*. London: Cassell.

Ashford, M. with Ribbins, P. (1998) 'Enabling "true" primary education', in Pascal, C. and Ribbins, P. (eds) *Understanding Primary Headteachers*. London: Cassell.

Atchison, J. (1993) 'Women and management training in the 1990s', in Ouston, J. (ed.), *Women in Education Management*. Harlow: Longman.

Atkinson, E. (2000) 'In defence of ideas, or why "what works" is not enough', *Management in Education*, vol. 14, no. 3, pp. 6–9.

Audit Commission (1989) *Losing an Empire, Finding a Role: The LEA of the Future*. London: HMSO.

Ball, S.J. (1981) *Beachside Comprehensive*. Cambridge: Cambridge University Press.

Ball, S.J. (1987) *The Micro-Politics of the School*. London: Routledge.

Ball, S.J. (1990a) *Politics and Policymaking in Education: Explorations in Policy Sociology*. London: Routledge.

Ball, S.J. (1990b) 'Management as moral technology: a Luddite analysis', in Ball, S.J. *Foucault and Education*. London: Routledge.

Ball, S.J. (1994a) 'Some reflections on policy theory: a brief response to Hatcher and Troyna', *Journal of Education Policy*, vol. 9, no. 2, pp. 171–82.

Ball, S.J. (1994b) *Educational Reform: A Critical and Post-Structuralist Approach*. Buckingham: Open University Press.

Ball, S.J. (1995) 'Intellectuals or technicians? The urgent role of theory in educational studies', *British Journal of Educational Studies*, vol. 43, no. 3, pp. 255–71.

Ball, S.J. (1997) 'Policy sociology and critical social research: a personal view of recent education policy and policy research', *British Educational Research Journal*, vol. 23, no. 3, pp. 257–74.

Ball, S.J. (1999) 'Performativities and Fabrications in the Education Economy: towards the performative society?' Keynote address to the AARE Annual Conference, Melbourne.

Barber, M. and Sebba, J. (1999) 'Reflections on progress towards a world class education system', *Cambridge Journal of Education*, vol. 29, no. 2, pp. 183–93.

Barker, B. (1999) 'Double vision: 40 years on', in Tomlinson, H., Gunter, H. and Smith, P. (eds), *Living Headship: Voices, Values and Vision*. London: Paul Chapman Publishing.

Barnett, B.G. (1995) 'Developing reflection and expertise: can mentors make the difference?', *Journal of Educational Administration*, vol. 33, no. 5, pp. 45–59.

Baron, G. (1979) 'Research in Educational Administration in Britain', in Bush, T., Glatter, R., Goodey, J. and Riches, C. (eds), *Approaches to School Management*. London: Harper Educational.

Baron, G. and Howell, D.A. (1974) *The Government and Management of Schools*. London: Athlone Press.

Baron, G. and Taylor, W. (eds), (1969) *Educational Administration and the Social Sciences*. London: Athlone Press.

Baron, G., Cooper, D.H. and Walker, W.G. (1969) *Educational Administration: International Perspectives*. Chicago: Rand McNally.

Barry, C.H. and Tye, E. (1975) *Running a School*. London: Temple Smith.

Bass, B.M. (1985) *Leadership and Performance Beyond Expectations*. New York: Free Press.

Bates, R. (1989) 'Leadership and the rationalization of society', in Smyth, J. (ed.) *Critical Perspectives on Educational Leadership*. London: Falmer Press.

Bates, R. (1993) 'On knowing: cultural and critical approaches to educational administration', *Educational Management and Administration*, vol. 21, no. 3, pp. 171–6.

Bates, Y. (1999) 'A vision for Lilian Baylis', in Tomlinson, H., Gunter, H., and Smith, P. (eds), *Living Headship: Voices, Values and Vision*. London: Paul Chapman Publishing.

Bateson, G. (1972) *Steps to an Ecology of Mind*. New York: Ballantine Books.

Beare, H., Caldwell, B. and Millikan, R. (1993) 'Leadership', in Preedy, M. (ed), *Managing the Effective School*. London: Paul Chapman Publishing in association with the Open University.

Becher, T. (1989) *Academic Tribes and Territories*. Buckingham: SRHE and Open University Press.

Beck, J. (1999) 'Makeover or Takeover? The strange death of educational autonomy in neo-liberal England', *British Journal of Sociology of Education*, vol. 20, no. 2, pp. 223–38.

Beeson, S. with Ribbins, P. (1998) 'From Tigger to Eeyore: a headteacher's life?', in Pascal, C. and Ribbins, P. (1998) *Understanding Primary Headteachers*. London: Cassell.

Bell, L. (1999) 'Back to the future: the development of educational policy in England', *Journal of Educational Administration*, vol. 37, no. 3, pp. 200–28.

Bell, L., Halpin, D. and Neill, S. (1996) 'Managing self-governing primary schools in the locally maintained, grant-maintained and private sectors', *Educational Management and Administration*, vol. 24, no. 3, pp. 253–61.

Benaim, Y. and Humphreys, K.A. (1997) 'Gaining entry: challenges for the novice headteacher', *School Leadership and Management*, vol. 17, no. 1, pp. 81–94.

Benn, C. and Chitty, C. (1997) *Thirty Years On*. London: Penguin.

Bennett, A. (1997) *Writing Home*. London: Faber and Faber.

Bennett, H. (1999) 'One drop of blood: teacher appraisal mark 2', *Teacher Development*, vol. 3, no. 3, pp. 411–27.

Bennett, N. (1995) *Managing Professional Teachers, Middle Management in Primary and Secondary Schools*. London: Paul Chapman Publishing.

Bennett, S.J. (1974) *The School: An Organizational Analysis*. Glasgow: Blackie.

Bennis, W. and Nanus, B. (1985) *Leaders*. New York: Harper and Row.

Bentley, T. (1998) *Learning Beyond the Classroom*. London: Routledge.

Bentley, T. (2000) 'Learning Beyond the Classroom', *Educational Management and Administration*, vol. 28, no. 3, pp. 353–64.

Bernstein, B. (1971) 'On the classification and framing of educational knowledge', in Young, M.F.D. (ed.), *Knowledge and Control*. London: Cassell and Collier Macmillan.

Best, R., Ribbins, P., Jarvis, C. with Oddy, D. (1983) *Education and Care*. London: Heinemann.

Beveridge, M. (1998) 'Improving the quality of educational research', in Rudduck, J. and McIntyre, D. (eds), *Challenges for Educational Research*. London: Paul Chapman Publishing.

Bezzina, C. (1998) 'The Maltese primary school principal', *Educational Management and Administration*, vol. 26, no. 3, pp. 243–56.

Bhindi, N. and Duignan, P. (1997) 'Leadership for a new century: authenticity, intentionality, spirituality and sensibility', *Educational Management and Administration*, vol. 25, no. 2, pp. 117–32.

Blackmore, J. (1989) 'Educational leadership: a feminist critique and reconstruction', in Smyth, J. (ed.), *Critical Perspectives on Educational Leadership*. London: Falmer Press.

Blackmore, J. (1996) ' "Breaking the silence": feminist contributions to educational administration and policy', in Leithwood, K., Chapman, J., Corson, D., Hallinger, P. and Hart, A. (eds), *International Handbook of Educational Leadership and Administration Part 2*. Dordrecht: Kluwer Academic.

Blackmore, J. (1999) *Troubling Women: Feminism, Leadership and Educational Change*. Buckingham: Open University Press.

Blackmore, J. and Sachs, J. (2000) 'Paradoxes of leadership and management in higher education in times of change: some Australian reflections', *International Journal of Leadership in Education*, vol. 3, no. 1, pp. 1–16.

Blair, T. (1999) *Speech to the London Conference for New Headteachers*. London: DfEE.

Blake, R.R. and Mouton, J.S. (1964) *The Managerial Grid*. Houston, TX: Gulf.

Blandford, S. (1997) *Middle Management in Schools*. London: Pitman.

Blase, J. and Anderson, G. (1995) *The Micropolitics of Educational Leadership*. London: Cassell.

Bogdanor, V. (1979) 'Power and participation', *Oxford Review of Education*, vol. 5, no. 2, pp. 157–68.

Bogotch, I.E. and Roy, C.B. (1997) 'The context of partial truths: an analysis of principals' discourse', *Journal of Educational Administration*, vol. 35, no. 3, pp. 234–52.

Bolam, R. (1997) 'Management development for headteachers: retrospect and prospect', *Educational Management and Administration*, vol. 25, no. 3, pp. 265–83.

Bolam, R. (1999) 'Educational administration, leadership and management: towards a research agenda', in Bush, T., Bell, L., Bolam, R., Glatter, R. and Ribbins, P. (eds), *Educational Management: Redefining Theory, Policy and Practice*. London: Paul Chapman Publishing.

Bolam, R., Clarke, J., Jones, K., Harper-Jones, G., Timbrell, T., Jones, R. and Thorpe, R. (1995a) 'The induction of newly qualified teachers in schools: where next?', *British Journal of In-Service Education*, vol. 21, no. 3, pp. 247–60.

Bolam, R., McMahon, A., Pocklington, K. and Weindling, D. (1995b) 'Mentoring for new headteachers: recent British experience', *Journal of Educational Administration*, vol. 33, no. 5, pp. 29–44.

Bone, T.R. (1982) 'Educational administration', *British Journal of Educational Studies*, vol. 30, no. 1, February, pp. 32–42.

Bone, T.R. (1992) 'Changing circumstances in the United Kingdom', in Miklos, E. and Ratsoy, E. (eds), *Educational Leadership: Challenge and Change*. Alberta: Department of Educational Administration, University of Alberta.

Booth, M. (1993) 'The effectiveness and role of the mentor in school: the student's view', *Cambridge Journal of Education*, vol. 23, no. 2, pp. 185–97.

Bottery, M. (1992) *The Ethics of Educational Management*. London: Cassell.

Bottery, M. (1996) 'The challenge to professionals from the new public management: implications for the teaching profession', *Oxford Review of Education*, vol. 22, no. 2, pp. 179–97.

Bottery, M. (1998) *Professionals and Policy: Management Strategy in a Competitive World*. London: Cassell.

Bottery, M. (1999) 'Global forces, national mediations and the management of educational institutions', *Educational Management and Administration*, vol. 27, no. 3, pp. 299–312.

Bottery, M. and Wright, N. (1996) 'Cooperating in their own deprofessionalisation? On the need to recognise the "public" and "ecological" roles of the teaching profession', *British Journal of Educational Studies*, vol. 44, no. 1, pp. 82–98.

Bourdieu, P. (1988) *Homo Academicus*. Cambridge: Polity Press in association with Blackwell.

Bourdieu, P. (1990) *In Other Words: Essays Towards a Reflexive Sociology*. Trans. M. Adamson. Cambridge: Polity Press in association with Blackwell.

Bourdieu, P. (1998) *Acts of Resistance*. Cambridge: Polity Press in association with Blackwell.

Bourdieu, P. (1999) 'Postscript', in Bourdieu, P., Accardo, A., Balazs, G., Beaud, S., Bonvin, F., Bourdieu, E., Bourgios, P., Broccolichi, S., Champagne, P., Christin, R., Faguer, J., Garcia, S., Lenoir, R., Œuvrard, F., Pialoux, M., Pinto, L., Podalydès, D., Sayad, A. Soulié, C. and Wacquant, L.J.D. *The Weight of the World*. Cambridge: Polity Press, in association with Blackwell.

Bowe, R. and Ball, S. with Gold, A. (1992) *Reforming Education and Changing Schools*. London: Routledge.

Boyd, W.L. (1999) 'Environmental pressures, management imperatives, and competing paradigms in educational administration', *Educational Management and Administration*, vol. 27, no. 3, pp. 283–97.

Brauner, B. (1997) 'Perspective on middle management in Israeli secondary schools', in Leask, M. and Terrell, I. (eds), *Development Planning and School Improvement for Middle Managers*. London: Kogan Page.

Bredeson, P.V. (1996) 'New directions in the preparation of educational leaders', in Leithwood, K., Chapman, J., Corson, D., Hallinger, P. and Hart, A. (eds), *International Handbook of Educational Leadership and Administration Part 1*. Dordrecht: Kluwer Academic.

Bridges, D. (1998) 'Research, dissent and the reinstatement of theory', in Rudduck, J. and McIntyre, D. (eds), *Challenges for Educational Research*. London: Paul Chapman Publishing.

Briggs, M. (1997) *Your Role as a Primary School Subject Co-ordinator*. London: Hodder & Stoughton in association with the Open University.

Brighouse, T. (1988) 'Politicising the manager or managing the politicians? – Can the headteacher succeed where the education officer failed?', *Educational Management and Administration*, vol. 16, no. 2, pp. 97–103.

Broadhead, P., Cuckle, P. Hodgson, J. and Dunford, J. (1996) 'Improving primary schools through school development planning', *Educational Management and Administration*, vol. 24, no. 3, pp. 277–90.

Brown, M. (1997) 'In conversation with Len Cantor', in Ribbins, P. (ed.), *Leaders and Leadership in the School, College and University*. London: Cassell.

Brown, M. and Rutherford, D. (1998) 'Changing roles and raising standards: new challenges for heads of department', *School Leadership and Management*, vol. 18, no. 1, pp. 75–88.

Brown, M. and Rutherford, D. (1999) 'A re-appraisal of the role of the head of department in UK secondary schools', *Journal of Educational Administration*, vol. 37, no. 3, pp. 229–42.

Brundrett, M. (1998) 'What lies behind collegiality, legitimation or control?', *Educational Management and Administration*, vol. 26, no. 3, pp. 305–16.

Brym, R.J. (1987) 'The political sociology of intellectuals: a critique and a proposal', in Gagnon, A.G. (ed.), *Intellectuals in Liberal Democracies*. New York: Praeger.

Burgess, R.G. (1983) *Experiencing Comprehensive Education*. London: Methuen.

Burgess, R.G. (1984) 'Headship: freedom or constraint?', in Ball, S.J. (ed.), *Comprehensive Schooling: A Reader*. Lewes: Falmer Press.

Burns, J.M. (1978) *Leadership*. New York: Harper and Row.

Bush, T. (1995) *Theories of Educational Management*. 2nd ed. London: Paul Chapman Publishing.

Bush, T. (1998) 'The National Professional Qualification for Headship: the key to effective leadership?', *School Leadership and Management*, vol. 18, no. 3, pp. 321–33.

Bush, T. (1999) 'Crisis or crossroads? the discipline of educational management in the late 1990s', *Educational Management and Administration*, vol. 27, no. 3, pp. 239–52.

Bush, T. and Coleman, M. (1995) 'Professional development for heads: the role of mentoring', *Journal of Educational Administration*, vol. 33, no. 5, pp. 60–73.

Bush, T., Bell, L., Bolam, R., Glatter, R. and Ribbins, P. (eds) (1999) *Educational Management: Redefining Theory, Policy and Practice*. London: Paul Chapman Publishing.

Busher, H. (1997) 'Principals and headteachers as chief executives', in Ribbins, P. (ed.), *Leaders and Leadership in the School, College and University*. London: Cassell.

Busher, H. and Harris, A. (1999) 'Leadership of school subject areas: tensions and dimensions of managing in the middle', *School Leadership and Management*, vol. 19, no. 3, pp. 305–17.

Busher, H. and Saran, R. (eds) (1995a) *Managing Teachers as Professionals in Schools*. London: Kogan Page.

Busher, H. and Saran, R. (1995b) 'Introduction: schools for the future', in Busher, H. and Saran, R. (eds), *Managing Teachers as Professionals in Schools*. London: Kogan Page.

Caldwell, B.J. (1998) 'Strategic leadership, resource management and effective school reform', *Journal of Educational Administration*, vol. 36, no. 5, pp. 445–61.

Caldwell, B.J. and Spinks, J.M. (1988) *The Self Managing School*. Lewes: Falmer Press.

Caldwell, B.J. and Spinks, J.M. (1992) *Leading the Self Managing School*. London: Falmer Press.

Caldwell, B.J. and Spinks, J.M. (1998) *Beyond the Self Managing School*. London: Falmer Press.

Callaghan, J. (1976) Ruskin College Speech, 18 October, 1976, from *The Times Educational Supplement*, 22 October 1976.

Carr, W. (1993) 'What is an educational practice?', in Hammersely, M. (ed.), *Educational Research: Current Issues*. London: Paul Chapman

Publishing.

Carr, W. and Hartnett, A. (1996) *Education and the Struggle for Democracy.* Buckingham: Open University Press.

Carvel, J. (2000) 'Poverty no excuse for failure, says Blunkett', *Guardian,* 2 March, p. 11.

Carvel, J. and Mulholland, H. (2000) 'Schools policy crisis as third superhead quits', *Guardian,* 15 March, p. 1.

Chubb, J.E. and Moe, T.M. (1990) *Politics, Markets and America's Schools.* Washington, DC: Brookings Institute.

Clark, P. (1998) *Back from the Brink.* London: Metro Books.

Clarke, B. (1997) 'In conversation with Lesley Anderson', in Ribbins, P. (ed.), *Leaders and Leadership in the School, College and University.* London: Cassell.

Clarke, M. and Stewart, J. (1992) 'Empowerment: a theme for the 1990s', *Local Government Studies,* vol. 18, no. 2, pp. 18–26.

Cochran-Smith, M. and Paris, C.L. (1995) 'Mentor and mentoring: did Homer have it right?', in Smyth, J. (ed.), *Critical Discourses on Teacher Development.* London: Cassell.

Cohen, M.D. and March, J.G. (1989) 'Leadership and ambiguity', in Bush, T. (ed.), *Managing Education: Theory and Practice.* Buckingham: Open University Press.

Cole, B. (1996) 'Pathways to headship: the role of mentoring in the training and development of headteachers' Unpublished MA thesis, Keele University.

Coleman, J.S., Campbell, E., Hobson, C., McPartland, J., Mood, A., Weinfeld, R. and York, R. (1966) *Equality of Educational Opportunity.* Washington, DC: Government Printing Office.

Collarbone, P. (1998) 'Developing a leadership programme for school leaders: an NPQH assessment centre manager reflects', *School Leadership and Management,* vol. 18, no.3, pp. 335–46.

Connell, R.W. (1983) *Which Way Is Up? Essays on Sex, Class and Culture.* Sydney: Allen and Unwin.

Constable, H. (1995) 'Developing teachers as extended professionals', in Busher, H. and Saran, R. (eds), *Managing Teachers as Professionals in Schools.* London: Kogan Page.

Coombe, C. and White, R. (1994) 'Improving the management and professional leadership skills of school heads in Africa: a development model', *Studies in Educational Administration,* no. 60, winter, pp. 3–14.

Cordingley, P. (1999) 'Pedagogy, educational management and the TTA research agenda', in Bush, T., Bell, L., Bolam, R., Glatter, R. and Ribbins, P. (eds), *Educational Management: Redefining Theory, Policy and Practice.* London: Paul Chapman Publishing.

Corson, D. (2000) 'Emancipatory Leadership', *International Journal of Leadership in Education,* vol. 3, no. 2, pp. 93–120.

Coulson, A.A. (1980) 'The role of the primary head', in Bush, T., Glatter, R., Goodey, J. and Riches, C. (eds), *Approaches to School Management.*

London: Harper and Row.

Court, M.R. (1998) 'Women challenging managerialism: devolution dilemmas in the establishment of co-principals in primary schools in Aotearoa/New Zealand', *School Leadership and Management*, vol. 18, no. 1, pp. 35–57.

Craig, P. with Rayner, S. (1999) 'Finite resource meeting infinite need: starting up an EBD support service', in Rayner, S. and Ribbins, P. (eds), *Headteachers and Leadership in Special Education*. London: Cassell.

Creemers, B.P.M. (1997) 'Departments in secondary schools in The Netherlands', in Leask, M. and Terrell, I. (eds), *Development Planning and School Improvement for Middle Managers*. London: Kogan Page.

Creissen, T. (1997) 'The introduction of the National Professional Qualification for Headship', in Tomlinson, H. (ed.), *Managing Continuous Professional Development in Schools*. London: Paul Chapman Publishing.

Creissen, T. and Ellison, L. (1998) 'Reinventing school leadership – back to the future in the UK?' *International Journal of Educational Management*, vol. 12, no. 1, pp. 28–38.

Cross, R. (1995) 'The role of the mentor in utilising the support system for the newly qualified teacher', *School Organisation*, vol. 15, no. 1, pp. 35–42.

Crowther, F. (1997) 'The William Walker Oration, 1996. Unsung heroes: the leaders in our classrooms', *Journal of Educational Administration*, vol. 35, no. 1, pp. 5–17.

Crowther, F. and Limerick, B. (1998) 'Leaders as learners: implications for postmodern leader development', *International Studies in Education Administration*, vol. 26, no. 2, pp. 21–9.

Crump, S. (1997) 'Organising leadership, schools, workplaces and government in Australia', *International Studies in Educational Administration*, vol. 25, no. 1, pp. 44–52.

Cuckle, P., Broadhead, P. Hodgson, J. and Dunford, J. (1998) 'Development planning in primary schools', *Educational Management and Administration*, vol. 26, no. 2, pp. 185–95.

Cutler, T. and Waine, B. (2000) 'Mutual benefits or managerial control? The role of appraisal in performance related pay for teachers', *British Journal of Educational Studies*, vol. 48, no. 2, pp. 170–82.

Dale, R. (1989) *The State and Education Policy*. Milton Keynes: Open University Press.

Danzig, A.B. (1997) 'Leadership stories: what novices learn by crafting the stories of experienced school administrators', *Journal of Educational Administration*, vol. 35, no. 2, pp. 122–37.

Danzig, A. (1999) 'How might leadership be taught? The use of story and narrative to teach leadership', *International Journal of Leadership in Education*, vol. 2, no. 2, pp. 117–31.

Daresh, J.C. (1995) 'Research base on mentoring for educational leaders:

what do we know?', *Journal of Educational Administration*, vol. 33, no. 5, pp. 7–16.

Daresh, J. and Male, T. (2000) 'Crossing the border into leadership: experiences of newly appointed British headteachers and American principals', *Educational Management and Administration*, vol. 28, no. 1, pp. 89–101.

Daugherty, R. (1997) 'National Curriculum assessment: the experience of England and Wales', *Educational Administration Quarterly*, vol. 33, no. 2, pp. 198–218.

Davidson, M.J. (1997) *The Black and Ethnic Minority Woman Manager*. London: Paul Chapman Publishing.

Davidson, M.J. and Cooper, C.L. (1992) *Shattering the Glass Ceiling*. London: Paul Chapman Publishing.

Davies, D. with Ribbins, P. (1998) 'Thriving in the face of insurmountable odds', in Pascal, C. and Ribbins, P. (eds), *Understanding Primary Headteachers*. London: Cassell.

Davies, L. (1990) *Equity and Efficiency? School Management in an International Context*. Lewes: Falmer Press.

Davies, L. (1995) 'Who Needs Headteachers?' Keynote lecture delivered to the Annual Conference of BEMAS, Oxford, September.

Day, C. (1995) 'Leadership and professional development: developing reflective practice', in Busher, H. and Saran, R. (eds), *Managing Teachers as Professionals in Schools*. London: Kogan Page.

Day, C. and Bakioğlu, A. (1996) 'Development and disenchantment in the professional lives of headteachers', in Goodson, I.F. and Hargreaves, A. (eds), *Teachers' Professional Lives*. London: Falmer Press.

Day, C., Harris, A., Hadfield, M., Tolley, H. and Beresford, J. (2000) *Leading Schools in Times of Change*. Buckingham: Open University Press.

de Lyon, H. (1989) 'Sexual Harassment', in de Lyon, H. and Widdowson Migniuolo, F. (eds), *Women Teachers*. Milton Keynes: Open University Press.

de Lyon, H. and Widdowson Migniuolo, F. (eds) (1989) *Women Teachers*. Milton Keynes: Open University Press.

Deakin, N. and Walsh, K. (1996) 'The enabling state: the role of markets and contracts', *Public Administration*, vol. 74, no. 1, pp. 33–47.

Deal, T.E. and Kennedy, A. (1982) *Corporate Cultures: The Rites and Rituals of Corporate Life*. Reading, MA: Addison-Wesley.

Dean, C. (2000a) '4,000 teacher jobs cannot be filled', *Times Educational Supplement*, 7 July, p. 1.

Dean, C. (2000b) 'Country has "run out" of teachers', *Times Educational Supplement*, 8, September, p. 4.

Deem, R. (1996a) 'Border territories: a journey through sociology, education and women's studies', *British Journal of Sociology of Education*, vol. 17, no. 1, pp. 5–19.

Deem, R. (1996b) 'The future of educational research in the context of the social sciences: a special case?', *British Journal of Educational Studies*, vol.

44, no. 2, pp. 143–158.

Deem, R. (1998) 'Educational research past, present and future: a feminist social science perspective', in Rudduck, J. and McIntyre, D. (eds), *Challenges for Educational Research*. London: Paul Chapman Publishing.

Deem. R., Brehony, K. J. and Heath, S. (1995) *Active Citizenship and the Governing of Schools*. Buckingham: Open University Press.

Dempster, N. and Logan, L. (1998) 'Expectations of school leaders: An Australian picture' in MacBeath, J. (ed.) (1998) *Effective School Leadership: Responding to Change*, London: Paul Chapman Publishing.

Dempster, N. and Mahony, P. (1998) 'Ethical challenges in school leadership', in MacBeath, J. (ed.), *Effective School Leadership: Responding to Change*. London: Paul Chapman Publishing.

Department for Education (DfE) (1993) *School Teacher' Pay and Conditions Document*, London: HMSO.

Department for Education and Employment (DfEE) (1998) *teachers: meeting the challenge of change*. London: DfEE.

Department for Education and Employment (DfEE) *National College for School Leadership: A Prospectus*. London: DfEE.

Department for Education and Employment (DfEE) (2000a) *Influence or Irrelevance: Can Social Science Improve Government?* Secretary of State's ESRC Lecture Speech, 2 February. London: DfEE.

Department for Education and Employment (DfEE) (2000b) *Autumn Package*. www.dfee.gov.uk/statistics/DB/AUT

Department of Education and Science (DES) (1985) *Better Schools*, London: HMSO.

Diggins, P.B. (1997) 'Reflections on leadership characteristics necessary to develop and sustain learning school communities', *School Leadership and Management*, vol. 17, no. 3, pp. 413–25.

Dimmock, C. (1998) 'Restructuring Hong Kong's schools', *Educational Management and Administration*, vol. 26, no. 4, pp. 363–77.

Doe, B. (1997) 'Identity crisis', *The Times Educational Supplement*, 13 June, p. 23.

Downie, R.S. (1990) 'Professions and professionalism', *Journal of Philosophy of Education*, vol. 24, no. 2, pp. 147–59.

Draper, J. and McMichael, P. (1996) 'I am the eye of the needle and everything passes through me: primary headteachers explain their retirement', *School Organisation*, vol. 16, no. 2, pp. 149–63.

Draper, J. and McMichael, P. (1998a) 'Preparing a profile: likely applicants for primary school headship', *Educational Management and Administration*, vol. 26, no. 2, pp. 161–72.

Draper, J. and McMichael, P. (1998b) 'Making sense of primary headship: the surprises awaiting new heads', *School Leadership and Management*, vol. 18, no. 2, pp. 197–211.

Duffy, E. (1999) 'Leading the creative school', in Tomlinson, H., Gunter, H. and Smith, P. (eds), *Living Headship: Voices, Values and Vision*. London: Paul Chapman Publishing.

Duke, D.L. (1998) 'The normative context of organizational leadership', *Educational Administration Quarterly*, vol. 34, no. 2, pp. 165–95.

Earley, P. (1992) *The School Management Competencies Project*. 3 vols. Crawley: School Management South.

Earley, P. (1993) 'Developing competence in schools: a critique of standards-based approaches to management development', *Educational Management and Administration*, vol. 21, no. 4, pp. 233–44.

Earley, P. and Fletcher-Campbell, F. (1989) *No Time to Manage? Department and Faculty Heads at Work*. London: NFER-Routledge.

Eden, D. (1997) 'The paradox of school leadership', *Journal of Educational Administration*, vol. 36., no. 3, pp. 249–61.

Edwards, A. (2000a), 'Evidence-based practice and the generation of knowledge about pedagogy in schools: enhancing practitioners' understanding of pedagogy in school – university research partnerships'. Paper presented at the AERA, New Orleans, April.

Edwards, A. (2000b) '*Researching pedagogy: a sociocultural agenda*'. Inaugural lecture, 7 November, School of Education, University of Birmingham.

Efficiency Unit (1988) *Improving Management in Government: the Next Steps*. Report to the Prime Minister. London: HMSO.

Ehrich, L.C. (1997) 'Professional development: its changing nature and implications for Australian principals', *International Studies in Educational Administration*, vol. 25, no. 1, pp. 12–19.

Engeström, Y. (1987) *Learning by Expanding: An Activity-Theoretical Approach to Developing Research*. Helsinki: Orienta-Konsultit.

Engeström, Y. (1999a) 'Activity theory and individual and social transformation', in Engeström, Y., Miettinen, R. and Punamäki, R. (eds), *Perspectives on Activity Theory*. Cambridge: Cambridge University Press.

Engeström, Y. (1999b) 'Innovative learning in work teams: analyzing cycles of knowledge creation in practice', in Engeström, Y., Miettinen, R. and Punamäki, R. (eds), *Perspectives on Activity Theory*. Cambridge: Cambridge University Press.

Engeström, Y. (2000) Opening address, Centre for Sociocultural and Activity Theory Research, University of Birmingham, 27 May.

Engeström, Y. (2001) *Cultural-History Activity Theory*, www.helsinki.fi/~jengestr/activity.

Engeström, Y. and Miettinen, R. (1999) 'Introduction', in Engeström, Y., Miettinen, R. and Punamäki, R. (eds), *Perspectives on Activity Theory*. Cambridge: Cambridge University Press.

Engeström, Y., Miettinen, R. and Punamäki, R. (eds), (1999) *Perspectives on Activity Theory*. Cambridge: Cambridge University Press.

Eraut, M. (1993) 'The characterisation and development of professional expertise in school management and in teaching', *Educational Management and Administration*, vol. 21., no. 4, pp. 223–32.

Esland, G. (1996) 'Knowledge and nationhood: the New Right, education and the global market', in Avis, J., Bloomer, M., Esland, G., Gleeson, D. and Hodkinson, P., *Knowledge and Nationhood*. London: Cassell.

Esp, D. (1993) *Competencies for School Managers*. London: Kogan Page.

Etzioni, A. (1969) *The Semi-Professionals and their Organisation*. New York: Macmillan.

Evans, J. with Ribbins, P. (1999) 'In praise of inclusivity: managing special education in a large secondary school', in Rayner, S. and Ribbins, P. (eds,) *Headteachers and Leadership in Special Education*. London: Cassell.

Evans, L. (1997) 'The effects of senior management teams on teacher morale and job satisfaction', *Educational Management and Administration*, vol. 26, no. 4, pp. 417–28.

Evers, C. and Lakomski, G. (1991a) *Knowing Educational Administration*. Oxford: Pergamon.

Evers, C. and Lakomski, G. (1991b) 'Educational administration as science: a post-positivist proposal', in Ribbins, P., Glatter, R., Simkins, T. and Watson, L. (eds), *Developing Educational Leaders*. Harlow: Longman.

Evetts, J. (1994) *Becoming a Secondary Headteacher*. London: Cassell.

Feintuck, M. (1994) *Accountability and Choice in Schooling*. Buckingham: Open University Press.

Fennell, H. (1999) 'Power in the principalship: four women's experiences', *Journal of Educational Administration*, vol 37, no. 1, pp. 23–49.

Fergusson, R. (1994) 'Managerialism in education', in Clarke, J., Cochrane, A. and McLaughlin, E. (eds), *Managing Social Policy*. London: Sage.

Ferlie, E., Ashburner, L., Fitzgerald, L. and Pettigrew, A. (1996) *The New Public Management in Action*. Oxford: Oxford University Press.

Fidler, B. (1997) 'School leadership: some issues', *School Leadership and Management*, vol. 17., no. 1, pp. 23–37.

Fidler, B. (1998) 'Editorial', *School Leadership and Management*, vol. 18, no. 3, pp. 309–15.

Fiedler, F.E., Chemers, M.M. and Mahar, L. (1977) *Improving Leadership Effectiveness: The Leader Match Concept*. New York: John Wiley.

Field, K., Holden, P. and Lawlor, H. (2000) *Effective Subject Leadership*. London: Routledge.

Fielding, M. (1996) 'Empowerment: emancipation or enervation?', *Journal of Education Policy*, vol. 11, no. 3, pp. 399–417. *

Fielding, M. (1999a) 'Target setting, policy pathology and student perspectives: learning to labour in new times', *Cambridge Journal of Education*, vol. 29, no. 2, pp. 277–87.

Fielding, M. (1999b) 'Radical collegiality: affirming teaching as an inclusive professional practice', *Australian Educational Researcher*, vol. 26, no. 2, pp. 1–34.

Fielding, M. (2001) 'Students as radical agents of change: a three year case study', *Journal of Educational Change*, forthcoming.

Fink, D. (1999) 'Deadwood didn't kill itself: a pathology of failing schools', *Educational Management and Administration*, vol. 27, no. 2, pp. 131–41.

Fitz, J. (1999) 'Reflections on the Field of Educational Management studies', *Educational Administration and Management*, vol. 27, no. 3, pp. 313–21.

Flynn, N. (1997) *Public Sector Management*. Hemel Hempstead: Prentice Hall/Harvester Wheatsheaf.

Foreman, K. (1995) 'Teacher professionality and the National Curriculum: management implications', in Busher, H. and Saran, R. (eds), (1995) *Managing Teachers as Professionals in Schools*. London: Kogan Page.

Foster, W. (1989) 'Towards a critical practice of leadership', in Smyth, J. (ed.), *Critical Perspectives on Educational Leadership*. London: Falmer Press.

Foucault, M. (1972) *The Archaeology of Knowledge*. Trans. A.M. Sheridan-Smith. London: Routledge.

Freire, P. (1972) *Pedagogy of the Oppressed*. Harmondsworth: Penguin.

Fullan, M. (1992) *What's Worth Fighting for in Headship?* Buckingham: Open University Press.

Fullan, M. (ed.) (1997) *The Challenge of School Change*. Arlington Heights, IL: Skylight.

Fullan, M. (1999) *Change Forces: The Sequel*. London: Falmer Press.

Fullan, M. and Hargreaves, A. (1992) *What's Worth Fighting for in your School?* Buckingham: Open University Press.

Fullan, M. with Stiegelbauer, S. (1991) *The New Meaning of Educational Change*. London: Cassell.

Gardner, H. (1998) 'Commentary. The intelligences of leaders', *International Journal of Leadership in Education*, vol. 1., no. 2, pp. 203–06.

Garrett, V. (1997) 'Principals and headteachers as leading professionals', in Ribbins, P. (ed.), *Leaders and Leadership in the School, College and University*. London: Cassell.

Garrett, V. and McGeachie, B. (1999) 'Preparation for headship? The role of the deputy head in the primary school', *School Leadership and Management*, vol. 19., no. 1, pp. 67–81.

Gasper, M. with Pascal, C. (1998) 'Demonstrating that learning is for life', in Pascal, C. and Ribbins, P. (eds), *Understanding Primary Headteachers*. London: Cassell.

Geijsel, F., Sleegers, P. and van den Berg, R. (1999) 'Transformational leadership and the implementation of large-scale innovation programs', *Journal of Educational Administration*, vol. 37., no. 4, pp. 309–28.

Gewirtz, S. and Ozga, J. (1990) 'Partnership, pluralism and education policy: a reassessment', *Journal of Education Policy*, vol. 5., no. 1, pp. 37–48.

Gewirtz, S., Ball, S.J. and Bowe, R. (1995) *Markets, Choice and Equity in Education*. Buckingham: Open University Press.

Gillborn, D. (1994) 'The micro-politics of macro reform', *British Journal of Sociology of Education*, vol. 15, no. 2, pp. 147–64.

Gipps, C. (1998) 'Some significant developments?', in Rudduck, J. and McIntyre, D. (eds), *Challenges for Educational Research*. London: Paul Chapman.

Glatter, R. (1972) *Management Development for the Education Profession*. London: Harrap.

Glatter, R. (1979) 'Education "policy" and "management": one field or two?', in Bush, T., Glatter, R., Goodey, J. and Riches, C. (eds), *Approaches to School Management*. London: Harper Educational.

Glatter, R. (1987) 'Towards an agenda for educational management', *Educational Management and Administration*, vol. 15, no. 1, pp. 5–12.

Glatter, R. (1997) 'Context and capability in education management', *Educational Management and Administration*, vol. 25, no. 2, pp. 181–92.

Glatter, R. (1999) 'From struggling to juggling: towards a redefinition of the field of educational leadership and management', *Educational Management and Administration*, vol. 27, no. 3, pp. 253–66.

Gleeson, D. (1996) 'Post-compulsory education in a post-industrial and post-modern age', in Avis, J., Bloomer, M., Esland, G., Gleeson, D. and Hodkinson, P., *Knowledge and Nationhood*. London: Cassell.

Gleeson, D. and Gunter, H. (2001) 'The performing school and the modernisation of teachers', in Gleeson, D. and Husbands, C. (eds), *The Performing School: Managing Teaching and Learning in a Performance Culture*. London: Routledge/Falmer.

Gleeson, D. and Shain, F. (1999a) 'By appointment: governance, markets and managerialism in further education', *British Educational Research Journal*, vol. 25., no. 4, pp. 545–61.

Gleeson, D. and Shain, F. (1999b) 'Managing ambiguity: between markets and managerialism – a case study of "middle" managers in further education', *Sociological Review*, vol. 47, no. 3, pp. 461–90.

Glickman, C.D. (1998) 'Educational leadership for democratic purpose: what do we mean?', *International Journal of Leadership in Education*, vol. 1, no. 1, pp. 47–53.

Glickman, C.D. (1999) 'Commentary. A response to the discourse on democracy: a dangerous retreat', *International Journal of Leadership in Education*, vol. 2, no. 1, pp. 43–6.

Glover, D., Gleeson, D., Gough, G. and Johnson, M. (1998) 'The meaning of management: the development needs of middle managers in secondary schools', *Educational Management and Administration*, vol. 26, no. 3, pp. 279–92.

Glover, D., Levačić, R., Bennett, N. and Earley, P. (1996a) 'Leadership, planning and resource management in four very effective schools. Part I: setting the scene', *School Organisation*, vol. 16, no. 2, pp. 135–48.

Glover, D., Levačić, R., Bennett, N. and Earley, P. (1996b) 'Leadership, planning and resource management in four very effective schools. Part II: planning and performance', *School Organisation*, vol. 16, no. 3, pp. 247–61.

Glover, D. and Miller, D. with Gambling, M., Gough, G. and Johnson, M. (1999) 'As others see us: senior management and subject staff perceptions of the work effectiveness of subject leaders in secondary schools', *School Leadership and Management*, vol. 19, no. 3, pp. 331–44.

Golby, M. (1996) 'Teachers' emotions: an illustrated discussion', *Cambridge Journal of Education*, vol. 26, no. 3, pp. 423–34.

Gold, A. (1993) 'The development of women managers in education, or, how to talk about it', in Ouston, J. (ed.), *Women in Education Management*. Harlow: Longman.

Gold, A. (1998) *Head of Department*. London: Cassell.

Goldring, E.B. (1992) 'System-wide diversity in Israel: principals as transformational and environmental leaders', *Journal of Educational Administration*, vol. 30, no. 3, pp. 49–62.

Goodson, I. (1995) 'Studying the teacher's life and work', in Smyth, J. (ed.), *Critical Discourses on Teacher Development*. London: Cassell.

Goodson, I. (1997) ' "Trendy theory" and teacher professionalism', in Hargreaves, A. and Evans, R. (eds), *Beyond Educational Reform, Bringing Teachers Back In*. Buckingham: Open University Press.

Grace, G. (1989) 'Education: commodity or public good?', *British Journal of Educational Studies*, vol. 37, no. 3, pp. 207–21.

Grace, G. (1995) *School Leadership: Beyond Education Management*. London: Falmer Press.

Grace, G. (1997) 'Critical leadership studies', in Crawford, M., Kydd, L. and Riches, C. (eds), *Leadership and Teams in Educational Management*. Buckingham: Open University Press.

Gramsci, A. (1971) *Selections from the Prison Notebooks*. Edited and trans. by Hoare, Q. and Nowell Smith, G. London: Lawrence and Wishart.

Gramsci, A. (1973) *Letters from Prison*. Sel., trans. and Intro. Lawner, L. New York: Harper and Row.

Gray, A. and Jenkins, B. (1995) 'From public administration to public management: reassessing a revolution?', *Public Administration*, vol. 73, no.1, pp. 75–99.

Gray, J. and Wilcox, B. (1995) *'Good School, Bad School': Evaluating Performance and Encouraging Improvement*. Buckingham: Open University Press.

Gray, J., Hopkins, D., Reynolds, D., Wilcox, B., Farrell, S. and Jesson, D. (1999) *Improving Schools: Performance and Potential*. Buckingham: Open University Press.

Gray, J., Reynolds, D., Fitz-Gibbon, C. and Jesson, D. (eds), (1996) *Merging Traditions: The Future of Research on School Effectiveness and School Improvement*. London: Cassell.

Gray, M. (1997) 'In conversation with Agnes McMahon', in Ribbins, P. (ed.), *Leaders and Leadership in the School, College and University*. London: Cassell.

Green, V.A. and Manera, E. (1995) 'Educational leadership: the practice of successful women administrators in the USA and Canada', *International Studies in Educational Administration*, vol. 23, no. 2, pp. 10–15.

Greenfield, T. (1978) 'Where does self belong in the study of organisation? Response to a symposium', *Educational Administration*, vol. 6, no. 1, pp. 81–101.

Greenfield, T. and Ribbins, P. (eds), (1993) *Greenfield on Educational Administration*. London: Routledge.

Grenfell, M. (1996) 'Bourdieu and initial teacher education – a post-structuralist approach', *British Educational Research Journal*, vol. 22, no. 3, pp. 287–303.

Grenfell, M. and James, D. with Hodkinson, P., Reay, D. and Robbins, D. (1998) *Bourdieu and Education*. London: Falmer Press.

Griffiths, D.E. (1958) 'Administration as decision-making', in Halpin, A.W. (ed.) *Administrative Theory in Education*. London: Macmillan.

Griffiths, D.E. (ed.) (1964) *Behavioural Science and Educational Administration*. The 63rd yearbook of the National Society for the Study of Education, part 2. Chicago: University of Chicago Press.

Griffiths, D.E. (1969) 'Theory in educational administration: 1966', in Baron, G., Cooper, D.H. and Walker, W.G. (eds), *Educational Administration: International Perspectives*. Chicago: Rand McNally.

Griffiths, D.E. (1979) 'Intellectual turmoil in educational administration', *Educational Administration Quarterly*, vol. 15, no. 3, pp. 43–65.

Griffiths, M. (1998) *Educational Research for Social Justice*. Buckingham: Open University Press.

Gronn, P. (1983) 'Talk as work: the accomplishment of school administration', *Administrative Science Quarterly*, vol. 28, no. 1, pp. 1–21.

Gronn, P. (1985) 'After T. B. Greenfield, whither Educational Administration?', *Educational Management and Administration*, vol. 13, no. 1, pp. 55–61.

Gronn, P. (1993) 'Administrators and their talk', *Educational Management and Administration*, vol. 21., no.1, pp. 30–9.

Gronn, P. (1996) 'From transactions to transformations', *Educational Management and Administration*, vol. 24, no. 1, pp. 7–30.

Gronn, P. (1999a) *The Making of Educational Leaders*. London: Cassell.

Gronn, P. (1999b) 'Leadership from a distance: institutionalizing values and forming character at Timbertop, 1951–1961', in Begley, P.T. and Leonard, P.E. (eds), *The Values of Educational Administration*. London: Falmer Press.

Gronn, P. (2000) 'Distributed properties: a new architecture for leadership', *Educational Management and Administration*, vol. 28, no. 3, pp. 317–38.

Gronn, P. and Ribbins, P. (1999) 'The salvation of educational administration: better science or alternatives to science?', in Strain, M., Dennsion, B., Ouston, J. and Hall, V. (eds), *Policy, Leadership and Professional Knowledge in Education*. London: Paul Chapman Publishing.

Guat Tin, L. and Lee Hean, L. (1997) 'Singapore – Heads of department and school improvement', in Leask, M. and Terrell, I. (eds), *Development Planning and School Improvement for Middle Managers*. London: Kogan Page.

Gunter, H. (1997) *Rethinking Education: The Consequences of Jurassic Management*. London: Cassell.

Gunter, H. (1999a) 'An intellectual history of the field of education management from 1960'. Unpublished PhD. thesis, Keele University.

Gunter, H. (1999b) 'Contracting headteachers as leaders: an analysis of the NPQH', *Cambridge Journal of Education*, vol. 29, no. 2, pp. 249–62.

Gunter, H. (1999c) 'Researching and constructing histories of the field of education management', in Bush, T., Bell, L., Bolam, R., Glatter, R. and Ribbins, P. (eds), *Educational Management: Redefining Theory, Policy and Practice*. London: Paul Chapman Publishing.

Gunter, H., McGregor, D. and Gunter, B. (2001) 'Teachers as leaders: a CASE study', *Management in Education* vol. 15, no. 1, pp. 26–28.

Hall, V. (1993) 'Women in educational management: a review of research in Britain', in Ouston, J. (ed.), *Women in Education Management*. Harlow: Longman.

Hall, V. (1996) *Dancing on the Ceiling*. London: Paul Chapman Publishing.

Hall, V. (1997a) 'Leadership and team learning in secondary schools', *School Leadership and Management*, vol. 17, no. 3, pp. 327–29.

Hall, V. (1997b) 'Dusting off the phoenix', *Educational Management and Administration*, vol. 25, no. 3, pp. 309–24.

Hall, V. (1998) 'We are all adult educators now: the implications of adult learning theory for the continuing professional development of educational leaders and managers'. Paper presented to the to the ESRC Seminar Series: Redefining Educational Management, Milton Keynes. June.

Hall, V. (1999a) 'Review symposium', *Educational Management and Administration*, vol. 27, no. 1, pp. 99–103.

Hall, V. (1999b) 'Gender and education management: duel or dialogue', in Bush, T., Bell, L., Bolam, R., Glatter, R. and Ribbins, P. (eds), (1999) *Educational Management: Redefining Theory, Policy and Practice*. London: Paul Chapman Publishing.

Hall, V. and Southworth, G. (1997) 'Headship', *School Leadership and Management*, vol. 17, no. 2, pp. 151–69.

Hall, V. and Wallace, M. (1996) 'Let the team take the strain: lessons from research into senior management teams in secondary schools', *School Organisation*, vol. 16, no. 3, pp. 297–308.

Hall, V., Mackay, H. and Morgan, C. (1986) *Head Teachers at Work*. Milton Keynes: Open University Press.

Hallinger, P. (1992) 'The evolving role of American principals: from managerial to transformational leaders', *Journal of Educational Administration*, vol. 35, no. 3, pp. 35–48.

Hallinger, P. and Heck, R.H. (1996a) 'The principal's role in school effectiveness: an assessment of methodological progress, 1980–1995', in Leithwood, K., Chapman, J., Corson, D., Hallinger, P, and Hart, A. (eds), *International Handbook of Educational Leadership and Administration Part 2.* Dordrecht: Kluwer Academic.

Hallinger, P. and Heck, R. (1996b) 'Reassessing the principal's role in school effectiveness: a review of empirical research, 1980–1995', *Educational Administration Quarterly,* vol. 32, no. 1, pp. 5–44.

Hallinger, P. and Heck, R. (1999) 'Can leadership enhance school effectiveness?', in Bush, T., Bell, L., Bolam, R., Glatter, R. and Ribbins, P. (1999) *Educational Management: Redefining Theory, Policy and Practice.* London: Paul Chapman Publishing.

Halpin, A.W. (ed.) (1958) *Administrative Theory in Education.* London: Macmillan.

Halpin, D. (2001) 'Hope, Utopianism and Educational Management' *Cambridge Journal of Education* vol. 31, no. 1, pp. 103-118.

Hammer, M. (1996) *Beyond Reengineering.* New York: Harper Business.

Hammersley, M. (1996) 'Post mortem or post modern? Some reflections on British sociology of education', *British Journal of Educational Studies,* vol. 44, no. 4, pp. 395–407.

Hammersley, M. (2000) 'The sky is never blue for modernisers: the threat posed by David Blunkett's offer of "partnership" to social science', *Research Intelligence,* no. 72, June, pp. 12–13.

Hannon, P. (1998) 'An ecological perspective on educational research', in Rudduck, J. and McIntyre, D. (eds), *Challenges for Educational Research.* London: Paul Chapman Publishing.

Hansard Society (1990) *The Report of the The Hansard Society Commission on Women at the Top.* London: Hansard Society for Parliarmentary Government.

Harber, C. and Davies, L. (1997) *School Management and Effectiveness in Developing Countries.* London: Cassell.

Hargreaves, A, (1994) *Changing Teachers, Changing Times.* London: Cassell.

Hargreaves, A. (1995) 'Beyond collaboration: critical teacher development in post-modern age', in Smyth, J. (ed.), *Critical Discourses on Teacher Development.* London: Cassell.

Hargreaves, A. (1998) 'The emotional politics of teaching and teacher development: with implications for educational leadership', *International Journal of Leadership in Education,* vol. 1, no. 4, pp. 315–36.

Hargreaves, A. and Evans, R. (1997) *Beyond Educational Reform: Bringing Teachers Back In.* Buckingham: Open University Press.

Hargreaves, A. and Fullan, M. (1998) *What's Worth Fighting for in Education?* Buckingham: Open University Press.

Hargreaves, A. and Goodson, I. (1996) 'Teachers' professional lives: aspirations and actualities', in Hargreaves, A. and Goodson, I. (eds), *Teachers' Professional Lives.* London: Falmer Press.

Hargreaves, D.H. (1967) *Social Relations in a Secondary School.* London:

Routledge and Kegan Paul.

Hargreaves, D.H. (1996) 'Teaching as a research-based profession: possibilities and prospects'. Teaching Training Agency annual lecture.

Hargreaves, D.H. (1998) 'A new partnership of stakeholders and a national strategy for research in education', in Rudduck, J. and McIntyre, D. (eds), *Challenges for Educational Research.* London: Paul Chapman Publishing.

Hargreaves, D.H. and Hopkins, D. (1991) *The Empowered School: The Management and Practice of Development Planning.* London: Cassell.

Harries-Jenkins, G. (1984) 'Education management: part 1', *School Organisation and Management Abstracts,* vol. 3, no. 4, pp. 213–33.

Harries-Jenkins, G. (1985) 'Education management: part 2. A bibliography', *School Organisation and Management Abstracts,* vol. 4, no. 1, pp. 5–16.

Harris, A. (1998) 'Improving ineffective departments in secondary schools: strategies for change and development', *Educational Management and Administration,* vol. 26, no. 3, pp. 269–78.

Harris, A., Jamieson, I. and Russ, J. (1995) 'A study of "effective" departments in secondary schools', *School Organisation,* vol. 15, no. 3, pp. 283–99.

Harrison, R. and Williams, J. (1993) 'A training initiative', in Ozga, J. (ed.), *Women in Educational Management.* Buckingham: Open University Press.

Hart, A.W. (1999) 'Educational leadership: a field of inquiry and practice', *Educational Management and Administration,* vol. 27, no. 3, pp. 323–34.

Hartley, D. (1997) 'The new managerialism in education: a mission impossible?', *Cambridge Journal of Education,* vol. 27, no. 1, pp. 47–58.

Hartley, D. (1998) 'In search of structure, theory and practice in the management of education', *Journal of Education Policy,* vol. 12, no. 1, pp. 153–62.

Hartley, D. (1999) 'Marketing and the "re-enchantment" of school management', *British Journal of Sociology of Education,* vol. 20, no. 3, pp. 309–23.

Harvey, M. (1994) 'Empowering the primary school deputy', *Educational Management and Administration,* vol. 22, no. 1, pp. 26–38.

Harvey, M., Clarke, R., Hill, S. and Harrison, B. (1999) 'Preparing the way for partnership in establishing a centre for school leadership', *Educational Management and Administration,* vol. 27, no. 2, pp. 155–66.

Hatcher, R. (1994) 'Market relationships and the management of teachers', *British Journal of the Sociology of Education,* vol. 15, no. 1, pp. 41–63.

Hatcher, R (1998) 'Social justice and the politics of school effectiveness and improvement', *Race, Ethnicity and Education,* vol. 1, no. 2, pp. 267–89.

Hatcher, R. and Troyna, B. (1994) 'The "policy cycle": a Ball by Ball account', *Journal of Education Policy,* vol. 9, no. 2, pp. 155–70.

Hayes, D. (1995) 'The primary head's tale: collaborative relationships in time of rapid change', *Educational Management and Administration*, vol. 23, no. 4, pp. 233–44.

Hayes, D. (1996) 'Taking nothing for granted', *Educational Management and Administration*, vol. 24, no. 3, pp. 291–300.

Healy, M. (1994) *The Experience of Headteacher Appraisal.* London: Kogan Page.

Heck, R.H. (1991) 'Towards the future: rethinking the leadership role of the principal as philosopher-king', *Journal of Educational Administration*, vol. 29, no. 3, pp. 67–79.

Hegarty, S. (1998) 'A response from outside the university system', in Rudduck, J. and McIntyre, D. (eds), *Challenges for Educational Research.* London: Paul Chapman Publishing.

Helsby, G. (1999) *Changing Teachers' Work.* Buckingham: Open University Press.

Hersey, P. and Blanchard, K. (1982) *Management of Organizational Behavior: Utilizing Human Resources.* 4th ed. Englewood Cliffs, NJ: Prentice-Hall.

Hillage, J., Pearson, R., Anderson, A. and Tamkin, P. (1998) *Excellence in Research on Schools.* London: DfEE.

Hinchliffe, A. with Ribbins, P. (1999) 'Empowerment through communication: an integrated approach to special needs', in Rayner, S. and Ribbins, P. (eds), *Headteachers and Leadership in Special Education.* London: Cassell.

Hirst, P. (1974) *Knowledge and the Curriculum.* London: Routledge and Kegan Paul.

Hodgkinson, C. (1978) *Towards a Philosophy of Administration.* Oxford: Blackwell.

Hodgkinson, C. (1991) *Educational Leadership: The Moral Art.* Albany, NY: State University of New York.

Hodgkinson, C. (1993) 'Foreword', in Greenfield, T. and Ribbins, P. (eds), *Greenfield on Educational Administration.* London: Routledge.

Hodgkinson, C. (1996) *Administrative Philosophy.* Oxford: Pergamon.

Hodgkinson, C. (1999) 'The triumph of the will', in Begley, P.T. and Leonard, P.E. (eds), *The Values of Educational Administration.* London: Falmer Press.

Hopkins, D. and MacGilchrist, B. (1998) 'Development planning for pupil achievement', *School Leadership and Management*, vol. 18, no. 3, pp. 409–24.

Hopkins, D., West, M., Ainscow, M., Harris, A. and Beresford, J. (1997) *Creating the Conditions for Classroom Improvement.* London: David Fulton.

Howell, D.A. (1978) *A Bibliography of Educational Administration in the UK.* Windsor: NFER.

Hoyle, E. (1982) 'Micropolitics of educational organisations', *Educational Management and Administration*, vol. 10, no. 2, pp. 87–98.

Hoyle, E. (1986) 'The management of schools: theory and practice', in Hoyle, E. and McMahon, A., *World Yearbook of Education 1986: The*

Management of Schools. London, Kogan Page.

Hoyle, E. (1995) 'Changing conceptions of a profession', in Busher, H. and Saran, R. (eds), *Managing Teachers as Professionals in Schools.* London: Kogan Page.

Hoyle, E. (1999) 'The two faces of micropolitics', *School Leadership and Management,* vol. 19, no. 2, pp. 213–22.

Hsieh, C. and Shen, J. (1998) 'Teachers', principals' and superintendents', conceptions of leadership', *School Leadership and Management,* vol. 18, no. 1, pp. 107–21.

Hughes, M. (1978) *Education Administration: Pure or Applied?* Birmingham: University of Birmingham.

Hughes, M. (1985) 'Leadership in professionally staffed organisations', in Hughes, M., Ribbins, P. and Thomas, H., *Managing Education: The System and The Institution.* Eastbourne: Holt, Rinehart and Winston.

Hughes, M. (1997) 'From bulletin to journal', *Educational Management and Administration,* vol. 25, no. 3, pp. 243–63.

Hughes, Martin. (1997) 'The National Curriculum in England and Wales: a lesson in externally imposed reform?', *Educational Administration Quarterly,* vol. 33, no. 2, pp. 183–97.

Hughes, M. and James, C. (1999) 'The relationship between the head and the deputy head in primary schools', *School Leadership and Management,* vol. 19, no. 1, pp. 83–95.

Hughes, M., Carter, J. and Fidler, B. (1981) *Professional Development for Senior Staff in Schools and Colleges.* A DES Supported Research Project. Birmingham: Faculty of Education, University of Birmingham.

Hughes, M., Ribbins, P., and Thomas, H. (1985) *Managing Education: The System and The Institution.* Eastbourne: Holt, Rinehart and Winston.

Hursh, D. (1995) 'It's more than style: reflective teachers as ethical and political practitioners', in Smyth, J. (ed.), *Critical Discourses on Teacher Development.* London: Cassell.

Hustler, D., Brighouse, T. and Rudduck, J. (eds) (1995) *Heeding Heads, Secondary Heads and Educational Commentators in Dialogue.* London: David Fulton.

Hutchinson, D. (1994) 'Competence-based profiles for ITT and induction: the place of reflection', *British Journal of In-Service Education,* vol. 20, no. 3, pp. 303–12.

Hutton, W. (1995) *The State We're In.* London: Jonathan Cape.

Hyde, H. (1997) 'In conversation with Peter Ribbins', in Ribbins, P. (ed.), *Leaders and Leadership in the School, College and University.* London: Cassell.

Inglis, F. (1985) *The Management of Ignorance.* Oxford: Blackwell.

James, C. and Whiting, D. (1998) 'The career perspectives of deputy head-teachers', *Educational Management and Administration,* vol. 26, no. 4, pp. 353–62.

Jayne, E. (1996) 'Developing more effective primary deputy (or associate) heads: enhancing the partnership', *Educational Management and Administration*, vol. 24, no. 3, pp. 317–26.

Jenkins, H. (1997) 'Leadership: a model for cultural change', in Fidler, B., Russell, S., and Simkins, T. (eds), *Choices for Self Managing Schools*. London: Paul Chapman Publishing.

Jenkins, R. (1992) *Pierre Bourdieu*. London: Routledge.

Jencks, C.S., Smith, M., Ackland, H., Bane, M.J., Cohen, D., Ginter, H., Heyns, B. and Michelson, S. (1972) *Inequality: A Ressessment of the Effect of the Family and Schooling in America*. New York: Basic Books.

Jephcote, M. with Salisbury, J., Fletcher, J., Graham, I., and Mitchell, G. (1996) 'Principals' responses to incorporation: a window on their culture', *Journal of Further and Higher Education*, vol. 20, no. 2, pp. 33–48.

Johnson, N. (1993) 'Preparing educational administrators: an Australian perspective', *Journal of Educational Administration*, vol. 31, no. 1, pp. 22–40.

Johnson, P. and Short, P.M. (1998) 'Principal's leader power, teacher empowerment, teacher compliance and conflict', *Educational Management and Administration*, vol. 26, no. 2, pp. 147–59.

Johnson, R. (1993) 'Pierre Bourdieu on art, literature and culture'. Editor's intro. in P. Bourdieu, *The Field Of Cultural Production*. Cambridge: Polity Press.

Jones, L. and Moore, R. (1993) 'Education, competence and the control of expertise', *British Journal of Sociology of Education*, vol. 14, no. 4, pp. 385–97.

Jones, M. (1990) 'The attitude of men and women primary school teachers to promotion and education management', *Educational Management and Administration*, vol. 18, no. 3, pp. 11–16.

Joyce, B., Calhoun, E. and Hopkins, D. (1997) *Models of Learning – Tools for Teaching*. Buckingham: Open University Press.

Joyce, B., Calhoun, E. and Hopkins, D. (1999) *The New Structure of School Improvement*. Buckingham: Open University Press.

Kam-Cheung, W. (1997) 'Early Chinese thinking and the moral education of educational leaders', *International Studies in Educational Administration*, vol. 25, no. 1, pp. 17–24.

Kasten, K.L. and Ashbaugh, C.R. (1991) 'The place of values in superintendents' work', *Journal of Educational Administration*, vol. 29, no. 3, pp. 54–66.

Kelly, B.E. and Bredeson, P.V. (1991) 'Measures of meaning in a public and in a parochial school: principals as symbol managers', *Journal of Educational Administration*, vol. 29, no. 3, pp. 6–22.

Kemp, R. and Nathan, M. (1989) *Middle Management in Schools, A Survival Guide*. Oxford: Blackwell.

King, A. (1976) 'The problem of overload', in King, A. (ed.), *Why is Britain Becoming Harder to Govern?* London: British Broadcasting Corporation.

Kirkham, G. (1995) 'Headlamp and the need for an enlightened view of mentoring for new school leaders', *Journal of Educational Administration*, vol. 33, no. 5, pp. 74–83.

Kirkham, G. (2000) 'Values and equity in headteacher recruitment and selection', *Management in Education*, vol. 14, no. 1, pp. 17–19.

Kitavi, M.W. and Van der Westhuizen, P.C. (1997) 'Critical skills for beginning principals in developing countries: a case from Kenya', *International Studies in Educational Administration*, vol. 25, no. 2, pp. 126–37).

Klein, S.R. and Dikert, R.M. (1999) 'Creating artful leadership', *International Journal of Leadership in Education*, vol. 2, no. 1, pp. 23–30.

Kogan, M. (1988) 'Normative models of accountability', in Glatter, R., Preedy, M., Riches, C. and Masterton, M. (eds), *Understanding School Management*. Milton Keynes: Open University Press.

Kuhn, T. (1975) *The Structure of Scientific Revolutions*. 6th imp. London: University of Chicago Press.

Kyle, N.J. (1993) 'Cara David: a leading woman in Australian education', *Journal of Educational Administration*, vol. 31, no. 4, pp. 80–99.

Lacey, C. (1970) *Hightown Grammar*. Manchester: Manchester University Press.

Ladwig, J.G. (1996) *Academic Distinctions*. London: Routledge.

Laible, J. and Harrington, S. (1998) 'The power and the possibility of leading with alternative values', *International Journal of Leadership in Education*, vol. 1, no. 2, pp. 111–35.

Lakomski, G. (1999) 'Against leadership: a concept without a cause', in Begley, P. and Leonard, P.E. (eds), *The Values of Educational Administration*. London: Falmer Press.

Lather, P. (1986) 'Research as praxis', *Harvard Educational Review*, vol. 56, no. 3, pp. 257–77.

Lauder, H. and Hughes, D. and Watson, S., Waslander, S., Thrupp, M., Strathdee, R., Simiyu, I., Dupuis, A., McGlinn, J. and Hamlin, J. (1999) *Trading in Futures, Why Markets in Education Don't Work*. Buckingham: Open University Press.

Le Grand, J. and Bartlett, W. (eds) (1993) *Quasi-Markets and Social Policy*. London: Macmillan.

Leask, M. and Terrell, I. (eds) (1997) *Development Planning and School Improvement for Middle Managers*. London: Kogan Page.

Leithwood, K., Jantzi, D. and Steinbach, R. (1999) *Changing Leadership for Changing Times*. Buckingham: Open University Press.

Leithwood, K., Steinbach, R. and Ryan, S. (1997) 'Leadership and team learning in secondary schools', *School Leadership and Management*, vol. 17, no. 3, pp. 303–25.

Leithwood, K., Tomlinson, D. and Genge, M. (1996) 'Transformational school leadership', in Leithwood, K., Chapman, J., Corson, D., Hallinger, P. and Hart, A. (eds), *International Handbook of Educational*

Leadership and Administration Part 2. Dordrecht, Kluwer Academic.

Leonard, P. (1998) 'Gendering Change? Management, masculinity and the dynamics of incorporation', *Gender and Education*, vol. 10, no. 1, pp. 71–84.

Leont'ev, A.N. (1981) *Problems of the Development of the Mind.* Moscow: Progress.

Lloyd, J. (1999) 'A new style of governing', *New Statesman*, 4 October, pp. 12–13.

Lodge, C. (1998) 'Training aspiring heads on NPQH: issues and progress', *School Leadership and Management*, vol. 18, no. 3, pp. 347–57.

Louis, K.S. and Miles, M.B. (1992) *Improving the Urban High School: What Works and Why.* London: Cassell.

Lukes, S. (1974) *Power: A Radical View.* London: Macmillan.

Luntley, M. (2000) *Performance, Pay and Professionals.* London: Philosophy of Education Society of Great Britain.

Lyons, G. (1974) *The Administrative Tasks of Heads and Senior Teachers in Large Secondary Schools.* Bristol: University of Bristol.

Lyons, G., Jirasinghe, D., Ewers, C. and Edwards, S. (1993) 'The development of a headteachers' assessment centre', *Educational Management and Administration*, vol. 21, no. 4, pp. 245–48.

Mac an Ghaill, M. (1994) *The Making of Men.* Buckingham: Open University Press.

MacBeath, J., Moos, L. and Riley, K. (1996) 'Leadership in a changing world', in Leithwood, K., Chapman, J., Corson, D., Hallinger, P., and Hart, A. (eds), *International Handbook of Educational Leadership and Administration Part 1.* Dordrecht: Kluwer Academic.

MacBeath, J., Moos, L. and Riley, K. (1998) 'Time for a change', in MacBeath, J. (ed.), *Effective School Leadership: Responding to Change.* London: Paul Chapman Publishing.

MacGilchrist, B., Mortimore, P., Savage, J. and Beresford, C. (1995) *Planning Matters.* London: Paul Chapman Publishing.

MacGilchrist, B., Myers, K. and Reed, J. (1997) *The Intelligent School.* London: Paul Chapman Publishing.

Macpherson, R.J.S. (1996) 'Accountability', *Educational Management and Administration*, vol. 24, no. 2, pp. 139–50.

Macpherson, R.J.S. (1999) 'Building a communitarian policy of educative accountability using a critical pragmatist epistemology', *Journal of Educational Administration*, vol. 37, no. 3, pp. 273–95.

Maguire, M. and Ball, S.J. (1994) 'Researching politics and the politics of research: recent qualitative studies in the UK', *Qualitative Studies in Education*, vol. 7, no. 3, pp. 269–85.

Mahony, P., MacBeath, J. and Moos, L. (1998) 'Who really runs the school', in MacBeath, J. (ed.), *Effective School Leadership: Responding to Change.* London: Paul Chapman Publishing.

Marland, M. (1993) 'Inspiration in administration', *Educational*

Management and Administration, vol. 21, no. 4, pp. 263–4.

Marsh, M. (1997) 'In conversation with Janet Ouston', in Ribbins, P. (ed.), *Leaders and Leadership in the School, College and University*. London: Cassell.

Martin, S. (1994) 'The mentoring process in pre-service teacher education', *School Organisation*, vol. 14, no. 3, pp. 269–77.

Matthew, S. with Pascal, C. (1998) 'Raising children's expectations', in Pascal, C. and Ribbins, P. (eds), *Understanding Primary Headteachers*. London: Cassell.

Maxcy, S.J. (1998) 'Preparing school principals for ethno-democratic leadership', *International Journal of Leadership in Education*, vol. 1, no. 3, pp. 217–35.

Maxcy, S.J. and Caldas, S.J. (1991) 'Moral imagination and the philosophy of school leadership', *Journal of Educational Administration*, vol. 29, no. 3, pp. 38–53.

McConnell, J. with Ribbins, P. (1998) 'Leading an "excellent primary school" ', in Pascal, C. and Ribbins, P. (eds), *Understanding Primary Headteachers*. London: Cassell.

McCrea, N. and Ehrich, L. (1999) 'Changing leaders' educational hearts', *Educational Management and Administration*, vol. 27, no. 4, pp. 431–40.

McCulloch, G., Helsby, G. and Knight, P. (2000) *The Politics of Professionalism*. London: Continuum.

McEwen, A. and Salters, M. (1997) 'Values and management: the role of the primary school headteacher', *School Leadership and Management*, vol. 17, no. 1, pp. 69–79.

McGregor, D. and Gunter, B. (2001) 'Changing pedagogy of secondary science teachers: the impact of a two year professional development programme', *Journal of Teacher Development*, in press.

McGuinness, C. (1999) *From Thinking Skills to Thinking Classrooms*. DfEE Research Brief No. 115. London: DfEE.

McIntyre, D. (1998) 'The usefulness of educational research: an agenda for consideration and action', in Rudduck, J. and McIntyre, D. (eds), *Challenges for Educational Research*. London: Paul Chapman.

McPherson, A. and Raab, C.D. (1989) *Governing Education: A Sociology of Policy since 1945*. Edinburgh: Edinburgh University Press.

McTaggart, R. (1990) 'Action research for Aboriginal pedagogy: beyond "both ways" education?', in Zuber-Skerritt, O. (ed.), *Action Research for Change and Development*. Griffith University, Brisbane: Centre for the Advancement of Learning and Teaching.

McTaggart, R. (1991) 'Western institutional impediments to Australian Aboriginal education', *Journal of Curriculum Studies*, vol. 23, no. 4, pp. 297–25.

Menter, I., Muschamp, Y., Nicholls, P., Ozga, J., with Pollard, A. (1997) *Work and Identity in the Primary School*. Buckingham: Open University Press.

Mercer, D. (1996) ' "Can they walk on water?": professional isolation and the secondary headteacher', *School Organisation*, vol. 16, no. 2, pp. 165–78.

Mercer, D. (1997a) 'The secondary headteacher and time-in-post: a study of job satisfaction', *Journal of Educational Administration*, vol. 35, no. 3, pp. 268–81.

Mercer, D. (1997b) 'Job satisfaction and the secondary headteacher: the creation of a model of job satisfaction', *School Leadership and Management*, vol. 17, no. 1, pp. 57–67.

Merson, M. (2000) 'Teachers and the myth of modernisation', *British Journal of Educational Studies*, vol. 48, no. 2, pp. 155–69.

Mewborn, D.S. (1999) 'Creating a gender equitable school environment', *International Journal of Leadership in Education*, vol. 2, no. 2, pp. 103–15.

Miller, H. (1995) 'Review essay: dons, domination and the state', *British Journal of Sociology of Education*, vol. 16, no. 2, pp. 259–66.

Moll, L.C. and Greenberg, J.B. (1990) 'Creating zones of possibilities: combining social contexts for instruction', in Moll, L.C. (ed.), *Vygotsky and Education*. Cambridge: Cambridge University Press.

Møller, J. (1997) 'Some moral dilemmas in educational management,' in Kydd, L., Crawford, M. and Riches, C. (eds), *Professional Development for Educational Management*. Buckingham: Open University Press.

Moos, L and Dempster, N. (1998) 'Some comparative learnings from the study', in MacBeath, J. (ed.), *Effective School Leadership: Responding to Change*. London: Paul Chapman Publishing.

Morgan, C. (1979) 'Management education – dissimilar or congruent?', *Open University Course 321, Management in Education Unit 1*. Milton Keynes: Open University Press.

Morgan, C. (1999) 'Rediscovering the joy of learning: managing inclusion and EBD in a primary school', in Rayner, S. and Ribbins, P. (eds) *Headteachers and Leadership in Special Education*. London: Cassell.

Morgan, C., Hall, V. and Mackay, H. (1983) *The Selection of Secondary School Headteachers*. Milton Keynes: Open University Press.

Morgan, C., Hall, V. and Mackay, H. (1984) *A Handbook on Selecting Senior Staff for Schools*. Milton Keynes: Open University Press.

Morley, L. and Rassool, N. (1999) *School Effectiveness: Fracturing the Discourse*. London: Falmer Press.

Mortimore, P. and Mortimore, J. (eds) (1991a) *The Primary Head: Roles, Responsibilities and Reflections*. London: Paul Chapman Publishing.

Mortimore, P. and Mortimore, J. (eds) (1991b) *The Secondary Head: Roles, Responsibilities and Reflections*. London: Paul Chapman Publishing.

Mortimore, P., Sammons, P., Stoll, L., Lewis, D. and Ecob, R. (1988) *School Matters: The Junior Years*. Wells: Open Books.

Morris, E. (1998) *Speech to the Seventh British Appraisal Conference, 26th January: Appraisal: Effective Teachers, Effective Schools*. London: DfEE.

Mulkeen, T.A. and Cooper, B.S. (1992) 'Implications of preparing school administrators for knowledge work organisations: a case study', *Journal of Educational Administration*, vol. 30, no. 1, pp. 17–28.

Murphy, J. (1990) 'Principal instructional leadership', in Thurston, P. and Lotto, L. (eds), *Advances in Educational Leadership.* Greenwich, CT: JAI Press.

Murphy, J. (1998) Preparation for the school principalship: the United States' story', *School Leadership and Management*, vol. 18, no. 3, pp. 359–72.

Murphy, R. (1998) 'Misleading prognoses? Educational research in action', in Rudduck, J. and McIntyre, D. (eds), *Challenges for Educational Research.* London: Paul Chapman Publishing.

Myers, K. (ed.) (1996) *School Improvement in Practice: The Schools Make a Difference Project.* London: Falmer Press.

Nash, R. (1999) 'Bourdieu, 'habitus', and educational research: is it all worth the candle?', *British Journal of Sociology of Education*, vol. 20, no. 2, pp. 175–87.

Nias, J. (1987) 'One finger, one thumb: a case study of the deputy head's part in the leadership of a nursery/infant school', in Southworth, G. (ed.), *Readings in Primary School Management.* Lewes: Falmer Press.

Nias, J. (1988) 'Reference groups in primary teaching: talking, listening and identity', in Glatter, R., Preedy, M., Riches, C. and Masterton, M. (eds), *Understanding School Management.* Milton Keynes: Open University Press.

Nias, J. (1996) 'Thinking about feeling: the emotions in teaching', *Cambridge Journal of Education*, vol. 26, no. 3, pp. 293–306.

Nixon, J. (1995) 'Teaching as a profession of values', in Smyth, J. (ed.), *Critical Discourses on Teacher Development.* London: Cassell.

Nixon, J. and Ranson, S. (1997) 'Theorizing "Agreement": the moral bases of the emergent professionalism within the "new" management of education', *Discourse: Studies in the Cultural Politics of Education*, vol. 18, no. 2, pp. 197–214.

Nixon, J., Martin, J., McKeown, P. and Ranson, S. (1997) 'Towards a learning profession: changing codes of occupational practice within the new management of education', *British Journal of Sociology of Education*, vol. 18, no. 1, pp. 5–28.

Novlan, J.F. (1998) 'New Zealand's past and tomorrow's schools: reasons, reforms and results', *School Leadership and Management*, vol. 18., no.1, pp. 7–18.

Oakley, A. (2000) *Experiments in Knowing.* Cambridge: Polity Press in association with Blackwell.

Ortiz, F.I. and Kalbus, J. (1998) 'Superintendent succession: prearrival and postarrival factors', *International Journal of Leadership in Education*, vol. 1, no. 4, pp. 337–56.

Ouston, J. (1993) 'Management competences, school effectiveness and education management', *Educational Management and Administration*, vol. 21, no. 4, pp. 212–21.

Ouston, J. (1997) 'Pathways to headship and pincipalship', in Ribbins, P. (ed.), *Leaders and Leadership in the School, College and University*. London: Cassell.

Ouston, J. (1998) 'Introduction', *School Leadership and Management*, vol. 18, no. 3, pp. 317–320.

Ouston, J. (1999) 'School effectiveness and school improvement: critique of a movement', in Bush, T., Bell, L., Bolam, R., Glatter, R. and Ribbins, P. (eds), *Educational Management: Redefining Theory, Policy and Practice*. London: Paul Chapman Publishing.

Owens, R.G. and Shakeshaft, C. (1992) 'The new "revolution", in administrative theory' *Journal of Educational Administration*, vol. 30, no. 2, pp. 4–17.

Ozga, J. (1987) 'Studying education policy through the lives of the policymakers: an attempt to close the macro-micro gap', in Walker, S. and Barton, L. (eds), *Changing Policies, Changing Teachers: New Directions for Schooling?* Milton Keynes: Open University Press.

Ozga, J. (1992) 'Review essay: education management', *British Journal of Sociology of Education*, vol. 13, no. 2, pp. 279–80.

Ozga, J. (ed.) (1993) *Women in Educational Management*. Buckingham: Open University Press.

Ozga, J. (1995) 'Deskilling a profession: professionalism, deprofessionalisation and the new managerialism', in Busher, H. and Saran, R. (eds), (1995) *Managing Teachers as Professionals in Schools*. London: Kogan Page.

Ozga, J. (2000) *Policy Research in Educational Settings*. Buckingham: Open University Press.

Ozga, J. and Lawn, M. (1988) 'Schoolwork: interpreting the labour process of teaching', *British Journal of Sociology of Education*, vol. 9, no. 3, pp. 323–36.

Park, S.H. (1999) 'The development of Richard Bate's critical theory in educational administration', *Journal of Educational Administration*, vol. 37, no. 4, pp. 367–88.

Pascal, C. and Ribbins, P. (eds) (1998) *Understanding Primary Headteachers*. London: Cassell.

Peters, R.S. (ed.) (1976) *The Role of the Head*. London: Routledge and Kegan Paul.

Peters, T. and Waterman, R. (1982) *In Search of Excellence*. Glasgow: HarperCollins.

Playko, M.A. (1995) 'Mentoring for educational leaders: a practitioner's perspective', *Journal of Educational Administration*, vol. 33, no. 5, pp. 84–92.

Pocklington, K and Weindling, D. (1996) 'Promoting reflection on headship through the mentoring mirror', *Educational Management and Administration*, vol. 24, no. 2, pp. 175–91.

Popkewitz, T.S. (1999) 'Introduction, critical traditions, modernisms and the "Posts" ', in Popkewitz, T.S. and Fendler, L. (eds), *Critical Theories in Education*. London: Routledge.

Poster, C. (1976) *School Decision-Making: Education Management in Secondary Schools*. London: Heinemann Educational.

Pring, R. (1988) 'Privatisation', *Educational Management and Administration*, vol. 16, no. 2, pp. 85–96.

Quicke, J. (2000) 'A new professionalism for a collaborative culture of organizational learning in contemporary society', *Educational Management and Administration*, vol. 28, no. 3, pp. 299–315.

Raab, C.D., Munn, P., McAvoy, L., Bailey, L., Arnott, M., and Adler, M. (1997) 'Devolving the management of schools in Britain', *Educational Administration Quarterly*, vol. 33, no. 2, pp. 140–57.

Radnor, H., Ball, S.J. and Vincent, C. (1997) 'Whither democratic accountability in education? An investigation into headteachers' perspectives on accountability in the 1990s with reference to their relationships with their LEAs and governors', *Research Papers in Education*, vol. 12, no. 2, pp. 205–22.

Ranson, S. (1993) 'Markets or democracy for education', *British Journal of Educational Studies*, vol. 41, no. 4, pp. 333–52.

Ranson, S. (1994) *Towards the Learning Society*. London: Cassell.

Ranson, S. (1995) 'Public institutions for cooperative action: a reply to James Tooley', *British Journal of Educational Studies*, vol. 43, no. 1, pp. 35–42.

Ranson. S. (1998) 'The future of educational research: learning at the centre', in Rudduck, J. and McIntyre, D. (eds), *Challenges for Educational Research*. London: Paul Chapman Publishing.

Ranson, S. (2000) 'Recognizing the pedagogy of voice in a learning community', *Educational Management and Administration*, vol. 28, no. 3, pp. 263–79.

Rayner, S. and Ribbins, P. (eds) (1999) *Headteachers and Leadership in Special Education*. London: Cassell.

Reay, D. and Ball, S.J. (2000) 'Essentials of female management', *Educational Management and Administration*, vol. 28, no. 2, pp. 145–59.

Reeves, J., Moos, L. and Forrest, J. (1998) 'The school leader's view', in MacBeath, J. (ed.), *Effective School Leadership: Responding to Change*. London: Paul Chapman Publishing.

Restine, L.N. (1997) 'Experience, meaning and principal development', *Journal of Educational Administration*, vol. 35, no. 3, pp. 253–67.

Reynolds, D. (2000) 'School effectiveness: the international dimension', in Teddlie, C. and Reynolds, D., *The International Handbook of School Effectiveness Research*. London: Falmer Press.

Reynolds, D., and Teddlie, C. (2000) 'The processes of school effectiveness', in Teddlie, C. and Reynolds, D., *The International Handbook of School Effectiveness Research*. London: Falmer Press.

Reynolds, D. and Teddlie, C. with Creemers, B., Scheerens, J. and Townsend, T. (2000a) 'An introduction to school effectiveness research', in Teddlie, C. and Reynolds, D., *The International Handbook of School Effectiveness Research.* London: Falmer Press.

Reynolds, D. and Teddlie, C. with Hopkins, D. and Stringfield, S. (2000b) 'Linking school effectiveness and school improvement', in Teddlie, C. and Reynolds, D., *The International Handbook of School Effectiveness Research.* London: Falmer Press.

Ribbins, P. (1985) 'The role of the middle manager in the secondary school', in Hughes, M., Ribbins, P. and Thomas, H., *Managing Education: The System and The Institution.* Eastbourne: Holt, Rinehart and Winston.

Ribbins, P. (ed.) (1997a) *Leaders and Leadership in the School, College and University.* London: Cassell.

Ribbins, P. (1997b) 'Leaders and leadership in the school, college and university: a prelude', in Ribbins, P. (ed.), *Leaders and Leadership in the School, College and University.* London: Cassell.

Ribbins, P. (1997c) 'Heads on deputy headship: impossible roles for invisible role holders?', *Educational Management and Administration*, vol. 25, no. 3, pp. 295–308.

Ribbins, P. (1999) 'Understanding leadership: developing headteachers', in Bush, T., Bell, L., Bolam, R., Glatter, R. and Ribbins, P. (eds), *Educational Management: Redefining Theory, Policy and Practice.* London: Paul Chapman Publishing.

Ribbins, P. and Marland, M. (1994) *Headship Matters.* Harlow: Longman.

Ribbins, P. and Sherratt, B. (1999) 'Managing the secondary school in the 1990s: new view of headship', in Strain, M., Dennison, B., Ouston, J., and Hall, V. (eds), *Policy, Leadership and Professional Knowledge.* London: Paul Chapman Publishing.

Richardson, E. (1973) *The Teacher, the School and the Task of Management.* London: Heinemann.

Riley, K.A. (1998) 'Creating the leadership climate', *International Journal of Leadership in Education*, vol. 1. no. 2, pp. 137–53.

Roach, M. (1993) 'The secondary deputy', in Ozga, J. (ed.) *Women in Educational Management.* Buckingham: Open University Press.

Rudduck, J. (1998) 'Educational research: the prospect of change . . .', in Rudduck, J. and McIntyre, D. (eds), *Challenges for Educational Research.* London: Paul Chapman Publishing.

Rudduck, J., Chaplain, R. and Wallace, G. (1996a) *School Improvement, What Can Pupils Tell Us?* London: David Fulton.

Rudduck, J., Chaplain, R. and Wallace, G. (1996b) 'Reviewing the conditions of learning in school', in Rudduck, J., Chaplain, R. and Wallace, G., *School Improvement, What Can Pupils Tell Us?* London: David Fulton.

Rutter, M., Maughan, B., Mortimore, P. and Ouston, J. with Smith, A. (1979) *Fifteen Thousand Hours: Secondary Schools and their Effects on Children.* London: Open Books.

Ryan, J. (1998) 'Critical leadership for education in a postmodern world: emancipation, resistance and communal action', *International Journal of Leadership in Education*, vol. 1, no. 3, pp. 257–78.

Ryle, A. (1999) 'Object relations theory and activity theory: a proposed link by way of the procedural sequence model', in Engeström, Y., Miettinen, R. and Punamäki, R. (eds), *Perspectives on Activity Theory*. Cambridge: Cambridge University Press.

Sammons, P. (1999) *School Effectiveness, Coming of Age in the Twenty-First Century*. Lisse: Swets and Zeitlinger.

Sammons, P., Hillman, J. and Mortimore, P. (1995) *Key Characteristics of Effective Schools: A Review of School Effectiveness Research*. London: Institute of Education for the Office for Standards in Education.

Sammons, P., Mortimore, P. and Thomas, S. (1996a) 'Do schools perform consistently across outcomes and areas?', in Gray, J., Reynolds, D., Fitz-Gibbon, C. and Jesson, D. (eds), *Merging Traditions: The Future of Research on School Effectiveness and School Improvement*. London: Cassell.

Sammons, P., Thomas, S. and Mortimore, P. (1996b) 'Promoting school and departmental effectiveness', *Management in Education*, vol. 10, no. 1, pp. 22–4.

Sammons, P., Thomas, S. and Mortimore, P. (1997) *Forging Links: Effective Schools and Effective Departments*. London: Paul Chapman Publishing.

Sapra, C.L. (1993) 'Towards 2000 and beyond: preparation of educational managers in India', *Journal of Educational Administration*, vol. 31, no. 4, pp. 51–66.

Saran, R. and Trafford, V. (eds) (1990) *Research in Education Management and Policy: Retrospect and Prospect*. London: Falmer Press.

Schein, E.H. (1985) *Organizational Culture and Leadership*. San Francisco: Jossey-Bass.

Scheurich, J.J. (1998) 'Commentary. The grave dangers in the discourse on democracy', *International Journal of Leadership in Education*, vol. 1, no. 1, pp. 55–60.

Schon, D. (1983) *The Reflective Practitioner: How Professionals Think in Action*. London: Temple Smith.

Sebba, J. (2000) 'Developing evidence informed policy and practice: a national perspective'. Paper presented to the BEMAS Research 2000: the sixth International Educational Management and Administration Research Conference, March, Cambridge.

Seddon, T. (1996) 'The principle of choice in policy research', *Journal of Education Policy,* vol 11, no. 2, pp. 197–214.

Seddon, T. (1999) 'On the politics of change: failed alternatives or creeping alternative counter-practices', *Education and Social Justice*, vol. 1, no. 3, pp. 32–7.

Sergiovanni, T.J. (1998) 'Leadership as pedagogy, capital development and school effectiveness', *International Journal of Leadership in Education*, vol. 1, no. 1, pp. 37–46.

Shain, F. and Gleeson, D. (1999) 'Teachers' work and professionalism in the post-incorporated further education sector', *Education and Social Justice*, vol. 1, no. 3, pp. 55–63.

Shayer, M. (1996) *The Long-Term Effects of Cognitive Acceleration on Pupils' School Achievement*. London: Centre for the Advancement of Thinking, King's College.

Shayer, M. (2000) *GCSE 1999: Added-Value from Schools Adopting the CASE Intervention*. London: Centre for the Advancement of Thinking. King's College.

Shipton, S. and Tatton, B. (1989) ' "Once your eyes are opened": initiatives in women's training by one teacher union', in de Lyon, H. and Widdowson Migniuolo, F. (eds), *Women Teachers*. Milton Keynes: Open University Press.

Simco, N. (1995) 'Professional profiling and development in the induction year', *British Journal of In-Service Education*, vol. 21, no. 3, pp. 261–72.

Simkins, T. (1999) 'Values, power and instrumentatility: theory and research in education management', *Educational Management and Administration*, vol. 27, no. 3, pp. 267–81.

Simon, H.A. (1945) *Administrative Behavior: A Study of Decision-Making Processes in Administrative Organization*. New York: Macmillan.

Skeggs, B. (1997) *Formations of Class and Gender*. London: Sage.

Slee, R. and Weiner, G. with Tomlinson, S. (eds), (1998) *School Effectiveness for Whom? Challenges to the School Effectiveness and School Improvement Movements*. London: Falmer Press.

Smulyan, L. (2000) *Balancing Acts*. Albany, NY: State University of New York.

Smyth, J. (1985) 'An educative and empowering notion of leadership', *Educational Management and Administration*, vol. 13, no. 4, pp. 179–86.

Smyth, J. (ed.) (1989a) *Critical Perspectives on Educational Leadership*. London: Falmer Press.

Smyth, J. (1989b) 'Preface', in Smyth, J. (ed.), *Critical Perspectives on Educational Leadership*. London: Falmer Press.

Smyth, J. (1989c) 'A "pedagogical" and "educative" view of leadership', in Smyth, J. (ed.), *Critical Perspectives on Educational Leadership*. London: Falmer Press.

Smyth, J. (ed.) (1993) *A Socially Critical View of the Self-Managing School*. London: Falmer Press.

Smyth, J. (1995) 'Devolution and teachers' work: the underside of a complex phenomenon', *Educational Management and Administration*, vol. 23, no. 3, pp. 168–75.

Smyth, J. (1996) 'The socially just alternative to the "self-managing school" ', in Leithwood, K., Chapman, J., Corson, D., Hallinger, P., and Hart, A. (eds), *International Handbook of Educational Leadership and Administration Part 2*. Dordrecht, Kluwer Academic.

Smyth, J. (1998) 'Reprofessionalising teaching: a university research institute engages teachers in creating dialogic space in schools', *Teacher*

Development, vol. 2, no. 3, pp. 339–49.

Smyth, J. and Dow, A. (1998) 'What's wrong with outcomes? Spotter planes, action plans, and steerage of the educational workplace', *British Journal of Sociology of Education*, vol. 19, no. 3, pp. 291–303.

Smyth, J. and Shacklock, G. (1998a) *Re-Making Teaching: Ideology, Policy and Practice.* London: Routledge.

Smyth, J. and Shacklock, G. (1998b) 'The politics and context of calls for cross-sectoral collaborative research', *Journal of Education Policy*, vol. 13, no. 2, pp. 265–73.

Smyth, J., Dow, A., Hattam, R., Reid, A. and Shacklock, G. (2000) *Teachers' Work in a Globalizing Economy.* London: Falmer Press.

Smyth, J., McInerney, P., Hattam, R. and Lawson, M. (1998) 'Teacher learning: the way out of the school restructuring miasma', *International Journal of Leadership in Education*, vol. 1, no. 2, pp. 95–109.

Snell, M. (1999) 'Schools' management and organisational restructuring: a survey of the disappearing deputy head.' Unpublished MA thesis, Keele University.

Southworth, G. (1993) 'School leadership and school development: reflections from research', *School Organisation*, vol. 13, no. 1, pp. 73–87.

Southworth, G. (1995a) *Looking into Primary Headship.* London: Falmer Press.

Southworth, G. (1995b) 'Reflections on mentoring for new school leaders', *Journal of Educational Administration*, vol. 33, no. 5, pp. 17–28.

Southworth, G. (1999a) 'Continuities and changes in primary headship', in Bush, T., Bell, L., Bolam, R., Glatter, R., and Ribbins, P. (eds), *Educational Management: Redefining Theory, Policy and Practice.* London: Paul Chapman Publishing.

Southworth, G. (1999b) 'Primary school leadership in England: policy, practice and theory', *School Leadership and Management*, vol. 19, no. 1, pp. 49–65.

Spaulding, A. (1997) 'Life in schools – a qualitative study of teacher perspectives on the politics of principals: ineffective leadership behaviors and their consequences upon teacher thinking and behavior', *School Leadership and Management*, vol. 17, no. 1, pp. 39–55.

Spooner, B. (1989) *Neither Up Nor Down.* Leeds: Gerbil Books.

Stålhammar, B. (1994) 'Goal-oriented leadership in Swedish schools', *Educational Management and Administration*, vol. 22, no. 1, pp. 14–25.

Stanley, L. and Wise, S. (1993) *Breaking Out: Feminist Consciousness and Feminist Research.* London: Routledge and Kegan Paul.

Starratt, R.J. (1999) 'Moral dimensions of leadership', in Begley, P.T. and Leonard, P.E. (eds), *The Values of Educational Administration.* London: Falmer Press.

Stodgill, R.M. (1974) *Handbook of Leadership.* New York: Free Press.

Stoll, L. and Fink, D. (1996) *Changing Our Schools: Linking School Effectiveness and School Improvement.* Buckingham: Open University Press.

Strachan, J. (1999) 'Feminist educational leadership in a New Zealand neo-liberal context', *Journal of Educational Administration*, vol. 37, no. 2, pp. 121–38.

Strain, M. (1995) 'Teaching as a profession: the changing legal and social context', in Busher, H. and Saran, R. (eds), *Managing Teachers as Professionals in Schools*. London: Kogan Page.

Strain, M. (1997) 'Records of achievement', *Educational Management and Administration*, vol. 25, no. 3, pp. 213–42.

Swartz, D. (1997) *Culture and Power: The Sociology of Pierre Bourdieu*. London: University of Chicago Press.

Swingewood, A.W. (1987) 'Intellectuals and the construction of consensus in postwar England', in Gagnon, A.G. (ed.) *Intellectuals in Liberal Democracies*. New York: Praeger.

Taylor, W. (1969) 'Simulation and the comparative study of educational administration', in Baron, G., Cooper, D.H. and Walker, W.G. (eds), *Educational Administration: International Perspectives*. Chicago: Rand McNally.

Taylor, W. (1973) *Heading for Change*. London: Routledge and Kegan Paul.

Taylor, W. (1976) 'The head as manager: some criticisms', in Peters, R.S. (ed.), *The Role of the Head*. London: Routledge and Kegan Paul.

Teacher Training Agency (TTA) (1997) *Report on the Outcomes of the NPQH Trials 1996–1997*. London: TTA.

Teacher Training Agency (TTA) (1998a) *National Standards for Headteachers*. London: TTA.

Teacher Training Agency (TTA) (1998b) *National Standards for Subject Leaders*. London: TTA.

Teacher Training Agency (TTA) (1998c) *National Standards for Qualified Teacher Status*. London: TTA.

Teddlie, C. and Reynolds, D. with Pool, S. (2000a) 'Current topics and approaches in school effectiveness research: the contemporary field', in Teddlie, C. and Reynolds, D., *The International Handbook of School Effectiveness Research*. London: Falmer Press.

Teddlie, C., Reynolds, D. and Sammons, P. (2000b) 'The methodology and scientific properties of school effectiveness research', in Teddlie, C. and Reynolds, D., *The International Handbook of School Effectiveness Research*. London: Falmer Press.

Teddlie, C., Stringfield, S. and Reynolds, D. (2000c) 'Context issues within school effectiveness research', in Teddlie, C. and Reynolds, D., *The International Handbook of School Effectiveness Research*. London: Falmer Press.

Thomas, P. (1997) 'Leadership and team learning in secondary schools – some implications for schools: a headteacher's response', *School Leadership and Management*, vol. 17, no. 3, pp. 331–32.

Thrupp, M. (2000) 'Sociological and political concerns about school effectiveness research: time for a new research agenda'. Paper presented to the International Congress for School Effectiveness and Improvement Symposium, AERA, New Orleans, April.

Todd, R. and Dennison, W.F. (1980) 'The changing role of the deputy headteacher in English secondary schools', in Bush, T., Glatter, R., Goodey, J., and Riches, C. (eds), *Approaches to School Management*. London: Harper and Row.

Tolman, C.W. (1999) 'Society versus context in individual development: Does theory make a difference?', in Engeström, Y., Miettinen, R. and Punamäki, R. (eds), *Perspectives on Activity Theory*. Cambridge: Cambridge University Press.

Tomlinson, H., Gunter, H., and Smith, P. (eds) (1999) *Living Headship: Voices, Values and Vision*. London: Paul Chapman Publishing.

Tooley, J. (1995) 'Markets or democracy for education? A reply to Stewart Ranson', *British Journal of Educational Studies*, vol. 43, no. 1, pp. 21–34.

Tooley, J. (1996) *Education Without the State*. London: IEA.

Tooley, J. (1999) *Reclaiming Education*. London: Cassell.

Tooley, J. with Darby, D. (1998) *Educational Research, A Critique*. London: Office for Standards in Education.

Torrington, D. and Weightman, J. (1989) *The Reality of School Management*. Oxford: Blackwell Education.

Turner, C. and Bolam, R. (1998) 'Analysing the role of the subject head of department in secondary schools in England and Wales: towards a theoretical framework', *School Leadership and Management*, vol. 18, no. 3, pp. 373–88.

Turner, C.K. (1996) 'The roles and tasks of a subject head of department in secondary schools in England and Wales: a neglected area of research', *School Organisation*, vol. 16, no. 2, pp. 203–17.

Usher, R. and Edwards, R. (1994) *Postmodernism and Education*. London: Routledge.

Vulliamy, G. and Webb, R. (1995) 'The changing role of the primary school deputy headteacher', *School Organisation*, vol. 15, no. 1, pp. 53–64.

Vygotsky, L.S. (1978) *Mind in Society: The Development of Higher Psychological Processes*. Cambridge: Harvard University Press.

Walker, A.D., Chong, K. and Low, G. (1993) 'Principalship training through mentoring: the Singapore experience', *Journal of Educational Administration*, vol. 31, no. 4, pp. 33–50.

Walker, C. (1993) 'Black women in educational management', in Ozga, J. (ed.), *Women in Educational Management*. Buckingham: Open University Press.

Wallace, G. (1996a) 'Relating to teachers', in Rudduck, J., Chaplain, R. and Wallace, G., *School Improvement, What Can Pupils Tell Us?* London: David Fulton.

Wallace, G. (1996b) 'Engaging with learning', in Rudduck, J., Chaplain,

R. and Wallace, G., *School Improvement, What Can Pupils Tell Us?* London: David Fulton.

Wallace, M. and Hall, V. (1994) *Inside the SMT: Teamwork in Secondary School Management.* London: Paul Chapman Publishing.

Wallace, M. and Huckman, L. (1996) 'Senior management teams in large primary schools: a headteachers' solution to the complexities of post-reform management?', *School Organisation*, vol. 16, no. 3, pp. 309–23.

Watkins, P. (1989) 'Leadership, power and symbols in educational administration', in Smyth, J. (ed.), *Critical Perspectives on Educational Leadership.* London: Falmer Press.

Watts, J. (1980) 'Sharing it out: The role of the head in participatory government', in Bush, T., Glatter, R., Goodey, J., and Riches, C. (eds), *Approaches to School Management.* London: Harper and Row.

Watts, R. (1998) 'From Lady Teacher to professional', *Educational Management and Administration*, vol. 26, no. 4, pp. 339–51.

Webb, R. and Vulliamy, G. (1996) 'The changing role of the primary-school headteacher', *Educational Management and Administration*, vol. 24, no. 3, pp. 301–15.

Weick, K.E. (1989) 'Educational organisations as loosely coupled systems' in Bush, T. (ed.), *Managing Education: Theory and Practice.* Buckingham: Open University Press.

Weindling, D. (1999) 'Stages of headship', in Bush, T., Bell, L., Bolam, R., Glatter, R. and Ribbins, P. (eds), *Educational Management: Redefining Theory, Policy and Practice.* London: Paul Chapman Publishing.

Weldon, L. (1997) 'Australia: middle management in the Queensland Education system', in Leask, M. and Terrell, I. (eds), *Development Planning and School Improvement for Middle Managers.* London: Kogan Page.

West, A., Pennell, H. and Edge, A. (1997) 'Exploring the impact of reform on school-enrolment policies in England', *Educational Administration Quarterly*, vol. 33, no. 2, pp. 170–82.

Whinn-Sladden, R. (1997) 'In conversation with Viv Garrett', in Ribbins, P. (ed), *Leaders and Leadership in the School, College and University.* London: Cassell.

White, C. and Crump, S. (1993) 'Education and the three "P"s: policy, politics and practice. A review of the work of S.J. Ball', *British Journal of Sociology of Education*, vol. 14, no. 4, pp. 415–29.

Whitty, G. (1985) *Sociology and School Knowledge: Curriculum Theory, Research and Politics.* London: Methuen.

Whitty, G. and Power, S. (1997) 'Quasi-markets and curriculum control: making sense of recent education reform in England and Wales', *Educational Administration Quarterly*, vol. 33, no. 2, pp. 219–40.

Whitty, G., Power, S. and Halpin, D. (1998) *Devolution and Choice in Education: The School, The State, and The Market.* Buckingham: Open University Press.

Wildy, H. and Dimmock, C. (1993) 'Instructional leadership in primary and secondary schools in Western Australia', *Journal of Educational Administration*, vol. 31, no. 2, pp. 43–62.

Wildy, H. and Wallace, J. (1998) 'Professionalism, portfolios and the development of school leaders', *School Leadership and Management*, vol. 18, no. 1, pp. 123–40.

Williams, R.C. (1993) 'Review of educational leadership: the moral art of Christopher Hodgkinson', *Educational Management and Administration*, vol. 21, no. 4, pp. 255–8.

Willmott, R. (1999a) 'School effectiveness research: an ideological commitment?', *Journal of Philosophy of Education*, vol. 33, no. 2, pp. 253–68.

Willmott, R. (1999b) 'Structure, agency and school effectiveness: researching a "failing" school', *Educational Studies*, vol. 25, no. 1, pp. 5–18.

Willower, D.J. (1998) 'Work on values in educational administration: some observations', *Leading and Managing*, vol. 4, no. 4, pp. 232–42.

Winkley, D. with Pascal, C. (1998) 'Developing a radical agenda', in Pascal, C. and Ribbins, P. (eds), *Understanding Primary Headteachers*. London: Cassell.

Winter, R. (1989) 'Teacher appraisal and the development of professional knowledge', in W. Carr (ed.), *Quality in Teaching: Arguments for a Reflective Profession*. Lewes: Falmer Press.

Witziers, B., Sleegers, P. and Imants, J. (1999) 'Departments as teams: functioning, variations and alternatives', *School Leadership and Management*, vol. 19, no. 3, pp. 293–304.

Woodhead, C. (2000) 'Old values for the new age', *Times Educational Supplement*, p. 13.

Wragg, E.C., Wikeley, F.J., Wragg, C.M. and Haynes, G.S. (1996) *Teacher Appraisal Observed*. London: Routledge.

Yeatman, A. (1990) *Bureaucrats, Technocrats, Femocrats. Essays on the Contemporary Australian State*. Sydney: Allen and Unwin.

Yeatman, A. (1994) *Postmodern Revisionings of the Political*. London: Routledge.

Young, M.F.D. (1971a) 'Introduction', in Young, M.F.D. (ed.), *Knowledge and Control*. London: Cassell and Collier Macmillan.

Young, M.F.D. (1971b) 'An approach to the study of curricula as socially organized knowledge', in Young, M.F.D. (ed.), *Knowledge and Control*. London: Cassell and Collier Macmillan.

Young, M.F.D. (1998) *The Curriculum of the Future*. London: Falmer Press.

Author Index

Subject Index